Restoring the
Christian Soul

Other Books by Leanne Payne

Real Presence
The Broken Image
Healing Homosexuality
Crisis in Masculinity
The Healing Presence
Listening Prayer

Restoring the Christian Soul

*Overcoming Barriers
to Completion in Christ
through Healing Prayer*

Leanne Payne

A Hamewith Book

Baker Books

A Division of Baker Book House Co
Grand Rapids, Michigan 49516

Published by Baker Books
a division of Baker Publishing Group
P.O. Box 6287, Grand Rapids, MI 49516-6287
www.bakerbooks.com

Paperback edition published 1996

Previously published in cloth in 1991 under the title *Restoring the Christian Soul through Healing Prayer: Overcoming the Three Great Barriers to Personal and Spiritual Completion in Christ* by Crossway Books

Printed in the United States of America

Library of Congress Cataloging-in-Publication Data

Payne, Leanne.
    [Restoring the Christian soul through healing prayer]
    Restoring the Christian soul : overcoming barriers to completion in Christ through healing prayer / Leanne Payne.
        p.   cm.
    Originally published : Restoring the Christian soul through healing prayer. Wheaton, Ill. : Crossway Books, c1991.
    "Companion volume to The healing presence"—CIP pref.
    Includes bibliographical references and index.
    ISBN 10: 0-8010-5699-3 (pbk.)
    ISBN 978-0-8010-5699-4 (pbk.)
    1. Spiritual life—Christianity. 2. Spiritual healing. 3. Self-acceptance—Religious aspects—Christianity. 4. Forgiveness of sin. 5. Forgiveness—Religious aspects—Christianity. I. Payne, Leanne. Healing presence. II. Title.
    [BV4501.2.P3625   1996]
    234—dc20   95-50955

Excerpts from *God in the Dock* by C. S. Lewis © 1970 by C. S. Lewis Pte Ltd are reprinted by permission of Curtis Brown Ltd and HarperCollins Publishers.

Excerpts from *Letters to Malcolm: Chiefly on Prayer* by C. S. Lewis, copyright © 1964, 1963 by the Estate of C. S. Lewis, reprinted by permission of Harcourt Brace Jovanovich, Inc.

Excerpts from *Letters of C. S. Lewis*, edited by W. H. Lewis, copyright © 1966 by W. H. Lewis and the Executors of C. S. Lewis, reprinted by permission of Harcourt Brace Jovanovich, Inc.

Excerpts from *Reflections on the Psalms*, copyright © 1958 by C. S. Lewis and renewed 1986 by Arthur Owen Barfield, reprinted by permission of Harcourt Brace Jovanovich, Inc.

Excerpts from *That Hideous Strength* by C. S. Lewis used by permission of The Bodley Head, London.

Unless otherwise indicated, Scripture is taken from the HOLY BIBLE, NEW INTERNATIONAL VERSION®. NIV®. Copyright © 1973, 1978, 1984 by International Bible Society. Used by permission of Zondervan. All rights reserved.

Scripure marked NEB is taken from *The New English Bible.* Copyright © 1961, 1970, 1989 by The Delegates of the Oxford University Press and The Syndics of the Cambridge University Press. Reprinted by permission.

To Mario Bergner, Jean Holt, and Clay McLean,

beloved colleagues in this ministry
who are taking forward the message and ministry
of healing in ways that break new ground.

Table of Contents

Acknowledgments   xi
Preface   xiii

Part I: The Virtue of Self-Acceptance

1: Self-Hatred: The Traitor Within When Temptation Comes   19
2: First Great Barrier to Wholeness in Christ: Failure
   to Accept Oneself   25
3: Struggling Through to Self-Acceptance   31
4: Affirmation: What It Is and How It Is Received   45
5: Listening Prayer: The Way of Grace and the Walk in the Spirit   57

Part II: The Forgiveness of Sin

6: Healing of Memories: The Forgiveness of Sin   67
7: Second Great Barrier to Wholeness in Christ:
   Failure to Forgive Others   81
8: Prolonged Healing of Memories:
   Abandonment Issues and the Repression of Painful Emotions   103
9: Third Great Barrier to Wholeness in Christ:
   Failure to Receive Forgiveness   141
10: Conclusion to Healing of Memories   153

Part III: Spiritual Warfare and the Gift of Battle

11: The Use of Holy Water and Other Powerful Christian
    Symbols and Agencies   163
12: The Gift of Battle   183
13: Cosmic Dimensions of Spiritual Warfare
    in Christian Organizations   191
14: Wrong Ways to Do Battle   201
15: Restoring the Christian Hope of Heaven and
    the Grace to Persevere   217
Notes   233
Index   243

Is anything too hard for the Lord?

(Genesis 18:14)

Pastoral Care is defective unless it can deal thoroughly with the evils we have suffered as well as with the sins we have committed.

(Frank Lake, *Clinical Theology*)

Acknowledgments

Restoring the Christian Soul is a book about prayer and its awesome power as we gather in Christ's name. The school of prayer is surely one from which none of us ever graduates in this life. There is always more to experience and learn about prayers of praise, thanksgiving, intercession, supplication, and faith. The kind of prayer we are most concerned with in these pages is prayer for healing of the soul, the forgiveness of sin. This prayer work is not peripheral to Christian practice and the gospel message. It should be and indeed is part of the work of baptism and our initiation into Christ. It has long been neglected, however, and professionals in the healing arts are now dealing with the consequences of this neglect.

To pray effectively for the healing of souls is to see the work of the cross (Christ's passion) made fully manifest in lives and the gifts and fruit of the Holy Spirit flourish within the Body of Christ. It is to see people come into maturity and wholeness and thereby the power to evangelize and to succor a world starving for love, truth, and light. To gather as prayer partners and teams, therefore, is the most exciting thing in the world, for God waits to hear and respond to those who seek His mind on how to pray.

> Again, I tell you that if two of you on earth agree about anything you ask for, it will be done for you by my Father in heaven. For where two or three come together in my name, there am I with them. (Matthew 18:19, 20)

This book then, like my others, is born out of many years of learning to pray with and for others. Therefore, I want to acknowledge first of all the Pastoral Care Ministries Team made up of my prayer partners who also travel with me in the ministry. They are (Revs.) William and Anne Beasley, Mario Bergner, Lynne and Paul Berendsen, (Rev.) Conlee and Signa Bodishbaugh, Connie and Bob Boerner, Patsy Casey, John Fawcett, Jean Holt, Clay McLean, Mary Pomrenning, and Ted and Lucy Smith. What extraordinary fellow pilgrims and prayer partners they are! I thank them for who they are and all that they are. For their courageous, loving hearts and faith, I continually thank God.

A prayer group within the larger prayer team is made up of Lynne, Connie,

Lucy, and Patsy. For over twelve years now, they have met regularly with me for prayer, and I cannot think of many things we haven't faced and prayed through together in these sessions. The faith, love of truth, honesty, and sheer stamina of these remarkable women never fail to bless and sustain me and the other team members. Only eternity will tell what their husbands have given (and suffered!) for this ministry. For a period of time Bob Boerner, for example, stayed home with five teenage daughters and prayed for us while Connie went several times a year to lead the music ministry and pray for others in our healing missions. Now that the children are grown, he joins us on the team when he can manage time off from work. Paul Berendsen, besides doing the huge job of trying to stretch our dollars and keep our accounts in order, has never failed to bless his wife as she, year in and year out, has brilliantly managed the affairs of this ministry. Ted Smith has become the father figure for the whole group, blessing us and everybody else with his gifts of wisdom, guidance, and special faith in prayer.

The Rev. Andrew Comiskey and his Desert Stream team are so often with us that we consider them a part of the PCM family, as is the Rev. Jerry Soviar of Toledo, Ohio. They too are vital prayer partners with us. From thirty or more years ago, I want to recognize Lenora Runge, and from twenty-five years ago, Elinor Price. These precious ones, though long separated by distance, have remained with me in prayer. Gayle Sampson and Carol Kraft, more accessible geographically, are two more whose fellowship in prayer spans the decades. Mike Casey, Dr. Bernie Klamecki, Ivy Upton and John and Mary Stocking are others who never forget to love and pray for this ministry, and they provide a more unique and healing support for me than they realize. We have special prayer partners, translators, and teams overseas, some listed in the acknowledgments to *The Healing Presence*, but the list grows long, and they know who they are. We are so grateful for everyone who prays for and with us. Together we have a wealth of answered prayer, and I could fill books with the miracle of it all.

I trust the Father is magnified and the cross of His Son lifted high in the following pages. If so, His Holy Spirit will bless and heal through them. For this, we thank God the Father, Son, and Holy Spirit in advance.

Preface

But I, when I am lifted up from the earth, will draw all men to myself.

(Jesus, quoted in John 12:32)

*T*his work is the companion volume to *The Healing Presence*, and although it can easily be read on its own, it builds on the theological and psychological foundation laid in that book. These books are not twins. This volume is a continuation of the first, and together they constitute the main body of work and ministry presented in our healing seminars and Pastoral Care Ministry Schools.

In the ministry of prayer for healing of the soul, we are continually helping Christians to hurdle one or another of the three great barriers to personal and spiritual wholeness in Christ. They are 1) the failure to gain the great Christian virtue of self-acceptance, 2) the failure to forgive others, and 3) the failure to receive forgiveness for oneself.

Every time we more fully understand *and accept* our true identities in Christ, forgive another, or confess a sin, barriers to our becoming mature disciples—all we were created to be—fall down. But at times we are unable on our own to understand what is blocking us, much less how to remove it. Then we need the ministry of others in order to walk in freedom. God's love is blocked and unable to flow freely into our brokenness; one of his servants must therefore help us to receive the healing. Part of the discipling process is to help others discern what their barriers are and then through healing prayer to lead them out of the prison house and into the freedom of maturity in Christ.

Our work begins where God's grace has laid the foundation; we are not to save souls, but to disciple them. Salvation and sanctification are the work of God's sovereign grace; our work as His disciples is to disciple lives until they are wholly yielded to God.[1]

The First and Primary Healing

True religion is the union of the Spirit of God with the human spirit, and this is effected in and through Jesus Christ. "He that is joined to the Lord is one Spirit." Jesus is the Mediator between God and man. He reveals the Father, unites us with the Father, and comes with the Father to make His home with us (John 14:21-23).[2]

As Oswald Chambers and F. B. Meyer remind us, the first and primary healing out of which all other healing proceeds is the new birth. Once Christ abides within, one with our spirits, then His life can radiate throughout our souls—that is, our minds and hearts—including our memories, our willing (volitional), feeling, intuitive, and imaginative faculties, and beyond that, even to our sensory and physical being. Then, as His light encounters dark places of unforgiveness and woundedness within us, healing can take place.

I will start with the failure to accept oneself, for so many Christians today are stuck at this very point. Once this stumbling block is hurdled, we can then forgive and receive forgiveness from the mature standpoint of who we are *in Christ*. To accept oneself is to be enabled to live out of one's true center, that is, out of the "new man" or the true self in Christ. The true center is the place where we *abide* in Christ. One who dwells there "walks in the Spirit" and is out from under the control of the sinful nature; he *abides* in union with the One who completes him. Such a man or woman wears the robe of Christ's righteousness; he deeply understands his justification and his at-one-ment in Christ and can therefore most truly glory always in the cross of Christ. He or she knows, beyond all shadow of a doubt, that "there is now no condemnation for those who are in Christ Jesus, because through Christ Jesus the law of the Spirit of life set me free from the law of sin and death" (Romans 8:1-2).

Today, there is a multitude of Christians whose failure to accept themselves is accompanied by a needless and ongoing sense of guilt and shame, or even more critically, an intense and even pathological self-hatred. Often these persons have come to Christ out of dysfunctional homes and environments, places where evil has, whether overtly or more subtly, run rampant, ravaging their spirits and souls, if not their bodies as well. These have been robbed of even the most basic childhood pleasures, indeed, of the experience of childhood itself. The problems of shame and self-hatred can be so intense that these persons can hardly receive teaching or even prayer for healing until we have helped them to acknowledge before Christ this self-hatred. It is then in His Presence that the large step of renouncing this hatred is taken. Once this infirmity of soul is faced and dealt with, these persons are able to open their hearts and begin to receive from God the healing they need.

For that reason then—so that *all* can enter into the teaching on self-acceptance and take the necessary steps toward achieving it—I will begin with self-hatred and prayer for renouncing it.

The cross, with its forgiveness of sin and transmission of the very life of God to us through the shed blood of Christ, is the doorway to the removal of all three barriers. Indeed, it is the doorway to all that is authentically Christian.

PART I

THE VIRTUE OF
SELF-ACCEPTANCE

*It is often said today . . . that we must love ourselves
before we can be set free to love others. This is certainly
the release which we must seek to give our people. But no
realistic human beings find it easy to love or to forgive
themselves, and hence their self-acceptance must be
grounded in their awareness that God accepts them in
Christ. There is a sense in which the strongest self-love
that we can have, in the sense of agape, is merely the
mirror image of the lively conviction we have that God
loves us. There is endless talk about this in the church, but
little apparent belief in it among Christians, although they
may have a conscious complacency which conceals the
subconscious despair which Kierkegaard calls "the
sickness unto death."*

(Richard Lovelace, *Dynamics of Spiritual Life:
An Evangelical Theology of Renewal*)[1]

CHAPTER 1

Self-Hatred: The Traitor Within
When Temptation Comes

*The old Puritan idea that the devil tempts men had this remarkable effect,
it produced the man of iron who fought; the modern idea of blaming his
heredity or his circumstances produces the man who succumbs at once.*[1]

(Oswald Chambers)

*B*efore a large overseas Pastoral Care Ministries (PCM) conference, Clay
McLean was driving across the country toward a city where he was to hold
what proved to be very important and fruitful meetings. These were just prior
to his joining the rest of the team for the overseas meetings. He was not long
on the road when he suddenly found himself enmeshed in spiritual warfare. It
was coming in the form of an intense temptation to fall into sexual sin. He actually saw in his spirit dark figures that he thought were not just ordinary demons,
but large dark "powers" following him.

On this occasion Clay had to travel alone, something that had always been
hard for him. He had gotten into his car for the long journey feeling somewhat
anxious. Some of his old feelings of intense loneliness and rejection were plagu-
ing him. He had particularly suffered from self-hatred in the past, and some of
this old behavior had returned.

Although Clay wasn't thinking rationally at this point and couldn't see
clearly what was happening, the enemy was tempting him to once again wal-
low in self-hatred and the devastating self-pity that had accompanied it. The
accuser of his soul was also reminding him of past hurts and rejections, of sins
and grievous failures that had occurred before God began to heal him emotionally and set into him a sense of psychological well-being.

This temptation to fall was a powerful last-ditch attempt to rob Clay of the possessions unique to himself as a person—first, his *oneness* with God and his new self inherent in that oneness, and second, his creative capacity to collaborate with God to bring forth lasting fruit in the Kingdom of God. Oswald Chambers had a firm hold on this phenomenon: "Temptation is," he says, "the testing by an alien power of the possessions held by a personality."

> In the temptation (of Christ) the devil antagonized the same thing that he antagonized in the first Adam, viz., oneness with God.[2]

> Satan does not tempt us to do wrong things; he tempts us in order to make us lose what God has put into us by regeneration, viz., the possibility of being of value to God.[3]

Why Temptation?

There is another side to these occurrences, and that is the sure knowledge that God not only knows about them, but has (even as with Job) allowed them. Why does God allow the Devil to tempt us? First of all, in a fallen world, we are necessarily tempted, not only by the sin without, but the (albeit unconscious) sin within. As Christians who are not sinning consciously and willfully, it is all too easy for us to forget the depth of sin in the human heart. Also, as moderns who are fed on a steady diet of secular psychological wisdom, it is even easier for us to rationalize our own sins and deficiencies and to transfer the blame for them onto others. When we are rationalizing our sins, we are not looking up to God, trusting in Him, and listening for the healing word. It is therefore necessary that temptation and trial compel us to face honestly what is in our hearts. This is, as Chambers says, "in order that a higher and nobler character may come out of the test."[4]

No one with a ministry worth having has escaped this testing, and the tests differ according to our weaknesses—those very things within us that need healing. This is one more reason why, with the greatest of joy and no hesitancy or apology whatsoever, we call people to a radical obedience to Christ.[5] Such obedience requires that we confront, acknowledge, and repent of our sin and propensity toward sin immediately as it becomes conscious. We are thereby spared dreadful suffering, humiliating falls, and perhaps even a lifetime of regret. Too, we discover for ourselves the truth of St. Paul's words: "No temptation has seized you except what is common to man. And God is faithful; he will not let you be tempted beyond what you can bear. But when you are tempted, he will also provide a way out so that you can stand up under it" (1 Corinthians 10:13).

Surely, one of the greatest benefits of learning to undergo the kind of testing that reveals our inner weaknesses is that, if we can correct them early, we can avoid misleading others. David's prayer, offered after acknowledging sin in his life, occupies a prominent place in my prayer journal. Should I forget to pray it, then I will often be reminded: "Let none of those who look to thee be shamed on my account, O Lord God of Hosts; Let none who seek thee be humbled through my fault, O God of Israel" (Psalm 69:6, NEB).

The Way of Escape

In our conferences, I say a lot about creativity. We see people mightily affirmed in their capacity to collaborate with God, and thereby enabled to be the "maker"[6] God has created them to be. This always runs counter to the demonic temptation to self-hatred, self-pity, and to a debilitating sense of shame and inferiority. I have learned to instruct people, as soon as temptation strikes, to invoke the Presence, saying, "Come, Lord Jesus," and then to *practice the Presence of God,* with, within, and all about them. In this way, they immediately get themselves centered; they *abide* in God. They know and affirm their position in God—that they are *in Christ* and He *in them.* Then sometimes immediately, and always amazingly, the demonic force and spiritual warfare recedes. What at first seems overwhelming in its power to overshadow, slime, and hold us in its foul clutches simply fades backward, declawed and whimpering. Oswald Chambers expresses it this way:

> When temptation comes, stand absolutely true to God no matter what it costs you, and you will find the onslaught leaves you with affinities higher and purer than ever before.[7]

This is what Clay did. All this occurred just before God poured out blessing after blessing upon him and paved the way for two more remarkable healings which I will refer to later. In fact, his battle with temptation was all a prelude to the more powerful and effective ministry he now exercises.

The renunciation of self-hatred is no small step to take, especially for those whose personalities have been formed by these attitudes from early on. It requires that we open ourselves wide to the full spectacle and meaning of the cross, that we allow ourselves to be confronted by Christ crucified, not only for our sin but for the evils we have suffered. We cry out, "Lord, I believe! Help thou mine unbelief!" and then go on to receive fully into ourselves all that flows out of His Atonement: justification, sanctification, a full incarnation (baptism or indwelling) of the Holy Spirit, authority in personal and spiritual conflict: i.e., redemption, healing, and full affirmation of who we are in God.[8]

The renunciation of self-hatred is a deliberate (volitional) step we take, and we keep our eyes on the Source of our salvation, not on our subjective feelings, which are unreliable and even "diseased" due to the habitual attitudes we've formed. As we do this, God honors our transaction and showers His grace upon us. We then do battle with all the diseased and negative thoughts and imaginings, lifting them up to Him as they arise in our hearts and minds.

Of course, it takes longer for some Christians—for example, those suffering with over-scrupulousity or perfectionism, or with gross sin and/or perversion in their backgrounds—to finally come out of self-hatred. For them, the root causes underlying their self-hatred, psychological as well as spiritual, are simply more complicated and entangled. As they move toward self-acceptance, these things surface to be spread out before God in prayer.

When Clay first attended a PCM, he sat on the very back row. After about the fifth or sixth one he attended, I asked him to move up front. That is when I found out how he, even as a Christian, "felt about" himself. Though a minister of the gospel who helped those who were the neediest, he felt himself so foul as to fear he would contaminate the ministry team if he sat too close to them.

There are usually (as in Clay's case) several key healings that take place before these deeply wounded ones enter into a full and secure acceptance of themselves as persons. In the meantime, we as ministers and counselors have to help them understand how dangerous and even sinful self-hatred is and how the evil one uses the failure to accept and celebrate the new self in Christ to tempt them to sin. Self-hatred, with its shame and self-pity, is a powerful and compelling means the enemy uses to tempt these precious, gifted souls to step entirely outside the true self and into the old with all its uncreative behavior and sin.

Clay had been delivered out of the hands of Baal, the idol god of sexual orgy, compulsion, and neurosis.[9] Had Clay succumbed to temptation and fallen sexually in his testing, he would once again have found himself in the clutches of Baal. Because of the emotional injuries and deprivations of his childhood, his battle with that loathsome idol had been fierce beyond description and almost claimed his life. And it was these very injuries and circumstances that caused his severe self-hatred. Not only would he have had to once again fight for his sanity, he would also have had the matter of idolatry to deal with, for "temptation yielded to is lust deified."[10]

It is tragic to see Christian leaders fall. There is, even as St. Paul has said, no need to live from the lower self, obeying its drives: "So then, my brothers, there is no necessity for us to obey our unspiritual selves or to live unspiritual lives. If you do live in that way, you are doomed to die; but if by the Spirit you put an end to the misdeeds of the body you will live" (Romans 8:12-13, *Jerusalem Bible*). Christians must, however, acknowledge their need for emotional healing and seek it. Failure to deal with inner insecurities and self-hatred, thereby failure to gain a secure identity in Christ, is the most common underlying weakness in these falls.

Clay has learned the practice of the Presence of Christ, and thereby his at-one-ment with Him. To learn this is to understand the great and grave doctrine of our justification in Him. In a joy that still takes him by surprise, Clay now often phones me from different parts of the globe just to exclaim something like the following: "I'm the happiest man in all Texas. No, in all the world, I'm the most blessed of men!" This is the way one so gifted in Christ and now free to allow that creativity to flow will feel; this is the way any man or woman will feel once released from the hell of self-hatred. This healing is ours in the cross of Christ; it has already been accomplished by Christ's death and resurrection.

We need only receive it, as the full message and efficacy of His cross is applied to our wounds as well as to our sins.

PRAYER OF RENUNCIATION OF SELF-HATRED

For God caused Christ, who himself knew nothing of sin, to *be* sin for our sakes, so that in Christ we might be made good with the goodness of God. (2 Corinthians 5:21, *J. B. Phillips,* emphasis in Phillips's text)

Prayer of Thanksgiving

Holy Father, I thank You that I am reconciled to You through the death of Your Son, and that through faith in Him as my Savior from sin, my heart is not only washed clean from my own sin, but it can be delivered from its grievous reactions to the sins and shortcomings of others around and against it. Because of Your Son, Father, I can look straight up to You and dare to let all these feelings surface, and I do so now, knowing that Christ is ready to take them and give me in exchange His Life and Your perspective on myself and others. Accept my thanksgiving, O God our Father. I thank You for Christ who has redeemed me from sin and death and who is even now pouring His eternal life into me.

Lord Jesus Christ, Son of the Father, in whom I am to abide, to fully live, move, and have my being (my true and new self), I direct my thanksgiving to You. I bow before You as Lord of my life, and I thank You, Precious Holy One, crucified for me, that Your blood justifies me, that in oneness with You, Your goodness is mine.

Holy Spirit, Thou who dost so constantly and faithfully mediate to us the love of both Father and Son, I thank You now for the grace to receive all that is mine as a child of God. Empower me now as I renounce the sin of self-hatred and as I move toward the goal of wholly accepting my true identity as a child of God the Father, Son, and Holy Spirit.

Pray quietly, giving thanks. If diseased feelings start to surface, simply allow them to flow, one at a time up and out of your heart and mind and into the Crucified One. Note them later in your prayer journal, not only so you can converse with God about them, but recognize and refuse them if and when they return asking readmittance to your heart. Now see Him dying on the cross to take those things into Himself. Then see Him risen again, ascending to the Father, there to intercede to the Father for you, to pour out upon you His Spirit, to send to you words of life that engender in you new and wholesome feelings and attitudes. And give thanks.

Prayer of Petition

You may want to lift, simply and clearly, petitions to the Lord at this time. A prayer such as the following might be in order. It will better prepare you to make your renunciation of self-hatred.

Well you know, O Lord, that I have been unable to appropriate Your holiness and righteousness as I wish; I have been unable to practice Your Presence because my feelings about myself are so diseased. I have looked to You, just now, as my dying Savior, taking into Yourself my sin and darkness, my diseased feelings about You, others, myself. I thank You that You have done this and that in time even my feeling self will reflect this. Heretofore, Lord, I have taken my eyes from You and from objective truth and have descended into and lived out of my unhealed feeling self. This, with Your help, Lord, I will cease doing, and I will note the very moment I am "living out of" that subjective, hurting place and will look straight up to You for the healing word You are always sending. I confess to You the sin of pride that is bound up in my self-hatred. I thank You for Your forgiveness and for full release from it.

For greater understanding of the humility that replaces this pride, see page 49.

Prayer of Renunciation

*Now, Lord, in Your Name and with the grace You shower upon me,
I renounce the sin of self-hatred.*

Quietly give thanks for God's forgiveness.

With this renunciation, a multitude of accusing thoughts or maybe even root causes behind the self-hatred may begin to surface. Simply write them down in your prayer journal, acknowledging them, and then listen for the thought or the illumination God is sending you, for this will be the word from Him that not only replaces the diseased thought pattern but will flood you with understanding.

CHAPTER 2

First Great Barrier to Wholeness in Christ: Failure to Accept Oneself

Jesus then said to His disciples: "If anyone wishes to be a follower of Mine, he must leave self behind; he must take up his cross and come with Me. Whoever cares for his own safety is lost; but if a man will let himself be lost for my sake, he will find his true self. What will a man gain by winning the whole world at the cost of his true self? Or what can he give that will buy that self back?"

(Matthew 16:24-26, NEB)

If you are led by the Spirit, you are not under law.

(Galatians 5:18)

*T*here is a line over which many of us never step. That is the line between

Immaturity
───────────
Maturity

Being under the Law, a law, or many laws
─────────────────────────────────────
The walk in the Spirit

Listening to many voices: those within our
unhealed hearts, and of the world, the flesh, the devil
───
Listening to God

It is the line between bondage and freedom. Accepting oneself is the vital step to be taken in order to cross this line.

One sensitive, loving priest said to me, "I seem to have many who—after making full confession of sin, after healing of memories, after a release of the Spirit in their lives—yet look to me for *something* else. They look up from the Communion cup, from laying-on-of-hands. . . . What is it they are straining for?" I knew the answer: They are straining to come into the freedom that is in fact theirs—but they've been unable to cross over the line. They are still dependent, immature, in some way. They are looking for permission to act, to be.

These folk need to get through the formidable barrier of failure to accept themselves; they need to cross over into the maturity to which Christ calls them.

A person may not accept himself when he is very self-centered, selfish, and has not died to the old self. He experiences real guilt, and it is a good thing that he is sorely afflicted with it. He cannot say with St. Paul and the Christian: "For we know that our old self was crucified with Him so the body of sin might be done away with, that we should no longer be slaves of sin" (Romans 6:6).

It is therefore a mercy that he heartily dislikes and fails to accept that self, that he has honest negative thoughts about himself. But we must differentiate between the self that collaborates with the principle of evil and selfishness, and the self that abides in Christ and collaborates with Him. That is the true self. That is the justified new creation, the soul that is saved and lives eternally. The former self we deliberately and continually die to; the other we joyfully and in great humility and thankfulness accept.

It is true that once we are able to accept and celebrate the new self, we tend to forget this new creation as such, for we are focused on Christ who is our Lodestar, who is (beyond what we can now think or imagine) our life. We are simply too engaged in looking to Him, in obeying and collaborating with Him in His mission to love the world through us. And we say, along with St. Paul: "To me to live is Christ." But it is only with the full acceptance of this new self that we find our true center, that place of quiet strength and solid *being*, that center from which we know and see ourselves to be white-robed in the very righteousness of Christ Himself. It is from this center of oneness with Christ that we can cry out with Isaiah and the saints of old: "I delight greatly in the Lord; my soul rejoices in my God. For he has clothed me with garments of salvation and arrayed me in a robe of righteousness, as a bridegroom adorns his head like a priest, and as a bride adorns herself with her jewels" (Isaiah 61:10).

We need to recognize when this outward focus on Christ has been seriously blocked by the failure to accept ourselves.[1] We need to recognize and do something about the diseased attitudinal patterns toward the self, those formed in the crucible of the various accidents and deprivations of our past.

I can be a Christian filled with the Spirit of God, but if I hate myself, the light of God is going to emanate through me in distorted ways. I will still be seeing myself through the eyes of others around me, those who perhaps could not love or affirm me. I will not be seeing myself through the eyes of God; I will not be listening for the affirming as well as the corrective words He is always speaking to me, His beloved child. I will be dependent upon others, perhaps grievously bent toward them; I will be seeking their affirmation, their validation, and even their permission for my every move. Failing to accept myself, I will have no solid center, therefore I will "walk alongside myself."[2] I will suffer what the Scriptures name as lack of maturity and lack of freedom and will be a "man-pleaser" rather than a "God-pleaser." Truly, "it is for freedom that Christ has set us free" (Galatians 5:1), but I will know little of the walk in the Spirit; my spirit, unable to soar in the sunlight of all God has done for me, will flutter against the prisonhouse bars.

The other great blocks to wholeness in Christ—the failure to forgive others, and/or to receive forgiveness for ourselves—have to do with more or less specific memories and rejections. In contrast, the failure to accept oneself is an attitudinal block. It has to do with how we perceive and feel about ourselves and others. We develop immature, negative patterns of relating to God and to others when we've failed to come into a mature self-acceptance. Our inner vision of ourselves is diseased. This does not mean that we understand any better than the next Christian the depth of sin in the human heart; in fact, such a deficient view of the self cannot recognize, understand, and fully appropriate its justification in Christ, but is rather turned in on the self in a narcissistic way.[3]

Fr. Michael Scanlon, in his book *Inner Healing*, states that, "We have an attitudinal life which operates from the very core of our being. . . . This life determines broad general patterns of relating to others and to God." He then speaks of five different problem patterns that alert him to a need to pray for what he calls a "heart healing." These are:

1) A judgmental spirit that is harsh and demanding on self and others.
2) A strong perfectionist attitude demanding the impossible from self and others.
3) A strong pattern of fearing future events.
4) A sense of aloneness and abandonment in times of decision.
5) A preoccupation with one's own guilt and a compulsion to compete for position and success.[4]

Enveloping all of these patterns, or overarching them, is the inability to accept oneself and thereby go on to emotional and psychological freedom. In fact, even one of these patterns in a life indicates that the person has not achieved the important step of self-acceptance.

In the more painful cases, I hear remarks such as the following: "I have never liked myself; I hate myself; I was a mistake; I should never have been born; I just don't seem to fit in anywhere."

As Fr. Scanlon has noted, these patterns are present in an otherwise deeply religious life. Usually there is a constant expectation of growth or breakthrough to new spiritual freedom, but it doesn't happen. Why? Because, he says, the heart is hurting. It will continue to hurt so long as the diseased attitudinal patterns remain.

These dear ones often come to me or to some other minister of healing and ask for "one more prayer" for healing of memories. "Please," they will say, "there must be one more memory that needs healing." Their persistence and out-right tenacity in looking for healing (which for them would be the magic break-through) is amazing in that it seems almost endless. That is because the pain is endless, the heart is constricted, and the pain grows rather than lessens through the years due to the bonds that constitute the failure to be affirmed as a man or as a woman, as a person in one's own right.

How are these people healed? What is their need? Their crying need is to exchange old patterns of relating to life for new ones, to build in new patterns of thinking about themselves and others, of seeing themselves and others, of relating to themselves and others. In order to do this, they must learn to listen—to God and to their own hearts. There is nothing that will bring these souls through the failure to accept the self more quickly and thoroughly than the prac-tice of "listening prayer." Through it, they will begin seeing themselves through the eyes of the Master Affirmer, our Heavenly Father.

This listening involves, of course, coming into the Presence of God and there receiving His Word and illumination as to why we feel the way we do, why we do the things we do. It involves writing down every negative, untrue, and irrational thought and attitudinal pattern as we become aware of it. For some, this is almost a full-time task at first. I've had a number of people exclaim to me, "Oh, but you don't understand! Every thought I have is negative!" Oh yes, I do understand, and all the more reason why such a one has to get his pri-orities straight and enter into conversation with God as though it were his only lifeline. It probably is. The alternative, a failure to understand why we think or hurt the way we do, is too terrible to think about.

When we write down our diseased patterns of thought, we must always lis-ten to Him for the healing, positive, true words and patterns that are to replace the dark, negative ones! That is how we gain the mind of God and get rid of dis-eased patterns of thought. We first *acknowledge* we have them; then we find what they are rooted in and why we have them. Finally, we confess and get rid of them by yielding them up to God and taking in exchange the true word He is sending.

In the doing of this, we begin to realize that we are holding onto some of these old patterns, that we have a real resistance to letting them go. We find that they are often, in fact, defense mechanisms against the pain of growing up, of being vulnerable, of being responsible. At first, as Fr. Scanlon has said, we don't usually recognize them for what they are—old wounds used to escape reality, to justify failure, to gain attention and affection.

One of the saints has cautioned us: "Be wary of sickness." I personally have had to be very wary of physical weakness. Its siren song calls me to sit back, to "retire" just a little. Deep in the American psyche is this idea of retiring at a cer-tain age, of resting on our laurels, of "letting other folk do the work." We do indeed need to be wary of a little physical illness and note the ways we allow it to shape our existence. This is even more true, it seems to me, of emotional pain. Whether the weakness is physical, emotional, or spiritual, we need to seek God's face, asking, "What is this pain all about? What are You saying to me through this?"

It is remarkable how often the pain is merely a signal to listen in order that we might know what the next step toward wholeness should be. The following example illustrates this point. A certain young man from a family of high achievers had from early childhood suffered depression and was subject to deep anxiety. The roots of this anxiety and depression were uncovered, and he experienced great healing. He was, in fact, free from anxiety and depression for the first time since he could remember.

One day he got in touch with me, saying that his depression was back. I asked him, "What happened just before you began to be depressed?" With a moment's thought, he said it was after friends had asked him what he needed prayer for, and he couldn't think of a thing. He began to be depressed from that moment on. He was rather taken aback when I exclaimed, "Praise the Lord! We now know what to pray about!"

The next step in his recovery was the realization that he could relate to other people only as a sick person. He had already begun to recognize old coping mechanisms, those that gave him a ready defense against the pain of growing up, that justified his lack of responsibility, and that gained him sympathy and affection. But now this pain signified the valid need he had of learning to relate to others as a person, and not on the basis of his neediness—indeed, learning to accept himself as a whole person. When we learn to listen, we are wary of sickness. We learn to discern what the pain is and what it is saying to us.

CHAPTER 3

Struggling Through to Self-Acceptance

Sally, a young wife and mother, came up to me after I had been speaking on this matter of self-acceptance and told me her story. As a teen, she could not accept her "tall body," as she referred to it. She felt her unusual height would affect her chances of marrying. But she turned the right key early in life, a key every Christian has been given—*she struggled in prayer before the Lord until she accepted her height.* In other words, she came before the Master Affirmer and entered into deep and obedient conversation with Him. In His Presence, listening, she not only accepted her height but made other important decisions, one being that she would not marry at all unless it was to a man who met the qualifications for a good husband. She could not have made this decision had she not first accepted herself. She was lovely, poised, self-assured, and had an especially fine husband, a beautiful marriage, good-looking, tall sons! Others accept her height because she accepts it.

The acceptance of herself made all the difference in the world in her ability to accept the blessings in life God had to give her. When we reject ourselves or any part of ourselves, we communicate that view to others. They most often take us at our own evaluation. It is important to those in the healing ministry to see troubled people as God sees them (the *real* persons behind the phenomenal ones), not as they see themselves.

Romano Guardini, Catholic philosopher-theologian, in his essay "The Acceptance of Oneself," writes:

> The act of self-acceptance is the root of all things. I must agree to be the person who I am. Agree to have the qualifications which I have. Agree to live within the limitations set for me. . . . The clarity and the courageousness of this acceptance is the foundation of all existence.[1]

Nonacceptance ranges from the rejection of some physical aspect of our being to a wholesale hatred or rejection of oneself. Today this failure is being written about in terms such as low self-esteem, lack of affirmation, unmet emotional needs and love hunger as they emerge out of the dysfunctional family, and failing to like or to love oneself.[2]

I use the older term, *self-acceptance,* however, for several reasons. For one, the way I use the term, it includes all the above. Under its umbrella we look at the various traumas and unmet needs that have led to distorted thinking about oneself and others. In the ministry of healing prayer, we are concerned with basic love deficits, those that have rendered us unable to love others or receive love as we should. These gaping holes in people's souls are what God so yearns to gain admittance to, into which He longs to pour His healing life. But in addition, I use the term *self-acceptance* because it stands for a positive goal we as Christians are to reach. It denotes an authentic and necessary Christian virtue, one that is available to all who seek it.

There is yet another very practical reason. We live in a narcissistic age, one in which a sinful and blatant self-centeredness is the *in* thing and is being preached. Some who write on esteeming and loving oneself are confusing sinful and/or simplistic modes with healthy self-acceptance. Others are writing about *self-realization*—something that is not Christian. "We are not called to self-realization but to identification with Christ."[3]

A contemporary example of a mistaken attempt at self-realization is the search for "my lost child," i.e., the girl or boy that I was, or somehow could have been apart from the unhealthy circumstances I faced. There is something ephemeral about the self at any stage of our development. When the person who was neglected or abused in childhood looks to Christ, forgives others, and is forgiven, he or she can find healing of childhood memories. In this way, our Lord does in a very real way come present to the wounded "inner child." But He deals with people as the adults they are, and when He heals our memories (from any age), we simply find a greater integration of who we are in Him. But we will never find "our lost child" by looking for it. Our true self at any stage of our becoming is in Christ. He is the road out of the hell of the self-centered life.

> Your real new self will not come as long as you are looking for it. It will come when you are looking for Him. . . .[4]

In love we escape from our self into Him and into one another.[5]

This, the Christian view, is in contrast, indeed it is antithetical to the various worldly modes of self-actualization and self-realization.

On the other hand, the self-hatred and self-depreciation that accompanies our failure to accept ourselves is not Christian; it is utterly destructive toward the self. Totally pernicious, there is not one good thing in it. It is only after we have accepted ourselves that we are free to love others. If we are busy hating that soul that God loves and is in the process of straightening out, we cannot help others—our minds will be riveted on ourselves—not on Christ who is our wholeness. When we hate the self, we in fact practice the presence of the old self; we are *self*-conscious rather than *God*-conscious. Agnes Sanford, writer on healing prayer, said, "Jesus died for us, not that our souls should die but that they should live! It is only our inherited drive toward evil that is potentially destroyed."

Grievously erroneous and unchristian ideas concerning denying and hating oneself have long been propagated in one form or another in certain Christian circles. These ideas do not distinguish between the two selves—the old self which must be put to death and the new which is to be encouraged.[6] Persons holding these misunderstandings apparently try to combat the wrong kind of self-love by teaching people to love others but not themselves. These errors in thought are unscriptural but firmly entrenched, causing their adherents at times to lash out wildly at anyone who recognizes that there are beautiful as well as dark things within the human breast. The Apostle Paul is often quoted, "I know that within me dwells no good thing," and then, strangely, his qualifying phrase is omitted. Paul's subject here is the old sin nature, and he is saying that within *it* there is no good thing. "I know that nothing good lives in me, that is, *in my sinful nature*" (Romans 7:18, emphasis added).

The simple fact is that if we do not humbly accept ourselves, we cannot love and accept others. If we are hypercritical of ourselves, we will also criticize others. Walter Trobisch quotes the German psychotherapist Dr. Guido Groeger, who states that:

Because this affirmation is often withheld—especially in Christian circles— a type of Christian is created who loves out of duty and who in this way tortures not only others, but also himself.[7]

These erroneous perspectives not only influence people to disregard and downgrade what is right and good (talents and gifts from God), but train them in the tragic art of killing not the old but the new, creative self. The effects of these perspectives grow more telling with each successive generation.

As counselors, we have to know that:

At the root of every depression is the feeling of having lost something. . . . The deepest root of depression is the feeling that I have lost myself and have given up hope of ever finding myself again. There is nothing in me worth loving. . . . This means that self-acceptance and depression are closely related.[8]

Recently, after speaking on self-acceptance to a large group of deeply wounded people, we moved into prayer for healing. This particular Pastoral Care Ministries School was sponsored by Rev. Andrew Comiskey and those affiliated with Desert Stream, a ministry to sexually broken people. For a great many of these hurting ones there was a history of depression, the sort that can evolve out of the circumstances of a lost childhood. Then, as Andy Comiskey and Fr. William Beasley stood up with me to pray for them, anguished wails erupted from one young man, and then from others. The deepest root of their depression had been tapped, and the Holy Spirit began powerfully to minister into it. For many there that night, what had been an insurmountable barrier to wholeness was lifted. Christ came present to their worst memories, and they were enabled to yield these up to Him. They walked out of depression and into light.

From a neurotic fixation on the wounded "inner child," then, the suffering Christian's gaze becomes riveted upon the wounds of Christ. Therein is our healing. He takes upon and into Himself our darkness and depression and gives us in exchange His light and life.

In order to accept ourselves, we need to learn with C. S. Lewis the following lesson:

> Since I have begun to pray, I find my extreme view of personality changing. My own empirical self is becoming more and more important, and this is the opposite of self-love. You don't teach a seed how to die into treehood by throwing it into the fire: and it has to become a good seed before it's worth burying.[9]

I have prayed for persons whose parents have, as a matter of religious principle, withheld from them *all* affirmation. Only recently, I prayed with a man who is cut off from his feeling being. He can feel nothing—not sadness, not joy, not anger—though he is often sad, angry, and ever without joy. He learned to cope with his parents' methodical *disaffirmation* by dying utterly to his feeling being. He serves Christ as best he can, but without the power to name or feel emotion. I prayed for the healing of his feeling being, which could not have been more damaged had he been raised by alcoholic or sexually abusive parents.

Parents symbolize God to their young. If the Christian father who teaches his son or daughter about God is himself a stern and unfeeling judge, the child will, apart from some very unusual and happy circumstance, perceive God the Father in that way. If a child's Christian parents are impossible to please, the child will almost certainly perceive God in the same way. Until healing takes place and the damaged psyche is resymbolized,[10] such a one cannot hear God's "well done" spoken over him. He cannot understand and receive the affirmation the Father is continually pouring out upon His children or the promises that they shall have "glory"—meaning approval, favor, appreciation, and even fame with God!

> When I began to look into this matter, I was shocked to find such different Christians as Milton, Johnson and Thomas Aquinas taking heavenly glory quite frankly in the sense of fame or good report. But not fame conferred by our fellow creatures—fame with God, approval or (I might say) "appreciation" by God. And then, when I had thought it over, I saw that this view was scriptural; nothing can eliminate from the parable the divine *accolade*, "Well

done, thou good and faithful servant." With that, a good deal of what I had been thinking all my life fell down like a house of cards. I suddenly remembered that no one can enter heaven except as a child; and nothing is so obvious in a child—not in a conceited child, but in a good child—as its great and undisguised pleasure in being praised. Not only in a child, either, but even in a dog or a horse. Apparently what I had mistaken for humility had, all these years, prevented me from understanding what is in fact the humblest, the most childlike, the most creaturely of pleasures—nay, the specific pleasure of the inferior: the pleasure of a beast before men, a child before its father, a pupil before his teacher, a creature before its Creator.[11]

In his book *The Healing of Memories,* Dr. David Seamands has two chapters on distorted concepts of God, how they form, and the counselor's need to understand and deal aright with these infirmities within the soul. As he states, the key to understanding the "distorting of God's character" in those whose "love perceptors" are so skewed and damaged is to look at the

unhealthy interpersonal relationships, especially those which occurred during the early development years of childhood and adolescence. More than any other factor, these faulty relationships cause the emotional damages which distort spiritual perceptions.[12]

For those who need to deal with distorted perceptions of God, I recommend a prayerful reading of these chapters by Dr. Seamands, together with a Scriptural study of the love of God the Father. In addition to looking up the Scriptural references on the love of God, writing them in your prayer journal, and then personalizing them to yourself, you may want to read books such as Robert Frost's *Our Heavenly Father* or *Testaments of Love* (scholarly) by Leon Morris. To begin deliberately celebrating God as the divine Affirmer and the one who bestows favor on you, I recommend a small book entitled *Favor* by Bob Buess (P. O. Box 7110, Tyler, TX 75711) and C. S. Lewis's essay "The Weight of Glory," in his book by the same name.

Molly, Child of Divorce

She was fatherless and unaffirmed. A Christian wife and mother who had a successful ministry to others, Molly (not her real name) was in dire need of accepting herself. She had tried everything she knew to help herself, but had become increasingly mired in emotional and spiritual confusion. She also had serious physical problems which her doctors thought were related to her deep and continuing emotional unrest.

When she finally got quiet enough and gained the courage to face what was in her own heart, the key thing that came up was, "I have always hated myself." She was well versed in the Scriptures, but she could never get past the injunction to "die to the old man." This she had tried with all her might to do, but because she had never accepted herself, she succeeded only in dying to the *real self*.

Molly's parents were divorced when she was quite small. Her father had deserted the family. This was to her a terrible personal rejection that had affected her entire life, but she was largely in denial about it. Needing to maintain some kind of idealized image of the absent father, she projected the blame for her hurt and confusion onto her mother. For example, she charged her with "leaving me and going to work." When questioned, she realized this was irrational. Her mother was forced to work in order to gain their living.

A child takes the loss of a parent, whether through death, divorce, or however, as a personal rejection. Unhealed rejections become seedbeds of diseased "matter" such as bitterness, envy, rage, fear of rejection, and a sense of inferiority. When these things fester inside us, they greatly impact the way we hear and perceive others, who in turn become easy targets of the "missiles" these diseased attitudes and feelings project outward. Like poison-filled arrows, these darts of envy, bitterness, and so on find their mark in the minds and hearts of those we love the most. This is one of the reasons why, until we accept ourselves, we are dangerous to others as well as to ourselves. We are apt to misread their best intentions and slander them. This includes, of course, the way we see and speak of God as well.[13]

Stories like Molly's are legion. In our dysfunctional society, her story, with modifications here and there, is more the rule than the exception. Many children raised in single-parent homes "project" in this way onto the parent who is there to receive it. In Molly's home, the faithful parent was being scapegoated. In the worst way, Molly needed the healing of her early memories of rejection by her father. It is easy to see from this how the wounded child can sustain not only the loss of one parent but, in effect, the loss of both.[14]

For Molly, then, there was no father figure, no protecting, caring male with whom to identify. Every child needs a father to reach up to, and if the father is not there or fails to respond, the child is not lifted up and out of the "nest," up and out of the feminine milieu. The child is not lifted up and out of mother, the source of being on the natural plane. This is a large element in a young man's being unable to accept himself as a man, as well as in male homosexuality, for the young lad is unable to get his identity separated from that of his mother, the feminine. He is barred from the necessary identification with the masculine, and his own masculinity goes "begging." It is not called into life. He is unaffirmed in his gender identity. The young girl is also called up and out of infancy and girlhood and on into a fulfilling womanhood by her father's capacity to affirm her as a feminine person at each stage of her growth. In this way, he helps her separate her identity from her mother's, and he affirms her as a person in her own right. Without the father's help, the struggle is prolonged and heightened.

Dr. Daniel Trobisch says that the masculine principle is one of orientation, direction, order, and responsibility. In loving dialogue with his children, the father "calls them out and points the way to the greater world." The mother, he says, "is like a circle, and the father is the one who draws them out from that circle to a goal."[15] This process of being drawn toward a goal is a psychological reality for the "fathered" child, as well as a physical, spiritual, and intellectual one.

Dr. Trobisch goes on to point out an immensely important and vital truth that we in the twentieth century really do not comprehend: "The father draws the circle (the feminine) as well, into the greater world." In this day, we are chiefly in trouble because men are in full flight from feminine values. (For more on masculinity and femininity, see *The Healing Presence* and *Crisis in Masculinity.*) They are not, as it were, conveyors of meaning (all the feminine values) into the world at large. With a few notable exceptions, the way is barred for the true feminine to enter into and inform the more masculine powers of orientation, direction, order, and responsibility.

So very much of the stuff of psychological healing has to do with something amiss in the identification process. We've failed to bond or to identify with either mother or father or both. On the other hand, we may have internalized the "bad" mother or father and find ourselves so entwined and entangled with their diseased thoughts and attitudes as to be unable to separate our own from theirs. As a consequence, then, we are hurting emotionally, floundering in our relationships, and seriously unaffirmed as persons. This affects every part of our being. Unbalanced and unaffirmed in the masculine and the feminine facets of our personalities, we invariably suffer same-sex and/or other-sex ambivalence as well. In other words, we are irrationally prejudiced toward others and have difficulty relating to them on the basis of their sex. As Dr. Karl Stern points out:

> Compared with the objective reality in which we adults live, the persons of our early life are overcharged with emotional significance. They are larger than life-size. And they have the peculiar property of being able to stain the image of persons whom we encounter subsequently.[16]

Though Molly had little understanding of how the loss of her father figured into her self-hatred, she was all the same suffering the inner deprivation of never having been fathered. Nor could her impoverished, overworked, and unprotected mother provide her a stable home life. She reached adolescence with no affirmation as a woman and as a person in her own right by her own father or a father substitute.

These days it is all too easy for the search for love and affirmation to end in sexual permissiveness. That was the route Molly's need had taken. Because of this, she did things in adolescence that still colored her view of herself. She despised and distrusted herself for those things even though she had long since asked forgiveness and had turned from all consciously known unrighteousness. Yet, she perceived herself as inferior, even base—because of her past. She hated herself. She was trapped in the *unaffirmed position.* Though thoroughly converted to Christ, she was psychologically unhealed.

Obviously, there was a problem with her practical theology. She had failed to *receive* the forgiveness God had long been holding out to her. But she also had failed to accept herself—a psychological as well as a spiritual problem.

Self-Acceptance: A Christian Virtue

Self-acceptance was once taught as a virtue to be attained. Besides teaching the cardinal virtues (faith, hope, love, wisdom, justice, temperance, courage), our forefathers in the faith taught others such as *patience with the self*. Of this great virtue, Romano Guardini writes: "So he who wishes to advance must always begin again. . . . Patience with oneself . . . is the foundation of all progress." Among others taught were the virtues of truthfulness, loyalty, orderliness, disinterestedness, gratitude, recollection, silence, along with this vital one of self-acceptance.[17]

Why was the virtue of self-acceptance taught? Simply because no one is born with the capacity to accept himself. Self-acceptance is now taught (if at all) as a psycho-social developmental step in educational psychology. Psychologists point out progressions from infancy to maturity, which involve many steps of psycho-social development. When we miss a step, we are in trouble.

Ideally, the step of self-acceptance comes just after puberty. It can hardly occur if we have missed earlier important steps in the identification process or if at puberty the affirming masculine father figure is missing. (For more on this topic, see my books *Crisis in Masculinity* and *The Broken Image*.) In these cases, there are unmet basic love needs,[18] and healing and insight is needed in order to clear the way for self-acceptance to take place. There will most likely be serious unhealed memories of rejection in the past.

Puberty and adolescence is the narcissistic stage for all of us. We are mainly concerned about our bodies. We look at ourselves in the mirror, examining every little bump on our faces, every inch of our torsos. We want to know if we have the right kind of equipment for being male or female, and we fear that we don't. Girls don't like the size of their busts (either too small or too large), the shape of their legs, the color and texture of their hair, *ad infinitum*. Boys often focus on their size (their physiques and genitalia), their physical strength, and their competence in sports. In this culture they often suffer a severe sense of sexual inferiority as they compare themselves to others.

To whatever degree we fail to emerge from this adolescent, narcissistic stage, we will be stuck in some form or manifestation of the wrong kind of self-love. Failing to love ourselves aright, we will love ourselves amiss. The rampant morbid practice of introspection[19] is one of the most prevalent of these narcissistic manifestations, and the anxious practice of it can be as pernicious to personality development as masturbation (when carried past puberty) and homosexuality—two of the more obvious examples of a love turned inward.[20] To achieve a healthy personality, we must pass from this self-centered stage to the self-acceptance that is full, secure. Whoever does not accept himself is engrossed with himself.

The myth of Narcissus is the story of adolescence. The youth, Narcissus, looks at his own reflection in the water and falls in love with himself. His attention fixed on his own image, he tumbles into it and drowns. This myth is especially apropos to the twentieth century. The great majority of folk have not emerged out of the adolescent, narcissistic state that C. S. Lewis calls "the dark ages in every life"—that time when "the most unideal senses and ambitions have been restlessly, even maniacally awake." He laments the cessation of the "truly imaginative" as the soul is given over in adolescence to this auto-erotic period.[21]

But the fact that a Christian has not accepted himself, indeed, has not entirely emerged out of the immature, narcissistic state, is not always so apparent. A Christian man, for example, unaffirmed as a man, may very well be fixed on an image of himself as a successful businessman, priest, financial wizard, or whatever. Just as Narcissus of old, he has "fallen into his own image," and the authentic self (with all its authentic desires) is drowned. Such a man does not know his identity as a *person in Christ;* indeed, he does not know himself as an authentic person. He is a masked man, one whose worth and identity are tied up in his role or roles. How he is perceived socially is more important to him than who he *is* privately. His roles obscure his failure to accept himself, but his son or daughter is painfully aware of the truth. Such a father cannot affirm his son or daughter, cannot call them up and out of puberty and adolescence into maturity. He is himself unaffirmed.

Karl Stern writes about what happens to a son or daughter who can identify with a parent only in a role. This happens when there is

> a marked discrepancy between the person's social role and the true person. . . . Such a rift between outer appearance and inner character exists in many of us. Many psychologists have made a distinction between "social ego" and ego proper, between "role" and person. Jung called the social ego *persona* in contrast to the personality. The word *persona* is derived from the concept of the mask. The actors on the stage of ancient Rome wore masks with mouthpieces through which the words sounded (*per-sonare*). The person in his social role is often quite different from the person as he appears in his intimate life. Many people become more dependent on their own *persona*. Their social ego, their role as bank president or railway conductor, has the same function as the exterior skeleton in crustaceae. *They are so united to their social ideal that they would collapse, and very little would remain, if one robbed them of their position in society. Children's growing selves are quite sensitive to this discrepancy. By a number of factors they become identified with social ideals rather than with human beings of flesh and blood.*[22] (italics mine)

During the process of identification children absorb our sense of values as if by osmosis. If our scale of values is that of an external hierarchy, our children cannot grow. Nobody can grow on synthetic stuff.[23]

Needless to say, women in the church have long been taught, not by the Scriptures but by those who misunderstand the doctrine of the submission of women, to find their identity, not in Christ, but in their roles as wife and mother.[24] We have to deal continually with the sons and daughters of these mothers, as well as with the mothers themselves. When the mother is unaffirmed, and the rift between the real woman and the role-mask is too great, the child identifies not with the woman but with her social ideals about what a woman is. The following will, I trust, illustrate this point.

This woman, now up in years, could not relate to her mother as a flesh and blood person, a problem the other children in the family shared. She was fortunate in that she had a warm, caring father who nurtured his sons and daughters. At the same time, however, she was harmed by the fact that he idealized and idolized his wife as "socially" a step or two above himself. He must have taught his children these attitudes, for they all, though distant from her, respected her for the same reasons.

Later on in life, this daughter had a self-image that was idealized and superficial in spite of a good relationship with her father. This was because she had identified not with her mother, but with her mother's social ideals regarding what a woman is. She acted this out all her life. She could not see a man as a real person, but only as someone who acted out what she perceived as a proper role, in response to the false image she had of herself as woman. Her relationships with others askew, this woman, a devout soul, has struggled all her life to accept herself. Her loyalty to the way her parents saw reality, however, was so strong that she was never able to face the real truth about her need.

If we have failed to accept ourselves, it is vitally important for our children as well as ourselves that we seek and find the great Christian virtue of self-acceptance. To the extent we fail to gain it, we fail to get through the developmental step that ideally comes just after puberty. We will not graduate from the narcissistic period and will be stuck in a wrong form of self-love, if it is only the concern over our own "inferiority" or shortcomings. We will be unable to celebrate our inadequacy, our smallness, knowing Christ to be our full sufficiency. We cannot pass affirmation on to another if we have not received it ourselves. To the extent we cannot accept ourselves, we will be unable to affirm our sons or daughters; we will be unable to see and call forth the real person in others.

The Importance of Fathers to Self-Acceptance

So then, on the human level the key to stepping from adolescence into self-acceptance is the love and affirmation of a father. Sally with the "long body" had an affirming, loving, mature father in the home. He imaged (symbolized aright) God the Father to her. At the same time she was praying through her difficulties in accepting herself, she was receiving the blessing of a Christian father. He was doing what only a father or good father substitute can do—he was affirming her in her womanliness, that which is *other* than himself and therefore crucially complementary to himself and the true masculine everywhere. In so doing, he released her otherness and her "secret"—her true feminine giftedness and wisdom. This then made it infinitely easier for her to settle the whole matter of her unusual height with her Heavenly Father. She could respond to Him, serene in the knowledge that His ultimate blessing too was upon her, and that He had only good gifts for her.

In contrast, Molly's father left when she was an infant, and the few times she had seen him, he was unable to sustain interest in her. He had never in any way been a support to her. The masculine voice and giftedness which should have come through him—all that could first bless and then in awe *hallow* the true feminine within her—was missing. Her "secret" lay untouched by the masculine *other*; it was unawakened, unrecognized, unblessed. There would be no release of the inner being who joyfully responds, in trust and without anxiety, to God and to others. Until healed, she would fear abandonment and even expect that she deserved such.

For Molly, then, there was no release of the true feminine, no fatherly finger pointing the way up and out to the greater world and to a secure place within it. Even though she was Christian, there was little rest in God the Father for her— that which complements the unique feminine capacity to simply be. She had little real understanding that she could look up to Him and receive what had been missing in her life. On the other hand, she felt a compelling need to deny her past and her sinfulness and to transfer blame for it onto others. There was the painful striving to be perfect on her own in order to win God's love and acceptance, and that of others.

A mother, no matter how whole and affirming she is, cannot bridge the gap left by a missing father, or one who is present but unable to love or affirm, or one who is hostile, weak, overinvolved with business. It is extremely odd and irrational that some would think she could.

The father, by the same token, cannot fill the void left by a whole, loving mother. It is in the love of a mother, in a self-giving and secure nurturing by her, that we come to an all-important *sense of being* or of *well-being*. If this is missing, then the best of fathers cannot affirm the child in his or her personal and gender identity until healing takes place.[25] In such cases, there will be an intense sense of deprivation along with bouts of depression and separation anxiety. The painful sense of nonbeing must be addressed in the Presence of God the Father, for only He can create a sense of being where one has had such a difficult start in life.

But just as the mother is so vital to those first months and even years (the infant does not know itself to be separate from its mother, and it is in her love and acceptance that it comes to a secure sense of being), so the father is vital in affirming the child's gender identity.

This is not to say that the love and affirmation of both parents aren't vitally important all along. It is simply to say that in the developmental steps the child takes, the parents do not have the same function. There is a stage between three to six years that is also extremely important to gender identity, and here again, the father is vital. He then, even as later, calls the child up and out of mother—calls it up and points the way outward into the world. Many times when I've prayed with men suffering homosexual neurosis, I found it was at this very point that something traumatic had happened. The memory relived is that of a rejection by the father that impeded their coming up and out of the feminine milieu and gender identity. While achieving a sense of being in a mother's love, the child must separate its identity from her. And the role the father plays here is critical. Needless to say, if a father is present but has no relationship with the child, he will be ineffective in these developmental stages.

During and after puberty, if all goes well, the father must effectively "come between" the son and the mother. In this way he helps his wife to release the son (her main work of mothering is finished). In affirming the son *as a man*, the father enables him to completely separate his sexual and gender identity from his mother's. He does much the same for his daughter, only in the matter of gender identity her need is not so critical as her brother's, for she is the *same* as her mother. But he is key in affirming his daughter as a person in her own right, and with his affirmation she will be secure in her own feminine identity.

It is in dialogue with others that we are called to life.[26] Our parents are our first dialogue partners, and their communication with us from conception on through adolescence is crucial to our development. It either calls us into life or fails to. If our parents were uncommunicative or communicative in the wrong way, we must make up for this deficit in wholesome ways. Our reactions to a parental failure in communication are what we must observe and rectify. We cannot deny gross deficits, but must recognize and come to terms with them. It is essential of course that we forgive our parents.[27] It is our grievous reactions to the shortcomings and sins of others against us that make up so much of the matter to be dealt with in healing prayer. Once these subjective reactions are identified and we set out with the help of God to change them, we are on our way to wholeness. It is in great and good conversation with persons of wisdom, and above all, with our Heavenly Father, that we deal aright with these matters and begin to receive the healing we need. Our inner being, should it suffer a gaping chasm of emptiness and sense of nonbeing, waits to receive (above all) the Word, Christ Himself. And then, with Him, all the *words* of life. Truth, love, understanding, light, joy, faithfulness to the way things really are—all these good things and many more begin to flow into our souls on the wings of real communication with others. It is in conversation with God, with that which is other than ourselves, that we become.

The reason, then, so few come out of puberty and adolescence having accepted themselves has to do with the breakup of the home, the impaired ability of mothers to nurture their infants, and the absence of whole affirming fathers. Additionally, in the social environment of today—with its overheated, even pornographic media, its autonomous and thoroughly secularized public schools, and its culture actively hostile to Judeo-Christian morality and values—young people are called out from under their parent's influence before the necessary affirmation is set in. In these circumstances, the father loses his children to the peer group and to terrible psychological harm from drugs, sex, and so on, before they get through adolescence.

CHAPTER 4

Affirmation: What It Is
and How It Is Received

*I*t is in the love and affirmation of those around us as we are growing up that we gain a reasonably self-assured view of ourselves. If those who cared for us approved of us, then, being privileged to see ourselves through their eyes, we feel it is good and right to be ourselves. There are various degrees in the withholding of approval. Thus, the harm done varies.

In one sense we cannot overstate the importance of the loving acceptance and affirmation we need in order to accept ourselves. In another sense, this affirmation is never fully adequate to get the job done. Even if the love is there, the rejections we experience in a fallen world can hold us back from being able to receive it until we are healed. We are like the autistic baby who, no matter how loving his mother, is injured somehow and unable to receive her love; we are like the adopted child, the one so wounded due to loss of natural parents that he cannot love and appreciate the love and nurture his adopted parents long to lavish upon him.

We live in a fallen world; we are fallen. We cannot love as we would even those dearest to us. If we could, they would perhaps make idols of us; we would be their god. This happens even so, and it too is an evil. We all must eventually turn to the Master Affirmer, God the Father, for our true identity, our real, authentic selves. He heals the unaffirmed by sending His affirming word. And we all must receive this, those who are psychologically healthy due to affirmation on the natural plane, as well as those who were deprived of that. We are all unaffirmed in the higher sense until we find ourselves complete in Him.

You might ask yourself at this point: "What person in my life made me feel good about myself?" And then before reading further, write out in your prayer journal what that person did.

An ever-present and always affirming person in my life was my Aunt Rhoda. When I was a small child, an adolescent, and throughout my life, she never failed to make me feel good about myself. There was never a conscious effort on her part to affirm. In fact, the word was not part of her vocabulary. She herself loved to receive compliments, and she accepted them as a child would—with a kind of excitement: "My! That's a great thing to say about someone! Do you think it can be true!" There was joy and grace in the way she received them. In this way she taught me to pass on compliments—an important lesson, I think, and far more important than most people know. So she did not walk about thinking, *I need to affirm this or that person,* a mistaken route some parents take, and the children know it immediately. The act of affirming as a utilitarian method or duty simply doesn't work. It's far too shallow to get the job done.

Aunt Rhoda loved truth and goodness. The reason I always came away from her feeling encouraged was that she somehow managed to see *what was right and good in me* and praised it. Affirming persons praise the good wherever they see it, and they are always looking for it. In this way Aunt Rhoda was very Godlike, for that is surely what He does. Most people think He's looking for just the opposite in us, but in my many years of keeping a prayer journal, I've found He affirms with incredibly encouraging words. I have only the task of receiving them.

Something else characterizes affirming persons. There is not a mean, envious cell or bone in their bodies. Having accepted themselves, they help others do the same. They have no need to level others to a smaller size, thereby making themselves appear larger.

"Folly is bound up in the heart of a child," even as the Scriptures remind us (Proverbs 22:15). In order to see anything good in me, Aunt Rhoda had to look through bushels of foolishness (and God only knows what else) in my childish heart, and then later on in my adolescent and young adult heart. In "looking through" it, she didn't ignore it. She simply called foolishness (or whatever else) by its real name. But she never saw that as the real me.[1]

The truly affirming person, it seems to me, sees the good and the true in a person and calls it forth. Aunt Rhoda was always doing this, not only with me but with everyone fortunate enough to be in her orbit. She, an authentic person, always related to the authentic person in me. She called it forth.

Some may be thinking, "Ah, but Aunt Rhoda's circumstances in life must have been uncommonly good." As a matter of fact, few women would have psychologically or spiritually survived her particular situation. She was married to my Uncle Gus, who was as disagreeable and as prejudiced and as utterly pessimistic about people as my aunt was agreeable, big-hearted, and optimistic. They lived in close proximity to the household in which I grew up, one that consisted of my mother, sister, and grandmother. Because they were childless, they had time and interest to invest in my sister and me. We loved them dearly, but were aware at the same time that Aunt Rhoda was our haven of normalcy and safety from the irrationality that characterized our uncle. Never until I read Tolstoy's *War and Peace* did I ever glimpse another character such as my Uncle Gus. It was old Count Bolkonsky, a man who did everything (or so it seemed to me as I read the book) out of irritation and anger, at least where his daughter was concerned.

My Uncle Gus was far from being a prince, but in his own orbit, he lived as if he were one. Though at odds with the whole world, he was perfectly satisfied with himself. He owned and operated an automotive garage, and if a customer's appearance (for whatever reason) displeased him, he would not work on that person's car. Always too as if that treatment were not enough, he would roundly insult the person in the bargain. Uncle Gus was a "leveler." He leveled others clear to the ground, on principle.

When on occasion I as a child witnessed his irrational mistreatment of another, I was thoroughly mortified. Pained to the very core of my being for the person he wounded, I would press close to Aunt Rhoda for support. Seeing it all occur, she would simply look at him and say, "Now, Gus, if you want to be a jackass, you go right ahead. But Leanne and I, we are not going to let that ruin our day, are we, Leanne?" And at that, her arm around my shoulder, she would look down at me and in her lovely southern drawl say something like the following: "Now, child, you have to grow a niiice, thiiick alligator hide." And then, mixing her metaphors just a little, she'd say: "This is no skin off your nose, you know." Then she would look at Uncle Gus and the person he had just wounded, and she would leave Gus to shoulder the burden of his own asininity.

It was in this way, free from some painful subjective reaction, that she always handled such a situation. She put everything in its right perspective by speaking the truth that not only aptly named the problem, but reminded us that Gus did not have to live from his lower self. If he did, we were not responsible either for his act or to try to change him. It was in calling actions and situations by their real names, then, and not by trying to cover over or "fix" things that Aunt Rhoda ministered deeply to both the injured person and myself. She would then in one way or another give me a lesson in how to handle such things— always, as I realize now—with objectivity.

As the wife of Uncle Gus, it was her lot to live through this sort of scene over and over again. Always when I had been present, she would soon find the occasion to remind me of all my Uncle Gus's good points. "He's a moral man; he is a faithful husband," and so on, something that at the time seemed faint recommendation. My honest, unspoken reaction was, "Who cares that a man is faithful and honest if he's going to act like that!" She would go on to remind me that, "He loves you and your little sister, Leanne," and of course I would try to receive that.

Aunt Rhoda treated Uncle Gus as she treated everyone else—with respect, and never as less than a person. And though I realize this will strain the credulity of some, I never heard her speak a critical word about him or complain about the difficulties he caused. She simply called asininity what it was as it came out in Gus's behavior.

She saw and affirmed the good in him, and she loved him. She somehow saw the real Gus, the man God intended him to be. Therefore, she could forgive him his constant lack of feeling and intelligence. He was what I now know to be a "dry alcoholic."[2] Long before families of alcoholics were taught not to enable drinkers, Aunt Rhoda had a full grasp of the principle. Gus's father had been grievously alcoholic, and had it not been for Rhoda, Gus would have been too. But it was as an unhealed "dry alcoholic" that my Uncle Gus went to his grave. He never knew what normal is and was satisfied always that his mission in life was to level everyone. The miracle was that my aunt, whom he loved as much as he could love anyone, was never diminished by him. She never "bought into" his disease by taking responsibility for his behavior. She knew who she was. She had accepted herself. She stood tall, and even in joy, the whole of her life.

Gus was the one man who was always there in my growing-up years. Had Aunt Rhoda or my mother been at all codependent, i.e., had they subjectively reacted to him and found their lives shaped by his problems, they would have bent into him and crumpled under such a heavy weight. Had they listened to some of their pastors or teachers in that day, they would have tried as women to help him to wholeness through abdicating their true selves and becoming much less than God created them to be. They both knew far better than to put themselves into subjection to the spiritual and psychological darkness that had so diminished him. And because of this, they never sinned against him. Had they been less than who they were, it is questionable how things would have turned out for my sister and me. As youngsters, had we early come under the "leveler" or the "jackass" in my Uncle Gus, it is my belief that we would have been severely emotionally damaged. As it was, however, we had extraordinary models in our aunt and mother. We, like they, ended up loving and caring for Gus to the end of his days. He was a man with virtually no friends or intimates besides ourselves. Aunt Rhoda was able to love him, and then we in turn were— because we were never under any illusion about calling foolishness by its real name, sin by its real name, hard ignorant prejudice by its real name. We were not deceived by erroneous notions about submitting improperly to male sinfulness, and so did not sacrifice the new and true self on the altar of Uncle Gus's infirmity.

God, the Master Affirmer

In the Presence of God the Master Affirmer, the real self in union with Christ comes forward. He sees His Son in me. He calls us forward.

Though Aunt Rhoda, as well as my mother, were affirming, free, whole women who affirmed me in so very many ways, they could not affirm me as a woman and, therefore, as a person. They could not bring me out of puberty and into self-acceptance the way an affirming father or father-figure could have done. I was past thirty when I began working through the failure to accept myself. I learned to come to God the Father for affirmation. He then not only affirmed me as a woman and as a full person in my own right, but ministered into my life the masculine giftedness I lacked because of being fatherless. He gave me the power that enabled me to better contain the feminine world of meaning—to orient it, direct it, order it, and then to take full responsibility for my gift. God has called me, He has gifted me. I cannot deny the gift; I cannot project it onto others and demand they live it out for me. I have permission to be, to move, to walk with God.

Back to Molly

In the case of Molly, she was unable to receive the affirmation her mother and others held out to her. She was far too wounded due to the breakup in her family. As circumstances would have it, a young minister fell in love with her, and she married him. None of this pain had been resolved. She carried guilt and self-hatred over her sexual behavior into the marriage.

It so happened that her husband emphasized the "submission" (meaning subjection) of woman to her husband. He did not teach it as the Scriptures do, but simplistically, as those who have a faulty understanding of authority do. Because she hated herself, Molly willingly, even gladly embraced extreme teachings on submission to one's husband. It was in this way that she submerged her personality in his.

Her husband had been a model Christian boy, a model teenager. He was good, she was foul (or so her thinking went). A kind of spiritual schizophrenia took place: "As I grow more and more in ministry, I hate myself all the more. . . . There are two parts of me. . . . People don't realize this. I can't go on." Molly was trying to minister to others, to "give out," while at the same time she felt, in her own words, more and more split. Having missed the vital step of self-acceptance, she was paralyzed in immature and wrong-headed attitudinal patterns toward the self—to the point there was hardly a self from which to act, to be.

Do you have any idea how many Christian leaders are right here? How many go home after successful ministry and preaching services and suffer the throes of the damned as all the voices of self-hatred well up from their unhealed hearts to accuse them?

With Molly, the self-hatred was so great, her splitness so intense, that her physical body was now showing the effects. There was for her no true self—no solid sense of a center within from which to move.

I meet these Christians everywhere. They may know the Scriptures by heart; they may have their theological lessons down pat. And they can preach to others for a while. Then the pain becomes unbearable. They begin to break apart as the conscious mind wearies and loses its capacity to control and hold down the pain from the deeper levels of the mind and heart. This pain then, like the flame under a furnace, begins to erupt in smoky signals of compulsive behavior. There are falls into sinful, aberrant behavior in order to allay the pain of the unaffirmed, lost self. The failure to accept the self—this is the crisis of the unaffirmed.

Healing for the Mollys in This World

When Jesus read from the scroll of the prophet Isaiah these words: "The Spirit of the Lord is on me, because he has anointed me to preach good news to the poor. He has sent me to proclaim freedom for the prisoners," and so on, He was talking about the Mollys of this world. The good news for the Mollys is redemption, not only from sin, but from the effects of the sins of others. We proclaim this freedom to them in such a way as they can come running, flying, walking, or hobbling on crutches out of their prisonhouses. The pace varies, but the good news is that they are to be ushered out of the darkness of bondage and into the sunlight of identity and freedom.

Some would attempt to usher them into freedom apart from healing them, but this was never our Lord's way. He taught us to heal as well as to disciple His wounded ones. We must first bind up their wounds.

Molly needed healing of the "inner person" in the worst way, though her narrow religious background had prejudiced her against this kind of healing. She needed to understand why she was hurting so badly, and then she needed prayer for healing of memories—a thorough giving and receiving of forgiveness, as we will show in discussing the next two barriers to wholeness. She needed to forgive the very circumstances of her life—all those that went along with being the child of divorced parents and of severe economic hardship. But once this was done, she had to face the theological answer to her dilemma of being unable to accept herself.

Theological Solution to a Psychological and Spiritual Problem

> What our Lord wants us to present to Him is not goodness, nor honesty, nor endeavor, but real solid sin; that is all He can take from us. And what does He give in exchange for our sin? Real solid righteousness.[3]

Having addressed Molly's psychological need, we must now address her crying spiritual need: She would have to confess the sin of pride. Molly must come once again to the foot of the cross and there look up to the Crucified. She must say to Him, "Your death for my sin is sufficient." She would then have to acknowledge Him as her righteousness. "God made him who had no sin to be sin for us, so that in him we might become the righteousness of God" (2 Corinthians 5:21).

She would need to once again confess her sexual sins, but this time, receive the forgiveness. In rejecting and hating herself, she had fallen into pride. Herein is the pride: She wanted to be good enough on her own. It is so abominably hard for people to admit that they are not good enough—that the cross of Christ really was necessary, even for them. Molly would have to take a longer, broader look at the cross of Christ and incorporate into her emotional and spiritual life the great and utterly grave knowledge of our justification in and through the shed blood of Christ. In doing this, she would have to come to terms with the depths of sin in her heart and acknowledge her self-deception.

Just as sons or daughters often will try the rest of their lives to win the love of an unaffirming parent—by great exploits or accomplishments or whatever—so people try to keep the law on their own and thereby win God's love. They want to be righteous by having kept the law perfectly. They want, in short, their own righteousness, not His. And this is where the pride comes in.

The humility that acknowledges ourselves as truly fallen is a first priority in coming to accept ourselves. You may be asking, "Stress humility to the one who hates himself?" Yes, for self-hatred in the Christian is a substitute for humility; it belongs to pride.

I believe the confession of pride here at this point is the foundation of all progress, spiritual and otherwise. We all must confess the pride that refuses to acknowledge that we have indeed lost the divine splendor. We are indeed fallen and have acted out our fallenness.

> The greatest blessing spiritually is the knowledge that we are destitute; until we get there, Our Lord is powerless.[4]

Apart from God we have been and are in many ways monstrous; we do monstrous things. When we are properly related to God, we silence the accuser of our souls by admitting, "Yes, I am capable of the petty; I am capable of the monstrous; and if He should leave me but for a moment, I should do yet worse."

The humble acceptance of myself as fallen but now justified by Another who is my righteousness is the basis on which I can accept myself, learn to laugh at myself, be patient with myself. And then, wonder of wonders, be enabled for at least part of the time to forget myself. "Humble yourselves—feeling very insignificant—in the presence of the Lord, and He will exalt you. He will lift you up and make your lives significant" (James 4:10, *The Amplified Bible*).

St. Paul reminds us, "For [again from Scripture] 'No human being can be justified in the sight of God' for having kept the law: law brings only the consciousness of sin" (Romans 3:20, NEB). Molly was plenty conscious of her past sins—they colored her whole view of herself. Keeping the law (or having kept it!) does not exclude pride, but as the apostle says, "faith does" (Romans 3:27, NEB)—faith in Another who alone is my righteousness.

The Way of Self-Acceptance

> Give ear and come to me; hear me, that your soul may live. (Isaiah 55:3)

No one else can ever accept me for me, or you for you. All of us, like Molly, must confess our pride and then receive the healing word from God in order to accept ourselves. It is imperative that we begin earnestly listening to God the Father, the One who waits to bring us out of fearful, dependent relationships and into right relationship with Himself and others. This will occur quite naturally as we spread out before Him every diseased thought and attitudinal pattern. Then, as His precious chosen ones, we listen and receive the truth and reality He gives to replace them. That is how we bring dysfunctional, sinful, prideful patterns in the thought life and the imagination into submission to Christ. It is in this way that fleshly and demonic strongholds in the mind and imagination are torn down.

As for the Molly in our story, God the Father will in this process affirm her as a woman and as a person. The authentic self, the *real* Molly, will come to the fore quite naturally and more or less unconsciously. If Molly turns inward and introspectively tries to see this affirmation occurring, she will get in the way of her healing. At this point she is rather to note the bent, dependent behavior, especially in the many ways it manifests in her relationship to her husband, but she should not agonize over it. Rather, she is to spread this out before God and learn from Him and from others who are walking in freedom how to come out of what has been an unconscious idolatry. Her attention is to be directed outward in loving, listening-obedience to God, and it is in this stance that she will be receiving all the promises of God, even His everlasting covenant of faithful love and mercy. The hungry, thirsty, unaffirmed places within her will receive food and drink.

> Come, all you who are thirsty,
> come to the waters;
> and you who have no money,
> come, buy and eat!
> Come, buy wine and milk without money and without cost. . . .
> Listen, listen to me, and eat what is good,
> and your soul will delight in the richest of fare. (Isaiah 55:1-3)

In this stance of listening prayer, every thought of the mind, every imagination of the heart, is brought captive to Christ. Much will be utterly obliterated; what remains will be transformed. As her relationship to God is righted, her relationships to others will change, and this can be quite threatening and tumultuous. For example, Molly needed to realize that she had not seen her husband aright. She had idealized him as "the perfect Christian man," relating to him not as the man he really was, but to the "image" or "persona" he had been maintaining. She was fearful of being abandoned by him, while at the same time she was ambivalent toward him—both loving and hating him. This in turn left her open to the attentions of other men, a thing she hated and feared in herself.

Perhaps one of the most surprising things she learned was that he needed as much if not more help than she did. But he was far from acknowledging his need. Hadn't he kept the law perfectly? His rigid, even pharisaical attitudes became apparent as she straightened up from her bentness toward him and found her true identity in Christ. She had to come out of denial and acknowledge that he was emotionally remote and separated in large part from what it means to be human and caring, that he was well on his way to becoming a religious bigot, and that she has been affirming and enabling him in all this.

All this insight takes time, and mercifully, we are not usually required to come out of all of our denial overnight. In order to find wholeness for herself and her marriage, however, Molly had to face all this. She had to fully repent of her part in all of it, acknowledging her self-deception and her responsibility in their difficulties. Listening prayer is an essential for all of us. In the case of the Mollys, those who have in the name of religion put to death the real self, it is like a lifeline thrown to a drowning person. Once they have grasped it, they will come alive both psychologically and spiritually.

Catching Up with St. Paul

Christians, by and large, do not understand Romans and Galatians, which set out their freedom in Christ. Their tendency is either to remain or to come back under law and condemnation rather than to walk in the Spirit, listening to and obeying their Lord.

Paul cried out to the Romans: "There is no condemnation for those who are united with Christ Jesus, because in Christ Jesus the life-giving law of the Spirit has set you free from the law of sin and death" (Romans 8:1-2, NEB).

The occasion for his outcry—the Romans were tending to come back under the law rather than to walk in the Spirit because of the "Judaizers" among them. To walk in the Spirit is to cease striving in our own strength and goodness, and to walk in His. It is to celebrate our smallness, our inadequacy apart from Him. It is to admit that He alone is our righteousness. We cannot keep the law. *Another*, the Holy Other, must do it for us. To walk in the Spirit is to live in the present moment, always looking to Christ, always practicing His Presence, always moving in tandem with Him.

The Role of the Minister

As ministers we can never choose this freedom for another; the person needing it must choose it. We can pray for the healing of a passive and/or a rebellious will,[5] thereby freeing the person who so desires to choose aright. But we cannot coerce another. Jesus never did. As Oswald Chambers has said, "Christ never cajoled anyone." Christian counselors, like parental figures, are often sorely tempted to take such a responsibility upon themselves. But we can never change anyone. We can and must, however, speak the truth. The truth proclaimed in the power of the Spirit is what changes people. They then have the responsibility for listening and for preparing the ground of their hearts to receive the golden grain of truth God is always sowing.

The acceptance of oneself, like all that is great and valid in the Christian faith, can never be a secondhand experience. We must, each of us, apprehend Christ and the fullness of His salvation for ourselves. To so apprehend Him is to come into our full uniqueness. To help others apprehend Him is to point always and unswervingly to Him and to personal communication with Him.

It is in looking to Him that we become like Him! Tyrants, as C. S. Lewis has said, are monotonously alike—their minds are on themselves and their own aggrandizement. But as for the great saints, that is another matter. There is incredible diversity among them. We need think only of the twelve apostles, of Augustine, Luther, Ignatius of Loyola, St. Francis of Assisi, St. Theresa, Dwight L. Moody, C. S. Lewis, to name a few.

I want to be a disciple of Jesus. Adam Clarke, C. S. Lewis, Oswald Chambers, Agnes Sanford, F. B. Meyer, R. A. Torrey, Thomas à Kempis, and especially my own mother—all these (and many more) mean so much to me. I thank God regularly for them. Their faith, their keen minds, their very lives and wisdom have nourished me. They were, however, but ministers to bring me to Christ.

To be a disciple of a disciple is to be pale indeed. I do not want to be a pale Christian. With St. Paul, I say, "To me to live is Christ." With St. John, I lean my head on Christ's breast and hear what He says to me. This is the walk in the Spirit. This is the way we come out from under a law or many laws to abide in Christ. This is the way we cross over into a serene self-acceptance, no matter what our psychological needs have been and into the freedom of the realized true self in Christ.

Slaying Shame

> When you were slaves to sin, you were free from the control of righteousness. What benefit did you reap at that time from the things you are now ashamed of? Those things result in death! But now that you have been set free from sin and have become slaves to God, the benefit you reap leads to holiness, and the result is eternal life. (Romans 6:20-22)

For some, like Molly, once pride is confessed, there is the giant, shame, to deal with. In our Pastoral Care conferences over the years and in counseling, we've seen all manner of sexual brokenness. All of us know shame and have committed shameful deeds. But for the sexually abused and for those who have misused their bodies in promiscuous and/or perverted sex, the shame engendered can be a very large barrier to self-acceptance.

The good news is we have been given the antidote for shame. My prayer partners and I were in prayer, and the word *shame* had not been mentioned. But we were praying about the matter of self-hatred, the fact that so many Christians are stuck in it and fail to move on to a secure acceptance of themselves in Christ. As I was asking the Lord for grace to write of this in such a way that people could come free, Connie Boerner received a strong word from the Lord. It came in the form of a vision that expressed the full meaning of the cross. She shared it with us so vividly that we felt as if we too had seen it.

Connie saw two medieval soldiers in battle. One was filled with light, and his shield was illuminated. He held a sword in his left hand. The name over him was FORGIVENESS.

The other soldier was gray and illusory, almost a vapor, but very powerful. He also had a shield and a sword, but his shield was black. His name was SHAME.

FORGIVENESS stepped forward, plunged his sword into SHAME, and SHAME was slain.

This is precisely the way it is when we finally acknowledge our sin, crying out, "Lord, I have sinned against You and against my own body." We then open fully to receive to the very depths of our being His forgiveness for all our sin, and go on from there to just as deeply forgive and fully release others.

When people feel great shame, they usually also project considerable blame on others. King David, the man after God's own heart, is a great model for us in this respect. When confronted, he immediately accepted full responsibility for his sin.

> Against you, you only, have I sinned
> and done what is evil in your sight,
> so that you are proved right when you speak
> and justified when you judge.
> Surely I was sinful at birth,
> sinful from the time my mother conceived me.
> Surely you desire truth in the inner parts;
> you teach me wisdom in the inmost place. (Psalm 51)

Those struggling with pride and its consequent denial and transference of guilt onto others can be healed through praying the prayers of David in Psalm 51.

This is what the cross of Christ is all about. It causes us to acknowledge our sinful state and allows us to see His atoning death for our sin and His life in exchange for our death.

Several times recently in prayer with the team or alone, I've seen with my heart an exceedingly large cup brimming over (even aflame) with the LIFE of God that is to come to us. Even as we see Christ crucified for us and our sins flowing into Him as we confess them, so we in turn are to receive the eternal life, the eternal cup and bread, from the Risen Lord. We may want to see this huge cup with the eyes of our hearts, the cup he proffers to us even now, saying, "Take, and drink; this is My blood, given for you." This is My LIFE, eternal life, flowing into you, that which cleanses and washes away every stain, that which brings forgiveness and life. No matter how deep the wounding and horrendous the sin, the acknowledgment of ourselves as sinful from birth, the reception of Christ's forgiveness, and the extending of this forgiveness to others releases us from self-hatred and shame. Most truly,

FORGIVENESS slays SHAME.

CHAPTER 5

Listening Prayer: The Way of Grace and the Walk in the Spirit

Do not think that I have come to abolish the Law or the Prophets; I have not come to abolish them but to fulfill them. I tell you the truth, until heaven and earth disappear, not the smallest letter, not the least stroke of a pen, will by any means disappear from the Law until everything is accomplished. Anyone who breaks one of the least of these commandments and teaches others to do the same will be called least in the kingdom of heaven, but whoever practices and teaches these commands will be called great in the kingdom of heaven. For I tell you that unless your righteousness surpasses that of the Pharisees and the teachers of the law, you will certainly not enter the kingdom of heaven.

(Matthew 5:17-20)

*T*he extraordinarily wonderful thing about listening prayer is that it is not only the vital step we take toward self-acceptance, but it is also the same step that begins the walk in the Spirit for all of us, no matter what our psychological needs may be. Three chapters from my book *The Broken Image* deal with listening prayer, and these should be studied in conjunction with the crucial matter of self-acceptance. They are "Listening for the Healing Word" (chapter 6), "The Identity Crisis According to the Scriptures" (chapter 5), and the Appendix, "Listening to Our Dreams."

An Assignment to Help Us Get Started

Remember now that neither I nor anyone else can die to your old diseased attitudinal patterns for you; no one can pray over you the magical prayer that will do the instantaneous trick. But I can introduce you to miracle, that of the creature in holy converse with the Creator.

Once Molly confesses her pride, then she must keep her face turned upward (not toward me or any other human counselor, but to God). When she turns to me, I point her to God and teach her to listen to Him.

The first assignment I give a Molly is to go through the Gospels and personalize every promise and every command of Christ to His disciples. I ask her to write these out, addressed to her by name, in a fresh, new prayer journal. "Fresh" and "new" is stipulated because, if the person needing to accept herself has already been journaling, the pages of her journal will more than likely be filled with introspective musings. It will reflect more or less a "practice of the presence of self" in isolation from the Presence of God and the words He is speaking. It may reflect a losing battle with oppressive thoughts and merely be a record of all the old musings on diseased attitudinal patterns.

But the new journal will reflect true prayer. It will be a place where the person can bring the most diseased thoughts and patterns before God, look at them objectively, and then receive what God is speaking into the situation. The person will be exchanging old ways of seeing for God's way, old patterns for new ones. And the new ones are to be written out. This first exercise, besides bringing the needy one into a two-way conversation with God, will cause the person to deal with all the "I can'ts" in his or her life. It will bring the person into the radical obedience to Christ that prepares us for the other listening we must do.

The Power of Right Thinking

> If your self-acceptance rests on maintaining an image of yourself as a nice, good person who never did anything wrong on purpose, then you cannot allow much truth into your field of vision. True self-acceptance is in stark contrast to this self-delusion. Self-acceptance does not survive honesty; it rests on it. The Christian is not someone who is so brave or thick-skinned that he can face the truth about himself unafraid; rather he is a sinner who can face his sin because he has confidence that God has forgiven and accepted him in spite of it.[1]

When we need healing of our emotional and feeling being, we necessarily have negative, distorted thinking about ourselves and others. We do not ignore or deny it, but we write it out as specifically as we can, just as we do with our sins, and say to God, "Look at this. I don't want this. You take it!" We name it as the distorted thinking that it is. Then we replace it with right thinking—those light-filled thoughts and attitudes in line with truth and the way things *really* are. Remember, nature abhors a vacuum, and other negative patterns flood in when the old diseased ones are not replaced by the true.

Christians, of all people, are to think positively. We alone have reason never to despair. Faith and hope are ours, and they shine like beacons in the darkest circumstances. When our negative thoughts about ourselves are based in unremitted guilt, we immediately confess the sin and petition for cleansing. Then, as we hear what God is saying to us as cleansed souls, we make sure we do not continue to despise ourselves for past failures.

But negative thoughts toward the self that are not based in true guilt come from pride and rebellion rather than from humility (as some think and teach). Our consciences are to be cleansed, made holy and free. Guilt and negativity drive us toward sin and despair, not away from it. Freedom from guilt and full acceptance of forgiveness stop short of libeling the cross of Christ, of saying, "Jesus and His blood are not enough for me." Such is the "humility" of self-hatred, and it is rooted in something other than Christian theology.

In all this, we acknowledge the power of the mind, and we acknowledge the truth of Scriptures, "As a man thinketh in his heart, so is he." It is remarkable what we can do merely through the power of positive thinking toward changing our old negatives into positives.

Hopefully, we realize that we need to train our minds to think. Period. Let us hope, as well, we are not found among those Christians who seem to think that faith excuses them from thinking. Historically, Christians have been accused of *fideism*, the belief that faith *alone*, that is, apart from the exercise of reason, is the basis of knowledge (one of the misguided reactions of Christians to the schism between faith and reason. See *The Healing Presence*, chapter 10). But long before there were confused Christians, Socrates said, "Most are misologists"; in other words, most people hate to think. Some people are very sick indeed because they hate to think; they are too passive and lazy to think through their problems with God. This is mental sloth and should be confessed as such. But in the Scriptures we read: "Come let us reason together, saith the Lord."

And this remarkable invitation from God to reason with Him, when accepted, puts us a grand leap ahead of positive thinking alone. It brings us to the vital matter of listening prayer. We will think positively, all right, with all the faith and hope that is ours in Christ, but as we do this, we will be thinking through all the issues of our lives with God. Then, as we learn to hear God, we will receive from Him the true word, and we replace our old diseased negatives with the positive word He is always sending.

Sister Penelope Learns to Listen

The following example of listening prayer illustrates the way God so powerfully uses the Scriptures we've stored away in our hearts. We sometimes receive messages from Him that are not Scripture, *per se*, but they are always *scriptural*. That is, they are never in disagreement with the Scriptures, but are in full harmony with them and are always to be judged by them.

This story concerns Sr. Penelope, an attractive, saucy nun who had always been at odds with herself. There were, she said, certain sins in her life she had been unable to overcome. She wanted so very much to love God, to do His will ("I have dedicated my entire life to God; I would hold nothing back"), yet she felt rebellious and unlovable. She never felt close to the God she served. She and the other nuns met regularly for prayer in the convent. For twenty years her corporate prayers with the sisters, as well as her private prayers, were filled with negative thoughts about herself and her relationship to the God to whom she had chosen to give all.

She had gone through different kinds of "therapy" for her "problems" when I first met with her for prayer. I was definitely a last resort. She would have continued serving God the rest of her life the best she knew how, though thinking herself alienated from Him and full of hatred for herself.

I prayed with her, helping her to receive forgiveness, and asked her to consciously and deliberately practice the Presence of Christ. This she agreed to do. I then asked her to pay attention to and write out in a new prayer journal her negative thoughts and thought patterns, and then listen to the word God was speaking to her—those words from Him that would replace the negative, diseased patterns of thought. I asked her to discern where the diseased words were coming from—the world, the flesh, or the devil. This she agreed to do. I asked her to confess the pride that had kept her back from self-acceptance, and she did that. It wasn't long before I had a letter from her.

It didn't take more than a couple of minutes to write down ten negative thoughts to work on. I'm sure I can find more, but that's enough for the moment! I decided to take one a day for cancellation. Wonderful and happy chance! The first black thought to be dissolved was:

God will never speak to me.

Obviously, if that couldn't be erased, I'd have a lot of trouble doing anything else! The "answer" was not a direct refutation of the complaint, but rather it was sort of drowned out by that verse in Psalm 85, "I will listen to what the Lord is saying, for He is speaking peace to His faithful people and to those who turn their hearts to Him." The next was:

God can't do anything with me; I'm too selfish.

It melted before, "As many as received Him, to them gave He power to become sons of God," and "He will make your righteousness as clear as the light and your just dealing as the noonday."

But yesterday cut and healed at heart level. *I'll never be able to surrender to God* met Ezekiel 36:16-36, but especially verses 25-27. "I will sprinkle clean water on you, and you will be clean; I will cleanse you from all your impurities and from all your idols. I will give you a new heart and put a new spirit in you; I will remove from you your heart of stone and give you a heart of flesh. And I will put my Spirit in you and move you to follow my decrees and be careful to keep my laws."

The surrender issue is of long, long standing. I have felt as though my hands were hopelessly clamped onto my life, control, a driver's wheel, a rope—*something* that had to be let go, but I couldn't pry my grip loose, and confessors who demanded a verbal declaration of surrender made me feel only *more* guilty and frustrated and hypocritical because I knew the words couldn't effect the reality. And now—it doesn't matter anymore! It is God's responsibility. I can trust Him to give me the heart and spirit of surrender when it pleases Him. . . .

As soon as she got through the ten negative thoughts about herself, she wrote again, ecstatically:

Joy continues to well up in me. The negative thoughts just haven't any hooks to hang on any more, and I am becoming less Leah and more Rachel. . . .

Then, in a few more days, I received this remarkable word from her:

What you gave me was marriage counseling—you got me ready for a wedding!

I then got word from another nun in the convent. The message was this: "Sr. P. is so joyous, the convent is fairly rocking!"

The Mystical Wedding
Here we see the mystical wedding—the wedding of the soul to Christ. That is what listening prayer is all about. That is what any journaling worthy of the name Christian is all about. That is what happens when we decide to quit listening to all the other voices of the world, the flesh, and the devil—when we rightly discern and refute them where necessary and start really listening to God and receiving from Him. This Scriptural promise comes to pass—yes, even in *my* life!

I will betroth you to Myself forever, betroth you in lawful wedlock with unfailing devotion and love; I will betroth you to Myself to have and to hold, and you shall know the Lord. (Hosea 2:19-20, NEB)

The Crucifix and the Stained-Glass Window
The more we take our place in Christ, the more of our true selves there is to accept. Though the large step of self-acceptance enables us to cross over from immaturity and bondage into maturity and freedom, there is a very real sense in which we continue to die to the old self and accept the new.

To walk in the Spirit is, at the same time, to die to the old man. It is an automatic corollary. (Some people who strive so hard, year in and year out, to die to the old man, simply need to learn to walk in the Spirit! That is the way of getting "filled up" with God, and it spares us the tormenting job of having to "empty out" so often.) Even so, because we are both sinner and saint, we need to work into our lives a regular time for kneeling as sinner before God in preparation for rising anew in our prime identity as a child of God.

For our walk in the Spirit to remain vibrant and alive, then, we need to come present to our hearts, allowing the Spirit to search and reveal them. To do this is to take once again our place in Christ's death and dying. I will be writing more on this in a later chapter, but here would like to tie this in with the matter of self-acceptance and the ongoing necessity of dying to the old self and living to the new.

C. S. Lewis writes as well as anyone I know on the old man or self, that in us which wills to be put first, to be God. It is that gravitation away from God, "the journey homeward to habitual self." When we yield to it, we find ourselves living out of another spirit altogether. This, according to St. John, is the spirit and the nature of the devil at work in us, and if we yield, we will eventually have to hear Jesus say: "You belong to your father, the devil, and you want to carry out your father's desire" (John 8:44). The desire on the part of the created to be as the Creator is the deepest taproot of pride, and we have always to cry out to God to show us our pride that we might confess and yield it up to Him:

From the moment a creature becomes aware of God as God and of itself as self, the terrible alternatives of choosing God or self for the center open before it. This sin is committed daily by young children and ignorant peasants as well as by sophisticated persons, by solitaries no less than by those who live in society. It is the fall in every individual life and in each day of each individual life, the basic sin behind all particular sins. At this very moment you and I are either committing it or about to commit it or repenting of it.[2]

In love we escape from our self into one another. . . . The primary impulse of each is to maintain and aggrandize himself. The secondary impulse is to go out of the self, to correct its provincialism and heal its loneliness. In love, in virtue, in the pursuit of knowledge, and in the reception of the arts, we are doing this. Obviously this process can be described either as an enlargement or as a temporary annihilation of the self. But that is an old paradox: "He that loseth his life shall save it."[3]

A terrible thing to note about the old self is that it too can pray, as Lewis's verse so graphically points out:

> *Lord that made the dragon, grant me thy peace,*
> *But say not that I should give up the gold,*
> *Nor move, nor die. Others would have the gold.*
> *Kill rather, Lord, the Men and the other dragons;*
> *Then I can sleep; go when I will to drink.*

(C. S. Lewis, "The Dragon Speaks")[4]

This "fierce imprisonment in the (old) self is but the obverse of the self-giving which is absolute reality":

> For in self-giving, if anywhere, we touch a rhythm not only of all creation but of all being. For the Eternal Word also gives Himself in sacrifice; and that not only on Calvary. . . . From before the foundation of the world He surrenders begotten Deity back to begetting Deity in obedience. . . . From the highest to the lowest, self exists to be abdicated and, by that abdication, becomes the more truly self, to be thereupon yet the more abdicated, and so forever. This is not a heavenly law which we can escape by remaining earthly, nor an earthly law which we can escape by being saved. What is outside the system of self-giving is not earth, nor nature, nor "ordinary life," but simply and solely Hell.[5]

In a city where I once lived, there was a quiet little chapel built to the side of the main sanctuary of a church. It had a wonderful crucifix over its altar, and above that an exquisite old stained-glass window depicting the risen Christ. I had learned to walk in the Spirit and knew the joy of the Lord. The ministry He entrusted me with, however, was growing rapidly. It was then that I learned to work into my life, as Agnes Sanford refers to it, a rhythm of repentance and resurrection. I was so busy serving the Lord and helping others that I usually had little or no conscious knowledge of sin and pride in my heart, but I learned to set aside a time to be very quiet, letting Him show me the repenting I needed to do and the changes I needed to make in my life. At these times, I would go to this little chapel and there look up to the crucifix.

Then when I knew what to repent of, I would in prayer take my stand in His cross with Him and die to it. Sometimes this would take a while. Having died once again with Him to the old man or self, I would (before rising from my knees!) look up to the stained-glass depiction of Him as risen Savior and take my place in His rising, all the while exulting in my forgiveness and true identity in Him.

I no longer have access to this wonderful little chapel, but this practice is firmly planted in my heart. All of us have access to Christ's cross, and to build in such a rhythm of dying and rising with Christ is surely the way we stay spiritually and psychologically healthy. This is also the way we avoid burnout. We never forget that we are both sinner (albeit justified) and saint. Our main identity is that of saint, child of God, but we retain that only by remembrance that we are not yet who we will be when time is no more. Then we will no longer have to concern ourselves with daily dying to the old man. This is all a part of listening prayer and the walk in the Spirit.

That little chapel was a very meaningful place to me, and I think it was there that I learned to ask others to look up to Christ crucified and rising again for them as they confessed their sin and received their healing. Through this process of praying with others, I have become more and more certain of this—our hearts need to picture these great and grave actions of Christ aright, for they image the great story of our salvation. The head may well know Christian doctrine while at the same time the heart is starved for the story and the experience of love and forgiveness that comes with it. It's as if God has been waiting for us to once again be able to see with our hearts the great truths of our faith and receive the healing word and vision He is always sending.

The closer we come to God, the more fully we realize that He alone is our righteousness. To try to get good enough before we accept ourselves is to bypass the way of the cross.

Christ says ever and always, "Give me your pain, your sin, your sorrow. My Life I give in exchange for all that binds you." His vocation, indeed, was to become that sin, that sorrow that has hurt us so badly, whether buried away in our memories or occurring even now in the present moment. And as we take our place in His cross, that is, in His death and dying and forgive even as He forgave, then we become "the righteousness of God" in Him. It is in this way that we can release unto Him and into Him all that has ever beset us, all that has defiled. We can forgive the deepest, most painful rejections and deprivations. We do this, knowing that we too have grievously sinned against ourselves and others. We too are fallen, and we dwell in a fallen world. "I have hurt others, Lord; I have not loved You or others as I should; forgive me, O Lord, even as I forgive others, even as I forgive all the circumstances of my life." This prayer will continue to be part of the walk in the Spirit, and He continually renews us in His love and righteousness.

PART II

The Forgiveness of Sin

Forgiveness is the exclusive prerogative of Christianity. The schools of ancient morality had four cardinal virtues—justice in human relations, prudence in the direction of affairs, fortitude in bearing trouble or sorrow, temperance or self-restraint. But they knew nothing of mercy or forgiveness, which is not natural to the human heart. Forgiveness is an exotic, which Christ brought with Him from Heaven.[1]

(F. B. Meyer)

Therefore I tell you, whatever you ask for in prayer, believe that you have received it, and it will be yours. And when you stand praying, if you hold anything against anyone, forgive him, so that your Father in heaven may forgive you your sins.

(Mark 11:24-25)

CHAPTER 6

Healing of Memories:
The Forgiveness of Sin

The Spirit of the Sovereign Lord is on me,
  because the Lord has anointed me
  to preach good news to the poor.
He has sent me to bind up the brokenhearted,
  to proclaim freedom for the captives
  and release from darkness for the prisoners,
to proclaim the year of the Lord's favor
  and the day of vengeance of our God,
to comfort all who mourn,
  and provide for those who grieve in Zion—
to bestow on them a crown of beauty instead of ashes,
the oil of gladness instead of mourning,
and a garment of praise instead of a spirit of despair.
They will be called oaks of righteousness,
  a planting of the Lord for the display of his splendor.
They will rebuild the ancient ruins
  and restore the places long devastated;
they will renew the ruined cities
  that have been devastated for generations.

(Isaiah 61:1-4)

When you pray, say: "Father, hallowed be your name, your kingdom come.
Give us each day our daily bread. Forgive us our sins, for we also forgive
everyone who sins against us. And lead us not into temptation."

(Luke 11: 2-4)

*H*ealing of memories means forgiveness of sin. It is the heart's experience of forgiveness of sin at the precise sore spot where it is needed, one that impacts the soul in its totality—in its emotional, feeling, intuitive, imaginative capacities as well as in its more conscious, willing, thinking capacities. This place may be at any level of consciousness or unconsciousness. Nothing illustrates God's Healing Presence more wonderfully than His way of healing man's deepest hurts and memories.

Agnes Sanford coined the term at a time when very little healing was flowing through the church's formal confessional or informal prayer groups. The reason was that the central truth of God's forgiveness of sin, along with all the great spiritual realities of the Kingdom of God, had been largely relegated to the abstract. Victims of the schism between head and heart, we could "talk doctrine" but couldn't *experience* its healing power. We could not get it from our heads to our hearts.

Some could still preach great sermons about the forgiveness of sin, but could not *administer* it to the heart in need of it. In the church today, this is still largely true.

The soul in need of healing is suffering due to this same schism. The head and the heart simply are not working in a complementary fashion. The heart perhaps knows something the head does not, or conversely, the head needs to rightly comprehend and then critique what is in the heart.

The journey of life is, as Fr. Alan Jones has said, "for setting love in order."[1] A large part of that task has to do with setting our "two minds"[2] in order and in harmony, accomplished through forgiveness of sin:

> The truth is that any wound to the soul so deep that it is not healed by our own self-searching and prayers is inevitably connected with a subconscious awareness of sin, either our own sins or our grievous reactions to the sins of others. The therapy that heals these deep wounds could be called the forgiveness of sins, or it could be called the healing of memories. Whatever one calls it, there are in many of us wounds so deep that only the mediation of someone else to whom we may "bare our grief" can heal us.[3]

When someone bares his grief to us, no matter whether we are a priest, psychologist, minister, counselor, or layperson, we are to lead the person in confessional prayers. We may need to learn how to pray for the forgiveness of we know not what in the past history of his family. For example, Nehemiah and other Old Testament prophets offered prayers such as: "I confess the sins we Israelites, including myself and my father's house, have committed against you" (Nehemiah 1:6b). Or we may need to help the person forgive the circumstances of a lifetime. The point I want to stress is that we are hearing confessions of sin, and after these sins are acknowledged and repented of, we must never forget to proclaim the forgiveness of that sin as well as release from the bondage of the sins of others against us. This is the way souls find healing. It is perfectly appalling how seldom this is effectively done, even in the formal confessional.

Most often, the Holy Spirit leads very specifically in what to confess and who to forgive, but when the case is more nebulous (for example, a whole family is sick due to unconfessed sin that goes back through the generations), we need to look to God for direction in forming prayers of confession and forgiveness that will break the power of unconfessed sins over our lives. This is necessary because our woundedness and sin break our relationships. In order for these breaks to be set right, we must confess them. Is the break between myself and God? Myself and others? Within my own inner inner self am I at war? The fallen condition is a *crisis in separation,* and within the trauma of broken relationships resides our illnesses and identity crises. It is through prayer that relationships are mended (or at least forgiveness extended for the brokenness) and that our souls are healed of their grievous lacks due to failed relationships in the past.

King David understood this healing very well: "I acknowledged my sin to you, and my iniquity I did not hide. I said I will confess my transgressions to the Lord (continually unfolding the past till all is told) then You (instantly) forgave me the guilt and iniquity of my sin" (Psalm 32:5, *The Amplified Bible*).

Note the instantaneous nature of what happens when God forgives sin. Healings of the soul that have to do primarily with forgiveness at long last extended or received can be quite dramatic in that the relief is so instant, and in many cases, the joy so exquisite. C. S. Lewis, finally having received forgiveness for something that had bothered him for years, wrote his friend and confidante, Sr. Penelope:

As for me I specially need your prayers because I am (like the pilgrims in Bunyan) travelling across "a plain called Ease." Everything without, and many things within are marvellously well at present: Indeed . . . I realize that until about a month ago I never really believed (though I thought I did) in God's forgiveness. What an ass I have been both for not knowing and for thinking I knew. I now feel that one must never say one believes or understands anything; any morning a doctrine I thought I already possessed may blossom into this new reality.[4]

At such a time as this, we can think that there is little left for God to do in our souls. But most of us find, on coming back down to earth, that this is the first healing in a series—one that perhaps opens the way for the healing of deeply wounded emotions and/or diseased attitudes.

We need to understand prayer for the healing of memories in the context of prayer for healing in general. To pray for the healing of a person's memories is primarily to pray for the healing of his soul, and this differs from prayer for the healing of his spirit or body.[5]

Man's Spirit

The spirit is sick when alienated from God, and the healing of the spirit takes place when it is united to the Spirit of God. The evangelists, therefore, are the great healers of the spirit in that they broadcast continually the message of salvation. Anytime we introduce a person to Christ, we see this essential healing take place. God's Spirit descends into his spirit, linking the new believer with Himself. One is then "born from above" and now has a place within where the Holy Spirit lives, a holy and righteous base from which He radiates up through the soul as well as the physical body. From the moment of new birth, then, believers can and are to practice His Presence within. This is also the initial and primary healing of man's soul and the basis of his further becoming in Christ.

The Soul

> In reference . . . to man's psychical nature, "spirit" denotes life as having its origin in God and "soul" denotes that same life as constituted in man. Spirit is the inner depth of man's being, the higher aspect of his personality. Soul expresses man's own special and distinctive individuality. The *pneuma* (spirit) is man's nonmaterial nature looking Godward; the *psyche* is that same nature of man looking earthward and touching the things of sense.[6]

The Scriptures use the terms interchangeably, though they differentiate between spirit and soul. To speak of the soul is also to speak of the spirit in that the spirit of a man expresses itself through the soul. Conversely, of course, to speak of the spirit is also to speak of the soul, for the two are wed in man's makeup. We know nothing of a human spirit in isolation from a soul, or a soul in isolation from a human spirit.

To speak of prayer for the healing of the soul is, primarily, to speak of prayer for releasing someone from psychological sickness and emotional pain due to hurts and deprivations of the past. Prayer for healing of memories is in this category. When someone has such a need, he has a psychological barrier to freedom in Christ. Though the human spirit is united with Christ, God's Spirit cannot "radiate" through this problem area until the person gets help to understand and deal with it. This is where the gifts of counseling and healing come in, and people need to open up in prayer to receive them. Until one does, he is being determined by the difficulties of the past and lacks freedom.

There are other psychological barriers to freedom, and they also come under the heading of healing of the soul. They include, for example, the effects of ignorance and terrible poverty. Also, it is possible to be a Christian today and to be ignorant of necessary moral values and virtues—those necessary to our becoming as persons. Obedient to the best we know, we gain a moral self, moral character.

The Scriptures consider man as a whole, and we err if we fall into the trap of trying to separate and define too closely the differences between the faculties of the mind (e.g., conscious and unconscious), or where one leaves off and the other begins. And the same is true of spirit and soul. Spirit and soul differ, the faculties of the mind differ, but to try to differentiate them by separating them too closely is to do what the Scriptures do not do and what great Christian minds such as St. Augustine (in regard to spirit and soul) have failed to do.

Even so, all who pastor souls effectively, from St. Paul to this present day, have to deal with the essential makeup of man. To pray aright and to see healing take place, we have to discern where the need is. We will do a person no good and perhaps a lot of harm if we pray for his salvation (in effect, for the healing of his spirit) when he has in fact already accepted Christ, and his need is for emotional or physical healing. And we do live in a day when the church is in great confusion over these matters. One part of the church actually refuses to acknowledge the need for healing of the soul (as if full sanctification necessarily occurs at the moment of the new birth), while yet another denies, for all practical purposes, even the need for the new birth (the essential healing of man's spirit). To go even further, few Christians can discriminate between the psychological and the spiritual, and they think, like the pagans of old, that the mind is the highest element in man. This is only one more way of saying that we twentieth-century Christians have lost the understanding of Incarnational Reality.

With this in mind, I want to stress the following for all who pray for the healing of persons. It is essential that the Christian who needs healing realize and practice the Presence of Christ within. He must know and be reminded that his spirit is ingodded: it is the "whole place" within him, while the part of his soul that needs healing is coming into the light and being healed. The more wounded the person, the more necessary it is for him to understand and to continually affirm that Christ lives in him.

For example, the Christian who is being healed emotionally due to serious abuse or deprivation of some kind may know the most incredible pain and confusion as his soul is being healed. If he does not know the difference between his spirit and his soul, he may despair, thinking there is no hope for him. Every repressed feeling, memory, and emotion will be surfacing, along with all the dark voices involved. If he thinks of this storm-tossed part of his soul as his essential real self or spirit, rather than that wounded part of his soul that God is healing, then he will be unable to practice the Presence of God within. Indeed, he will think God very far from him. He will think God cannot possibly love such a confused and battered one as himself.

All this changes the moment we lead the person to the quiet place of affirming, "Another lives in me. My spirit is one with His. That is my whole place. All else is raging around me and within me, but I can stand now, confident, and watch as God heals this part of me that is so wounded." The point I am stressing here is that it is dangerous to say that certain things are amiss with the essential spirit of man when the real problem is a need for emotional and psychological healing. It leaves the person paralyzed, crippled, unable to move forward. Even more important, we are not recognizing the key to that person's healing—the practice of the Presence of the One who has redeemed and is even now in the process of healing him.

I've had several occasions recently to see people who are in despair about their lives and on the verge of suicide because they did not recognize this truth. When I asked them to practice the Presence of the Lord, they said, "I can't, my spirit is . . ." and then they would go on to describe some malady of their spirit. As soon as I ascertained they were in fact Christians, I said, "No. That is not so. Christ is within your spirit, ready to radiate up through your inner being. There is a whole place within you. You are the Lord's." They were then ministered to and enabled to withstand the batterings of facing deep woundedness in their souls and lives.

Recently, I prayed with a precious Christian leader who, though she had no conscious confusion over spirit and soul, was in the midst of tremendous psychological strain. From a seriously dysfunctional family, she had repressed her feelings in order to survive. She is now no longer able to repress all these feelings, and they are coming up in a most frightening manner. She was anxious, feeling bereft of God. Immediately I shared the above with her, and she eagerly grasped it, first writing it all down in her notebook. "God is in my spirit; my spirit is whole while my soul is being healed. I can practice the Presence of God, and I will." And she said, "That is exactly what I needed to hear," and her whole countenance changed. We all need to be reminded of this basic incarnational truth.

Ours is an incarnational view of man and reality. Christ is, as F. B. Meyer has said, "the living Fountain rising up in the well of our personality."[7] He is present now. He, our Healer, has already become flesh, has already accomplished the work of the cross, has already poured out the full gift of His Spirit upon us. As long as we dwell in time, there will never be more of Him available to us than now. Our walk with Him, our acknowledgment of Him with us, within us, while remaining fully sovereign—all this in the now—is what faith apprehends. God is available to us; Jesus is indeed, if we are born again of His Spirit, the living Fountain within. We practice His Presence. We keep this truth uppermost in prayer for the healing of the soul, that is, in the removal of blocks to our becoming in Christ.

Man's Body

When man is physically ill due to disease or accident, we pray differently than we would for the healing of the soul. The one effective principle for healing of spirit, soul, or body is invoking and affirming God's Presence with us. "And if the Spirit of him who raised Jesus from the dead is living in you, he who raised Christ from the dead will also give life to your mortal bodies through his Spirit, who lives in you" (Romans 8:11).

The sicknesses of spirit, soul, and body intertwine and overlap. It is not at all unusual to pray for the healing of a memory and see the body healed as well.

Or to pray for healing of the body and find matters of spirit and soul coming to the fore. Prayer for deliverance from demonic activity may (or may not) be needed with any one of these. Healing of spirit, soul, and body is simply, as John Gaynor Banks and Agnes Sanford have said, "answered prayer."

Healing of Memories
In prayer for healing of memories, we not only confess our sin, but we forgive those people and circumstances that have so grieved and wounded us. We often need to stop denying that we have been sinned against.

Sometimes the memories that need healing go far back in time, back before conscious memory. But the heart knows; it does not forget. It banks the memories. There sorrowful, shameful memories are suppressed. They do not disappear, but need healing.

The intellect and the heart, our "two minds," stand in antithesis. Opposite and complementary one to the other, they do not work in ways at all comparable. The heart, as the seat of the memory, is the "feeling mind." It is irrational only in that it "thinks" in symbols. "Feelings are," as Robert M. Doran, S. J., writes, "energy-become-conscious. Feelings are a matter of psychic energy." Furthermore:

Feelings always enter consciousness through being connected with *some* representation. Now, the most basic form of representation lies in symbols. A *symbol*, [Bernard] Lonergan says, is an image of a real or imaginary object that evokes a feeling or is evoked by a feeling; what this means is that there is never a feeling without a symbolic meaning; never a symbol without a feeling. To *name* one's feeling is to discover the dynamic images, the symbols that are associated with them. To have *insight* into one's feelings is to understand the symbolic association. To *tell one's story* is to narrate the course of one's elemental symbolizing.[8]

In my lectures and counseling I say less about feelings and how to deal with them than most others do. I think that is because I say so much about symbols and how to deal with them. To help a person become aware of and understand the images and pictures his heart is emitting automatically puts him in touch with his feelings. I find it is better to get a person's eyes on the symbol rather than the feeling. In this way, he objectifies the feeling and understands it more quickly. It can't seem bigger than life, "lording it over" him, so to speak.

The heart or "feeling mind," the seat of the memory, is subjective. We cannot reason with it or command it. All who have suddenly blocked on the name of a person they know well, or have been unable to give answers on tests for which they have thoroughly prepared, understand this facet of the unconscious well enough. We can try to reason with it or impatiently command it, and it simply balks.

Agnes Sanford called this, her subjective mind, "Junior," and delighted in teaching people how to treat it. If, she said, you are taking a test and can't remember the answer, just speak softly to Junior (at which point she would pat her hand over her heart as if soothing the balking mind) and say, "That's o.k., Junior, you just fish around and find the answer while I go on to the next question. Then I'll come back and you'll have it." And that is exactly what she would do. And sure enough, "Junior" would come up with it once she stopped trying to force the issue.

Medical missionary and psychiatrist Dr. James Stringham, lecturing on guilt and the need for confession in the healing of the *psyche*, speaks of the unconscious mind as the original computer. If fifty years of one's financial history were computerized, he says, the one time the person failed to pay a bill would be the first datum to come up. And so it is with guilt and experiences of rejection, as well as diseased or unnatural feelings, in the unconscious. The unconscious mind banks our emotions, our feelings of anger, hatred, desire, joy, and love, as well as our memories. And like the computer, it never forgets the "unpaid bill," the unforgiven or the unhealed. Desires or thoughts that the conscious mind has repressed are still very active in the subconscious, and as a further complication, the truly repressed materials come before the conscious mind only in disguised and unrecognizable (that is, symbolic) forms. Such images are not to be taken literally, but are to be read symbolically, in which case they are understandable. As Karl Stern says in his valuable book *The Third Revolution*:

> [T]hat vast dark universe of the "meaningless" which exists outside the world illuminated by logic becomes one meaningful structure once we have introduced certain tentative premises. Before we form concepts, before we think in words, and before we begin to think in logical abstractions, we go through an infantile phase in which the universe of our mind consists of sensation and imagery. The connection between that preconceptual rock bottom and the upper layer of logical conceptual thinking is mysterious. *But it is not unfathomable.*[9] (italics mine)

So the "feeling mind" or deep heart is, so to speak, the seat of the intuitive faculty, of the true imagination, and of the memory.

Memory

The power of the memory to make the past present to us in a very real way is extraordinary. *Anamnesis*, a Greek word used to explain eucharistic theology, best illustrates this phenomenon. It denotes bringing forward into the present an event from out of the past, and like our Lord's statement, "This is My body; this is My blood," it is not merely an act of psychological remembrance.

Even ancestral memories come up at times for healing, and at other times, they are simply, as I found out firsthand, experienced. The first time I went to Scotland, it was after a great deal of travel to the far-flung places of the earth. I happened to be traveling across the Highlands at a time when the mountains were solid purple with heather, and the smell of peat fires wafted across the land. In a profound experience, I somehow knew this place and that I had come home. It was as if my roots went down to the center of the earth there. On my return home, I looked into my genealogy and found that the great majority of my ancestors are Highland Scots. Since sharing this with others, any number of people have shared a like sort of thing with me.

Such an experience has nothing to do with reincarnation, a pagan way of explaining such phenomena. It may well have something to do with genetic imprinting, some basic "memory" written into the very cells of our being. A close friend and associate of mine has a female border collie, one that is now many generations removed from her ancestors who for centuries were bred to move zigzag fashion behind sheep—herding the entire flock forward in the direction the shepherd desired. This remarkable animal, so "humanized" I refer to her affectionately as Beastie just to remind myself she is one, still moves zigzag fashion, whether behind a person, a prey, or just when running in a field exploring. It's written somehow into her brain stem or genetic "memory." Perhaps some small part of what I experienced in Scotland I share with Beastie and the rest of the animal kingdom. But the greater part of the explanation lies in *the nature of time* and in the fact that we, though creatures of time, are made in the image of God. As Christians, these truths apply to us in a special way, for Christ indwells us. C. S. Lewis hints at all these things in this remarkable section on memory.

Memory, as we now know it, is a dim foretaste, a mirage even, of a power which the soul, or rather Christ in the soul (He went to "prepare a place" for us), will exercise hereafter. It need no longer be private to the soul in which it occurs. I can now communicate to you the fields of my boyhood—they are building-estates today—only imperfectly, by words. Perhaps the day is coming when I can take you for a walk through them.[10]

We now know that when surgeons operate on a certain portion of the brain, their fine instruments "touch off" old memories, memories in which the person relives incidences of the long forgotten past, replete with sounds, colors, smells. This illustrates in a concrete way that the mind does indeed bank the memories. But even more, it illustrates for me the fact that, if surgeons can, by accidentally touching the brain, find a memory, how much more readily can our God touch those memories that need forgiveness and healing.

The Holy Spirit is God's finger on sore memories. If the need for forgiveness of sin goes back generations, how easy it is for God to hear our prayer and touch that ancestral memory. He then lifts from us the burden of that thing that has so wounded our families.[11]

Time

Our memory helps us overcome the limitations we have as creatures of time. Time too is a creature. It is created. That is a mind-blowing concept, but it is true. Jesus, the infinite One, is outside of time, and all times are present to Him.

> To be God is to enjoy an infinite present where nothing has yet passed away and nothing is still to come.[12]

This means that all our times, together with all that we are, are eternally present to God.

Several years before learning how to pray for healing of memories, I had a very unusual experience, one that I did not share for a good number of years. I was on a camping trip in Oklahoma, and in the process of cleaning up the camp, I had walked out onto a huge boulder. The chore finished, I stepped back, and when I did, I stepped back in time. I saw two Indian men, and they saw me. I saw the terrain as it had been hundreds of years ago. I knew instantly that it was long before the white man had come, and that these Indian men had never before seen a white person. We were mutually astonished.

All this happened and was over in an instant. Amazed, I ran back to my old camper wagon and prayed. I asked the Lord what had happened, and I knew it was exactly as it seemed to be. I had looked down through time; they had looked up through time and seen me. I did not understand this experience for a long time, but as I prayed, the Lord assured me that He had allowed it and that it was in no way engineered by the powers of darkness.

At that point in my life, I was deeply perplexed over Edie, a young girl I had prayed for but been unable to help. She repeatedly fell into sexual sin, and then would repent with all her heart, at which times she would ask me to pray with her. I knew beyond all shadow of a doubt the power of God's forgiveness in my own life, and, knowing her desire to change, I couldn't understand her inability to stand in Christ. I did not understand her pain that ended in sexual compulsions, ones that drove her to throw herself away time after time with men.

Edie had been adopted as a young girl, and invariably when we prayed together for any length of time, a painful memory would surface. In it, she and her baby brothers were in a crib, and they were wet, filthy, and hungry. The police came, took her drunken mother one direction, her drunken father another. She never saw her parents or her baby brothers again. She agonized over this, and as the memory would surface, she would sob convulsively. She had taken this loss as the deepest kind of personal rejection. In her heart she felt that if they could not love her, no one could; if they abandoned her, all would. This was the root memory behind her compulsions. Had I known then what I learned later, she would have received a healing that would have enabled her to withstand the psychological storms that blew upon her as her soul was being healed of its deep deprivations.

While on this camping trip, I was asking the Lord why this girl remained so troubled, why she couldn't receive from Him what she needed. The Lord was showing me, both in this experience and in the one I had in Scotland, that all times are one with Him; that He is eternally present to all those moments where forgiveness and healing are needed.

Had I understood then the healing of memories, Edie could have been healed of her sexual compulsions, and then she could have gone on to full self-acceptance. I could have invited God in all His healing power into that memory. It not only contained the root trauma, but it most likely symbolized all the parental neglect and rejection she had ever known. The rejection had left her unable to accept love from God or from others. We would together have confessed the dreadful sins of alcoholism, of deprivation of parental love and care, and so on as the Holy Spirit led, and then, holding her tightly (the tiny infant in her was still crying out for a mother's arms), I could have helped her to forgive her mother, her father, her little brothers for leaving her. In helping her to forgive and then to receive from God both illumination and healing, God could have lifted from her the terrible burden of her parents' sins against her.

God had been with her in that worst of moments, that time when she lost her parents and brothers. Had someone been on the scene who knew how to take hold of God with one hand and her with the other, she could have been been comforted even then. As an infant, she had desperately needed someone to minister Christ's healing love to her, but so few Christians think or know to pray in this way even for the tiny baby. Several years later she was adopted by Christian parents, and under the hearing of the gospel, she had come to Christ. Now Christ lived within her, ready to heal those worst memories and to help her deal with the deep wounds in her soul. But she had needed the understanding and ministering hand of another—one who would not only direct her eyes upward to God, but who would then pray in such a way that Christ could enter into the root memories and bring healing. When that healing did not come, thinking herself fit only to be abandoned, she continued to try to get love, if only for a moment, through compulsively giving her body away to one stranger after another.

Was she responsible for her sin, the way she compulsively attempted to assuage the inner loneliness and pain? Yes. But as a Christian she desperately needed in her behalf the healing power that God has entrusted to the church. However, the church surrounding her had lost its power to heal the soul.

God heals even the traumas we can't remember. He wills to heal all. The good news is that He is present to all our times—past, present, and future. We must simply learn to collaborate with Him in prayer.

Time and Space

To be human is to be gifted with time and space, but it is also to be limited by time and space. We need to understand how the gift of prayer helps us overcome these obstacles. Prayer for healing of memories, that is, for in-depth forgiveness of sin, is the way we overcome our limitations as creatures of time. *Intercessory prayer,* something we are never to neglect, is the means given us to overcome the barriers of space. To intercede for another, no matter where he might be on the globe or even in space is to, in a manner of speaking, be present with him. "Though I am absent from you in body, I am present with you in spirit," said St. Paul, who prayed fervently for the Christians in his care (Colossians 2:5, see also, 1 Corinthians 5:3-5). I insert this admonition to intercessory prayer because it is easy, once we see the incredible results of prayer for healing of memories, to neglect this way of prayer. We then must correct the imbalance. But our illusion concerning time seems to be the most difficult, and C. S. Lewis effectively speaks to this ongoing blindness within the Christian community:

> We have a strange illusion that mere time cancels sins. I have heard others, and I have heard myself, recounting cruelties and falsehoods committed in boyhood as if they were no concern of the present speaker's, and even with laughter. But mere time does nothing either to the fact or to the guilt of sin. The guilt is washed out not by time but by repentance and the blood of Christ.[13]

Time, a creature, does not erase our sin. Only by our repentance and His blood is sin and guilt lifted from both past and present. It is for this reason that when a church, a nation, or an individual repents, *incredible* things happen.

A Warning Regarding False Doctrine

The awesome truth that Christ's atoning blood is sufficient to cancel the power of sin is being seriously obscured by certain ministers of inner healing today. While acknowledging the need for forgiveness and remission of sins, they put forward in their lectures and books something other than this great orthodox teaching. They add to this teaching occult doctrines unacceptable to any branch of the church—Catholic or Protestant. These teachings actually undermine the doctrine of repentance and forgiveness of sin, while at the same time they lead toward universalism and mediumistic practices.

Their main thesis? These teachers jump directly from the all-sufficient Christian truth of forgiveness of sin, especially as it is administered through the Christian liturgy of the Eucharist, to a world of ghosts—of unquiet spirits. The dead, they say, are trying to contact the living. The living have a responsibility to come into an ongoing relationship with the deceased. Rather than offer healing through forgiveness of sin by a holy and just God, they espouse a new *gnosis* (actually a new form of an old occultism) concerning familial spirits haunting the living—a thing that opens unwary people to spiritism and to familiar spirits—demons who impersonate the dead.

These doctrines introduce into the Christian community ideas that have long been part of the Anglo-American occult tradition. Edgar Cayce and Ruth Montgomery would be perfectly at home with what these ministers are practicing.

During World War II when our pilots were flying "The Hump" in the Far East, natives who had long been involved in ancestor worship would run out, getting as close to the propellers as they possibly could in order to relieve themselves of the "spirits" of their ancestors. Often these natives would be killed, and there was not one thing our flyers could do about it. The demonic hold that such practices have, not to mention all the superstitions that go along with them, are something that primitive and pagan races almost always have to be delivered from when they convert to Christ.

A lovely Chinese woman and her family came to one of my conferences. She was deeply distressed that these pagan teachings were flooding into her diocese and that her bishop did not discern the dangers, much less protect his people from them. As a young Christian from the Far East, she had (with great pain and suffering due to demonic oppression) come out of all the deluding practices that have to do with placating the spirits of the dead. She was now amazed to hear such things being taught and recommended in her Christian community.[14]

While this teaching has partially subsided, it still erupts periodically and subtly into Christian circles. We must be aware of it and simply affirm that repentance and forgiveness of sin alone releases us from the effects of our own sins and of others' sins, even when those offenses involve unconfessed sins, curses, and so on that come down through family lines. Christ's blood is enough. It is utterly sufficient. We need add nothing to that. We will then see the miracle of spiritual and psychological healing occur, and with it no bad fruit or seed from the tares sown among the wheat.

Doctrines of demons leave demonized souls in their wake. What we believe really matters. In an age when naturalism with its materialistic ideologies and epistemologies is breaking up and failing, we can expect the muddy mysticisms to flood in. The only protection against the false is the true—the power in the name of Christ that all Christians know as they learn to obey Christ and collaborate with His Spirit to preach, teach, and heal. We move in the *spirituals*, the gifts of the Holy Spirit, and we cease trying to do God's work in our own strength alone. To truly live and move obediently in the Kingdom of God is to move quite "naturally" and joyfully in the realm of *miracle*. But the church, in her capitulation to materialism and the ideologies of this world, has long failed to move as she should in the power that God gives. As this power is being restored, the power of true repentance and the remittance of sin, we will have to deal with the mysticisms that have flooded in to fill in the vacuum. These mysticisms will nearly always contain much of the true, and especially the truths the church is currently neglecting, but they will invariably be mixed and irreparably tainted with something other than *Incarnational Reality,* the reality of Christ with us, forgiving and releasing us from sin, thereby uniting us to the Father by His Spirit within, empowering us individually and corporately as the Body of Christ.

On the other hand, we will have to deal with the rise of the new anti-supernaturalists, dispensationalists, and what not, who are in terror of the true power of God and wildly lump the false and the true together. Christ's teaching on the wheat and the tares is apropos here. (See Matthew 13:36-43.) Such people, dishonestly quoting out of context, with no care for the full body of a fellow Christian's writings and works, are today ignorantly and recklessly pulling up the wheat with the tares. They are themselves sowers of bad seed. They are sowing fear and hatred (among other things) of the true imagination, being ignorant of it it and terrified of the false, and they are sowing fear and hatred of fellow Christians. They are slandering great servants of the Lord whose work and fruit of that work speaks for itself and needs no defense. They are also sowing the seeds of poor scholarship, poor theology, and poor psychology—like those putting forward the muddy mysticisms.

We can no longer naively fail to comprehend the ideologies of the day and the way that Christians who are trapped in them flail about trying to mend things. We can no longer ignore sound theology and the teaching of how truly to move in the power of God. Such was always harmful, but now the hour is critical. Surely there has never been a day when the people (leaders included) could be so easily and fatally led astray. May the Lord strengthen us all to do His will.

CHAPTER 7

Second Great Barrier to Wholeness in Christ: Failure to Forgive Others

For if you forgive men when they sin against you, your heavenly Father will also forgive you. But if you do not forgive men their sins, your Father will not forgive your sins.

(Matthew 6:14-15)

The failure to forgive another is a most formidable barrier to wholeness. One can only begin to comprehend its danger to the soul by meditating on Christ's words above. Most moderns, including Christians, have lost even the language with which to speak of the soul. Therefore, the soul's motions are largely lost to them. For that reason, I will write briefly of what seems to me to be the most common "categories" of this failure in order to help us identify our own needs to forgive, as well as to help us be of greater help to those for whom we pray.

Always, at the bottom of everything that is amiss, we will find pride. We need to confess it. And so it is in our failure to forgive the merely petty things in life. Let's look at that category first.

Forgiving Petty Offenses

We tend to overlook this category when we are praying for folks, but often the need to forgive will be just here. It's the *everydayness* of such irritations and transgressions that gets to us, and we can easily come to despise those who offend us in these ways.

Besides that, we should like to pick and choose those who are eligible to offend us. The implication here, of course, is that the offender is something of a snippet and grossly inferior to us in some way. The remedy is to confess the sin of *pride*, calling it precisely that, and then forgive the offender.

Christ does not see others as we see them. To stop for a moment, practice His Presence, and ask to see this person through His eyes can give us an entirely different perspective. In doing this, we often see strengths we've overlooked in the other person, while at the same time we may be painfully reminded of our own weaknesses and Christ's patience with the petty within ourselves.

I witnessed a remarkable physical healing in a woman who realized her need to forgive a petty offense. This woman was part of a prayer group that met regularly to pray for the healing of the sick. She had become increasingly crippled by arthritis, and no matter how often she received healing prayer, she slowly worsened. Several years into her illness, we were praying once again for her healing when the matter of her upstairs neighbor came forcibly before her. This neighbor was an invalid, and she took lunch to her every day at noon. Invariably, however, a few minutes before she could carry the steaming plate of food up the stairs, the phone would ring, and a whiny voice would moan, "Are you coming?"

Her thoughts toward this neighbor grew darker as this behavior continued, but rather than facing the poor soul with the fact that the daily phone call sorely tried her patience, she simply held her tongue with its growing list of unspoken retorts. But she "thought them" loudly enough. After several years of this, her insides were fairly shouting, "Don't I always come! Do I ever miss!" and so on. She got to the point that she would tense up just before the call came. So things went on, day in and day out.

On the day of her healing, she painfully bent her arthritic knees before the altar, and as we prayed with her, she realized her need to forgive the upstairs invalid and to ask God's forgiveness for her reactions. This she did, and she was instantly healed of her very painful arthritic condition. People who have never seen something like this have difficulty believing it. Such a healing dramatically illustrates the power of forgiveness and the way it can open us more fully to God's Healing Presence.

Humility and longsuffering, those great Christian virtues, are not often expounded or understood these days. Not all who seem to have them (by never thinking about themselves, for example), in fact, do have them. Christians bent toward one another in idolatrous and codependent ways sometimes mistake this condition for one of humility and service to others. In actuality, these conditions merely enable sick and sinful behavior in others.[1] "Humble yourselves—feeling very insignificant—in the Presence of the Lord, and He will exalt you. He will lift you up and make your lives significant" (James 4:10, *The Amplified Bible*).

To confess the sin of pride and to go on to forgive is marvelously simple, but many stumble right here. We find we must enroll in a primary level of the Holy Spirit's school of prayer. "Father, I am nothing apart from You, have mercy on me; I have been seeing *apart from You;* if you leave me for an instant,

I shall be even more prideful, more self-serving." When we learn to pray this prayer, without the least taint of the wrong kind of self-hatred on the one hand or a feeling of superiority on the other, we will be well on our way to maturity in Christ.

Where there are ongoing petty offenses, it is important that we forsake the subjective (reactionary) position and then—listening to God for instructions—step into the free air of an objective position. In this manner, my friend could have dealt honestly with her neighbor's daily whining question and phone call and then ministered Christ's love to the real problem—the invalid's intense loneliness and fear of abandonment.

Failure to Forgive Due to Being Out of Touch with One's Heart

In this day when people's heads are so out of touch with their hearts, many have unforgiveness and do not realize it until, in prayer for healing, the Holy Spirit reveals it.

Often when praying with such persons, I find that a memory of abusive or abnormal behavior by another will come up. The person will not know he needs to forgive the offender. I will have to say, "You must confess this as a sin against you, and you must name it specifically for the sin that it is, and then, before God, extend forgiveness to (offender's name)." The specific naming of the sin and of the offender is important. This is no abstract transaction, but a very real dealing before and with our God.

These persons will invariably be surprised, as if they have never thought about the matter in this light. This is especially true when the need to forgive another involves a parent. But once the deed or circumstance has been acknowledged as an offense, and forgiveness has been extended to that person, healing comes quickly.

Often these people do not know what normal is. They are from dysfunctional homes in which the members do not relate to one another in a healthy fashion. In addition, as children these persons usually were taught to deny their feelings. Even when normal thoughts and feelings were expressed, these were not validated. So there will be a deep inner knowledge of injustice and/or frustration and, at some level of their being, a knowledge of the need to forgive. I know this is so because when they restate (at my request) the offense and extend forgiveness, great anger begins to surface. I then have them raise their hands to Christ on the cross, and they "see" the anger and unforgiveness come up and out of them and flow into the One who, in our stead, takes and carries all our sin and darkness. After this is accomplished, we ask Christ to fill all those spaces where this pain, anger, and unforgiveness have been with His healing love and light.

Judy's story, recounted in chapter 6 of *Crisis in Masculinity*, is a good example of how emotionally sick and confused persons can be when they need to forgive another but do not realize it. The story also shows that we remain tied to parents in unhealthy ways until we extend forgiveness to those parents. In fact, we fail to fully separate our own identity from our parent's and end up hating ourselves.

Forgiving the Unforgiveable

> In all their distress he too was distressed, and the angel of his presence saved them. (Isaiah 63:9)

> Agony means severe suffering in which something dies—either the base thing, or the good. No man is the same after an agony; he is either better or worse, and the agony of a man's experience is nearly always the first thing that opens his mind to understand the need of Redemption worked out by Jesus Christ.[2]

Sometimes we must forgive actions that go far beyond the petty offenses to our pride and prejudice. For the young person, twisted in mind and spirit, robbed of even the simplest pleasures of childhood and youth due to the overbearing hatred and mistreatment of a crazed or perverted parent, forgiving can at first seem impossible. Many and varied too are the more subtle sins against the human spirit and soul that are equally hard to forgive. The minister errs who simply throws out the Scripture "forgive your enemy" to such persons without helping them into the Presence of God in such a way that they can both forgive and receive consolation and healing.

I have often had people say to me, "I cannot forgive." And when they tell me the circumstances, I fully understand their difficulty. In *The Healing Presence,* pages 88-90, I tell about my own experience of forgiving the "unforgivable," how through an entire afternoon I cried out to God for the power to forgive and knew only too well how helpless I was without His grace. As I wrote:

> There were terrible moments in that interminable afternoon when I wondered what I would do if God failed to help me, if I would simply have to cry out like this the rest of my life. Then came a moment when instantly my pleading was interrupted by an amazing awareness of Christ in me, and from that center where He and I were mysteriously one, forgiveness was extended to my enemy. It was as if Christ in and through me forgave the person (who can explain such a thing?)—yet I too forgave.[3]

Note here that it was not until I reached full identification with Christ that I was able to forgive. On the cross He identified Himself with my sin, my suffering—the very pain I was at that moment experiencing. In reaching that place of identification with Him, I could, as it were, stand in the cross and hurt—with Him.[4] One with Him in His dying, I was able to release my unforgiveness, with all its feelings of rage and woundedness, to Him in utter trust. In unison with

Him, I could pray: "Father, forgive them, they know not what they do." All my hurt, fear, inability to forgive flowed into Him, and in exchange He gave me freedom. Having taken my place in His dying, now one with Him still, I took my place in His rising. And I knew joy. There is no better theology than this. It's the message of the cross. And it applies to all of us. This is the way of Christian forgiveness.

On the basis of the Scriptures and from my own personal experience and that of helping many, many others with the worst imaginable situations, I can always assure these dear ones, "Oh yes, you can forgive. And I will gladly show you how. We will go to prayer, and 'you shall receive power' (Acts 1:8)— the power to forgive even your worst enemy." This enemy often will be your "beloved enemy." It is those nearest to us who have the greatest power to wound and maim us.

Johnny's story, first recounted in *The Broken Image*, pages 82-84, and now reprinted below, illustrates the way prayer for healing of memories can help a suffering soul to forgive the "unforgivable." This story also illustrates the vital part Johnny's will as well as his imagination (the way that, in the Presence of God, the heart is enabled to see) played in his being able to forgive an utterly reprobate father.

JOHNNY'S STORY

Johnny was married and in his mid-twenties when his father died. It was then that he, a very needy person, moved into homosexuality, a sexual behavior he practiced for two years.

His deep inner craving still unmet and his marriage in serious trouble, Johnny attempted to extricate himself from his homosexual activity. It was then that he found Christ and, thoroughly converted, became an ardent witness to the faith.

About ten years after his conversion, however, and all of them spent as a devout and wholly committed Christian, Johnny began falling apart. He feared his children would find out what he had been, he feared his wife would leave him, but most of all he had a dreadful fear of failure. In addition to these fears, his homosexual compulsions were once again too strong for his conscious mind to deny or repress, and he feared he was, in truth, deviant. He was in the midst of a nervous breakdown.

It was in this state of collapse that he responded to his wife's concerned urging and came for prayer. His conscious mind, so wearied with repressing all the old fears, denials, and bad memories, had ceased to do its job. Johnny would now have to face his inner loneliness, all the fears and darkness he had so long refused to see and acknowledge.

His story is a terrible one. It has to do with a brutalizing father, and with older brothers who practiced homosexuality as part of the pecking-order syndrome at work in the home.

His father had never had a smile or kind word for him, something he had yearned for all his life. As his sisters grew up, he had to live with the fact that his father was molesting them sexually, and that he could do nothing about it. He also watched his father choose girlfriends for his older sons, and then seduce them himself. These sons, brutalized by their father, spent time in prison, and became involved in the brute kind of homosexuality that prisons are rife with. They would then come home and abuse the younger boys in a similar fashion. Johnny, the youngest, seemed to catch the brunt of their dehumanizing behavior.

No wonder Johnny was breaking apart. All these memories were festering within, as yet unhealed. His masculinity had, of course, been seriously repressed in the environment he had grown up in.

After he had shared his story with me, one that he had never been able fully to tell before, we went to prayer. Although he knew that prayer was the only way, he at first resisted. This was because he thought prayer was more or less an exercise of the conscious mind, and that he would have to try to understand and deal with the whole problem consciously again. And that was precisely what he could no longer do, what he was worn out from attempting to do. That was when I asked him to relax completely and let me do the praying, while he simply looked up to Jesus with the eyes of his heart. His healing illustrates the inestimable value of "picturing" or imagining. Besides being a valid way of "seeing," it opens the heart to any pictures God would send. God sends us His help and truth, and often it comes as a "picture." Johnny's healing also illustrates how closely hate can be connected to love.

Realizing there was hatred toward his father, I asked him to picture his father standing next to Jesus. It is very difficult to look up and see Jesus when one's heart is filled with hate. And it is also difficult to picture the face of the one we hate. We tend to blot it out, annihilate it. Johnny couldn't look up to picture Jesus or his father, but yielding to the Presence of the Lord and with his head bent down almost to the floor, he began to sob uncontrollably as the deep-seated hatred toward his father welled up and out of his heart. He then had to forgive his father, and this forgiveness had to come from the deepest recesses of Johnny's wounded heart. It seemed to him an absolute impossibility. Even so, he knew he had to get through this impasse, for he could not go on in the old tormented way. I assured him that loving and forgiving another is a matter of the *will* rather than the emotions, and that his feelings naturally reflected the abuses of his early years with his father.

Praying that his *will* be strengthened, and insisting that he picture his father, I asked him to *will* to stretch up his hand and take the hand of his father. His head still bent, he slowly lifted his arm up as if to take the hand of his father, sobbing, "I *will* to forgive you, Dad. I *will* to forgive you." I asked him to look up into his father's face and say, "Father, I *do* forgive you." Then, to my astonishment, torrents of repressed love began to pour out. Johnny cried over and over and over, "Daddy, I love you, Daddy, I love you. I *do* forgive you. Jesus, forgive me for hating him. Jesus, forgive me. Jesus, help me." And then, to his dad, "If only you could have said one kind word to me." At this, he slowly looked up to see the face that in life had always appeared so stern and hostile to him. I shall never forget his amazement as he "saw" his dad's face. "My father is *smiling* at me! He is smiling at me!" he exclaimed.

I do not fully understand the smile that seemed to assuage a lifetime of yearning on Johnny's part, but I've seen this sort of thing happen far too often, along with the lasting wholesome fruit it bears, to ever doubt it. Can it be that there is something about forgiving that releases not only the living, but the dead as well? Can the dead know when they are released from another's unforgiveness? This is wonderful to speculate on, and of course we can only speculate. But this I know—when we heal in Jesus' name, He sends us healing pictures as well as healing words. Jesus was in charge of that smile. This also I know—in Johnny's prayer of forgiveness, he came into a relationship with his father, one that he had never been able to achieve in his dad's lifetime.

You will remember that Johnny began to search out homosexual partners only after his father's death. In his heart, he had always yearned to win his father's love and affirmation—that one smile. His dad's death, before any of this happened, left the injured little boy in Johnny crying out for that father-love, crying out for the masculine identity that could come with it. Perhaps he was in part looking for his father in these relationships. He was certainly searching for himself in another. He was in the grip of an acute identity crisis.

In forgiving his father, Johnny set the stage for his release from fear of failure. This fear was no mere weed in the garden of his heart, but a massive choking root that was threatening his entire inner life, and that is how it appeared in the picture that came as I prayed. Prayer for its removal seemed like prayer for the pulling up of an ugly old tree, roots and all. I prayed that the roots be loosened by God's love and power flowing in; and as this began to happen, I saw the fear come up and out of Johnny. I then asked for Jesus to fill with His freeing, healing love all the spaces where the awful root tentacles had been. We waited as we saw this happening, and until there was no fear left in his heart.

Like the lame man who when healed went into the Temple leaping and praising God, Johnny's reaction to finding himself set free was ecstatic. Having long sought the Lord and this healing, he was overwhelmed in its reality. His joy was a blessed thing to see.

In Johnny, we see the unhealed trauma of homosexual rape in childhood, the utter repression of masculinity by a hostile father and environment, and the terrible yearning for a father's love and his own identity all mixed in one. His major healing came as he was released from the repressed hatred toward his father and was enabled to forgive him.

The story of "The Doctor Who Hated His Face in the Mirror," first recounted in *Crisis in Masculinity,* pages 70-76, illustrates the way of helping others forgive the more subtle but equally devastating kinds of sins parents commit against them. In this story, we deal with the childhood oath, and the fear that forgiving may open oneself again to another's power to hurt.

THE DOCTOR'S STORY

A Christian physician, loved by everyone who knows him, had a most difficult time in accepting himself fully. Every morning, as he shaved, he was reminded of this need because he did not like to see his own face in the mirror. He is a man wonderfully used of God, and therefore one who has prayed continuously for the grace to overcome the problem of self-hatred, if for no other reason than in order to accept the vocation God has given him. Anointed by God to pray for the sick, he has *had* to live from the Center, at least part of the time. But he knows the danger of running from God's perfect will for himself when, judging himself unacceptable, he steps alongside and looks at himself with excessive distrust and unlove.

As he grew in the favor and admiration of others, and in success both as a physician and as a Christian serving in the public eye, his self-hatred pained him all the more. All kinds of new fears about himself set in: "Why do I seek out friendships with good-looking, handsome, athletic men?" Before his involvement in Christian ministry, he had kept his feelings, fears, yearnings, needs and loneliness to himself. In fact, before his experience of renewal in the Spirit, he had kept a stern authoritarian control over both himself and his family, a control that kept true conversation with them at a safe distance. Rarely, therefore, could he share meaningfully even with his wife. To do so might mean to look, even for a moment, at his fears, and then he would have to believe the worst of himself. But gradually, as he came present to the Lord, he came present to his own heart and gained the courage to look at his feelings and fears. After hearing me speak and reading *The Broken Image,* he realized and faced the fact that although he did not have a sexual neurosis, he was severely cut off from his masculine side. He simply could not accept himself as a man.

He came to talk to me about his fears, the main one being, "Why am I so desperate for male companionship? Is there really something wrong with me? I have never looked at myself as being masculine; by that I mean 'handsome, rugged, athletic.' I see myself as being different, odd, seeking male approval and companionship. I like to be creative, do gardening, read, travel, dress well, and I am 'people-oriented.' I'm a 'hugger.' And I feel I must apologize for being this way, that I must try to hide my creativity and my gifts."

As we talked, his agitation concerning his father quickly became apparent: "I have never felt loved or affirmed as a son or as a man by my father. I don't ever remember him holding me, telling me he loves me, that I am good, or that he is proud of me."

If ever a man needed to be lifted from the subjective to the objective position where his father was concerned, this good man did. He still yearned for his dad's love and affirmation; he still grew angry with him for not giving it. He looked for his father to change, and he went through all the gamut of emotions over and over again as he reached out to his father and as his father remained precisely the man he had always been: unloving, unreasonable, and always accusing others of neglecting him. At my suggestion that he, the physician, must gain the objectivity to see and accept his father as he in fact was, and that we would pray to this end, the pitch of his voice must have risen an octave: "But you don't know what you are asking! We can't accept him *that* way."

And out came the picture of what it had meant to try to grow up straight in the midst of an evil perversity. His father, a rich man, was also a miser. Although he owned thousands of acres of rich orchards in Oregon, he never gave anything to his wife or children that cost him anything—whether in the way of loving actions or even the lowliest gift. One of the doctor's most agonizing charges against his father was, "He never once gave me a gift. He is a rich man, and for my birthday he gives me coupons that cost him nothing." Throughout his school and college years, the son had spent vacations laboring in the father's orchards. Although he was well-paid, he had no sense of partnership with his father in this enterprise. His father remained as aloof toward him as toward the other workers. Through his work he came to know the magnitude of his father's holdings and remarked to me in bitterness, "My mother died without having even the most common labor-saving devices or a penny to jangle in her pockets. He even did the grocery shopping."

As he shared about his father's words and actions toward himself, I saw him as a miracle sitting before me. A "miracle," true enough, who was not yet affirmed in his masculine identity or as a person, and one who had yet to gain the objectivity needed to creatively handle the problem with his father. But few sons survive such a negation of themselves as this father was able to dish out. A man who negated life and love, this father had failed to snuff out the essential spirit, the *life* in his son. It was almost as if he had tried, albeit unconsciously. He had wounded him dreadfully, and if God had not helped this son, that son could have (by hating or failing to forgive his father) become a little more like him every year.

This is the problem with the childhood oath, with the childhood determination to "never be like my father." Apart from accepting and forgiving our parents *as they are,* we cannot get our identities separated from them and go on to accept ourselves. We are therefore in danger of becoming more and more like them. To fully forgive is divine, and divine intervention is required to do it. "Yes," said the doctor to this insight, "before I found Christ in a deeply meaningful way and began the work of forgiving, I was becoming more like him every year."

Nevertheless, the work of forgiveness to be done was not finished in Dr. L.'s life. He was now face to face with his need to receive the gift of divine objectivity, to be raised from the subjective little-boy position in relationship to his father to one of adult maturity with its capacity to stand above a problem, see it for what it is, name it before God, utterly forgive it, and no longer be grievously entangled in it. It's one thing to suffer a problem while looking down upon it from a free perch, and quite another to suffer it while still having one's feet, like a captive bird caught in the net. For Dr. L. to achieve the objective position, he must now accept his father as the man he in fact is and always has been. After explaining to him his need, I helped him to pray in the following fashion:

"I forgive you, Dad, for being unable to love me, unable to give to me or to my mother, my brother, and my sister. I face the illness and wickedness of your particular brand of miserliness, and I name it as the evil it is, as an evil with the power to wound my mother and my sister (even fatally perhaps, for they both died early of physical diseases), and myself. That you could never see or treat us as *persons,* that you could not affirm the life that was given us, but could only see everything in terms of your own small and even perverted desires, I forgive you. I forgive you for not becoming all God created you to be; I accept you as you have chosen to be, and I will no longer strive uselessly, demanding that you change, demanding that you love me, that you recognize me as a person with needs, feelings, aspirations, and desires. But because I can now truly forgive you, I will no longer give you the power to wound me or my own wife and children. We name the evil, and in the name of Him who is our light and life, we surmount it, we transcend it in the power of the Spirit. We can now bless you as you let us, expecting nothing in return. We do not accept your attempts to scapegoat us, but with the word of truth, that wisdom that comes from God, we turn your accusations and projections back upon your own head, and we leave you to deal with them. We know now that this is love, the love that 'is more stern and splendid than mere kindness.' It is the love, this word of truth, that will help you overcome the evil that binds you to yourself. We do not judge you, Dad, but we do judge the evil that has wounded us all.

"And now, Heavenly Father, I thank You for hearing this prayer, for enabling me to accept and fully forgive my father, and for enabling me to no longer subjectively flail under the evil that has afflicted us all, but to rise into that true objectivity that will perhaps someday enable me to be a channel of Your healing love to my father."

In this way, Dr. L. came into that green and spacious place where he began to know God the Father's affirmation of himself as a son and as a man. He began to hear the voice of the ultimate Affirmer. "On my first eight-day retreat, I heard the Father tell me He loved me, that I was precious in His eyes, and that He needed me to do His work. This permeated my entire being. . . . 'I love you and now call your sexuality [masculinity] into order so that you can grow in My love and then minister to men I call you to.'"

In this way, listening to the affirming words of God the Father, he began to "bond" with Him; he made contact with ultimate masculinity, which in turn struck fire to his own. And he began to gain, slowly at first, the gift of divine objectivity.

Dr. L. could now see that his deep desire for male relationships, never a bad thing in itself but rather needful and healthy for all men, was frightening to him because he had a fear of rejection by other men and such an over-whelming need for their affirmation of himself as a man. He had never bonded with his father and unconsciously sought this masculine bonding through other men. His need for masculine approval and love had been so great, therefore, that he had had to repress it, and rankling as it did, deep in his unconscious, it began to erupt as fear, guilt, odd thoughts, genital responses, impotency with his wife, and finally, as time went on, to an unhealthy fantasy life in order to perform sexually.

As Dr. L. came present to and understood his own heart, all repression of his need for father-love and masculine approval stopped. Then once it moved into the conscious where it could be laid before the Lord, it could no longer erupt in odd ways. He repented of and put to death the fantasy life he had adopted in response to his fears and guilt; his problems with impotency, inap-propriate genital responses, and odd thoughts subsided and disappeared.

From then on he could begin to relate to men. He was no longer afraid to put his arms around the man who needed his touch, hold him tight, and pray with him—whether this was in his capacity as a physician treating the ill and diseased, or as a layman called to pray with and for others. Dr. L. had a med-ical practice in a large West Coast port. His large medical practice brought him all conditions of men and women. As a specialist in his medical field, he is often called upon to treat medical problems that are specific to practicing homosexual males. Before his healing, these patients could bring to life the worst fears he had about himself. Now, however, in his own words, "I can talk with, pray with, cry with" the homosexual person. "I have become more lovingly authoritative or firm in speaking about sexual behavior to the men who come to me." Dr. L. now has, in fact, a most significant ministry to men suffering with sexual neuroses and, because of the cosmopolitan nature of his city, has helped people from many lands.

As infants snuggling in our mother's arms, sons and daughters alike are affirmed in their feminine side. We get in close touch with the feminine within our mothers and therefore within ourselves. Dr. L., having had a lov-ing, understanding mother, was highly developed in his feminine side. And this was a very good thing indeed. But, being insecure in his masculine side, he had been fearful and ashamed of his giftedness. He had even tried to hide the creativity that came directly out of being in close touch with his intuitive, feeling, compassionate self.

"As Leanne and I prayed about masculinity/femininity and their balance, I began to see myself differently. I began to see myself in the light of Jesus. I also saw the balance within Jesus; His masculinity/femininity became more obvious, and His relationships with both men and women." As this physician understood this, he recognized and accepted his own unique gifts.

An important prayer we pray over the one who has been so deeply wounded by the sins and sicknesses of others is one of "binding and loosing" (see Matthew 18:18). In the Scriptures these terms refer to loosing people from their sins and from the effects of being sinned against.

In the effective doing of this, we take an important principle from the prophets of old who, one with their people who had sinned, acknowledged their part in the corporate sin of the nation. Daniel's prayer (9:4-19) is one of the most beautiful illustrations of this principle, as is Nehemiah's prayer (1:5-11).

I confess the sins we Israelites, including myself and my father's house, have committed against you. (Nehemiah 1:6)

They stood in their places and confessed their sins and the wickedness of their fathers. (Nehemiah 9:2b)

When praying for someone who is grievously sinned against, we confess those sins before God that have so deeply pierced the soul of the one for whom we pray. This does not mean that the evildoer's sin is hereby remitted. It does mean that with this confession and our extension of forgiveness to the sinning one, the power of that sin to continue to wound and to shape the sufferer is broken.

An extreme instance comes to my mind just now. A woman had undergone the severest kind of ritual abuse as a child, abuse perpetrated by her mother who was involved in witchcraft. By the time she attended one of our conferences, she had received great help through the church, but she had come, hoping against hope, for release from the terror still connected with her memories of torture and abuse. Just to mention "forgiving the unforgiveable" to someone like this dear soul is to see the person begin to relive the terror. And this is what happened to her. She began to scream, saying, "I can't bear the pain; God has to release me," while her eyes, darting in every direction, had the look of an utterly terrorized animal. I held her as tightly as I could while she trembled from head to toe in this traumatized state. Knowing, however, that she had to forgive her mother before she could come into freedom, I pressed on to help her forgive, assuring her strongly of the following:

1) We do not forgive evil (per se).
2) We do not forgive Satan.
3) We do not forgive demons and evil principalities.

But we do forgive *persons* in the clutches of that evil. She calmed a little at that, and then we were able to confess specifically the sins of witchcraft and the sins of her mother's witchcraft against her. With this confession and her forgiveness of her mother (but not without an incredible battle), I was enabled to bind and lift from her the unspeakable sins perpetrated against her and loose her from them. She was freed that very day from the terror of a lifetime. Only in the Healing Presence of God are we enabled to pray this way. But this sin too He has already endured for us and experienced the awful turning of His Father's face from Him as he took upon Himself and into Himself the sin of a fallen world.

A Cleansing Grief

Truly, as Johnny, the doctor, and all of us find out, it is in being humbled to the ground with sorrow and loss that we as Christians can find both the grace and the option of mourning before Almighty God our sins, our sorrows, our grievous losses and injustices. From such a stance, we more deeply recognize the human condition, that we too are sinners, that we too are capable of wounding others. We know that if we do not find the grace to forgive, within our hearts a coldness and a hardness will increase, and we will as sinners grow more monstrous. But if in this state of woundedness and mourning, we cry out to Him for the power to forgive, we receive healing and mercy. Our hearts softened and pliable now in a way for which our greatest successes could never have prepared us, we go on to true victory over the world, the flesh, and the devil. This is why it is not in our successes and victories, but in the fires of sorrow that we find our our truest selves. When we truly forgive (that vital principle at the very heart of Christ's cross and the Christian gospel), we find that He is with us (and has been all along) in the fiery affliction. If I fail to forgive, I turn from Him, and lose the real "I." An icy hardness begins to form in my heart, and I am the loser.

Though suffering is the way we can best learn, not all are helped by it. As Oswald Chambers has said, "it makes some people devils."

> We all know people who have been made much meaner and more irritable and more intolerable to live with by suffering. Suffering perfects only one type of person—the one who accepts the call of God in Christ.[5]

Johnny or the doctor or the woman so injured by witchcraft could have refused to forgive. Thanks be to God, I have seen very few who refuse to forgive once they understand that the grace to forgive and be forgiven is available to them. Once in a while, however, I do see it. It is not something one easily forgets, for of all that is tragic, this is the most. As Oswald Chambers reports:

> There is no suffering to equal the suffering of self-love arising from independent individuality which refuses to submit to God or to its nobler self.[6]

When the Need to Forgive Is at an Unconscious Level

"Forgive your father for dying." I shall never forget these words the Spirit spoke to me the first time I sat under the ministry of prayer for healing of memories.

My father died when I had just turned three, leaving my mother, myself, and my eighteen-month-old sister to grieve his loss.

I was with a group of ministers, religious (nuns, teachers, monks, deacons), and various professionals in the medical, health, and educational fields. We had gathered there as Christians to pray for one another and to learn more about healing prayer. I was already deeply involved in the ministry of praying with others. I had myself received the healing of all known hurts and even disappointments through confession of every known sin in every period of my life, through a wholehearted reception of God's forgiveness for these, through restitution where needed and possible, and through prayerful listening and waiting upon God.

But I was unaware of the deep sense of rejection I had felt at the loss of my father, that it was at the bottom of my need for healing in the first place. I was completely amazed by what happened to me in this healing of memories prayer. Even more important insofar as the healing ministry is concerned, the Lord proved to me beyond all shadow of doubt the validity of prayer for psychological healing—that He not only can, but delights in pointing out and bringing up the root traumas, no matter at what age in our lives they are experienced. And furthermore, it is not something *we* do; rather, it is what we allow *Him* to do!

The minister that day prayed for us, beginning in the present and going down through the years toward birth and conception. Since so much healing had already taken place in my life, nothing happened until we reached age three. Then up popped the clearest voice imaginable from my deep heart: "Forgive your father for dying!" *How ridiculous*, I thought, *to forgive one's father for dying*. But I did it just the same. Most fervently. The clarion quality of that command to me is something never to be forgotten, much less doubted or denied. The fact that children take the loss of parents, however it comes about, as a personal rejection was the subject of the minister's sharing with us on the following day—the very thing God had so clearly shown me.

I was totally unaware that I had experienced the loss of my father as a personal rejection in spite of the fact that throughout my childhood and adult life I had a recurring dream of searching for my father, of finding his casket, and of hoping against hope that he might somehow be alive. But once the memory of his death came to consciousness, the rejection was vividly clear in my mind and heart. Never, since the day Christ touched that memory, has the dream recurred.

With this healing, I finally understood what God was showing me in the camping-trip experience and in the uncanny experience of somehow knowing I had come home when in the Scottish Highlands. God is outside of time; all times are one with the Creator of time. This is a vital part of the Judeo-Christian truth system. It stands over and against pagan and/or occult ways of explaining like phenomena with the concepts of reincarnation, out-of-body-travel, and so on. God was finally able to answer my anguished queries over Edie, the young girl who repeatedly fell into sexual sin. I could see quite clearly how psychological wounds such as hers could be prayed for and healed. It is a wonderful thing to know that God is, even now at this very moment, present to any and all trauma we have suffered. As we learn to invite Him into these places, face the darkness, loneliness, and hurt with Him, and then set our hearts to forgive and receive forgiveness, He heals and sets us free. It is a profound ministry, vitally connected to the Christian confessional, whether formal or informal.

Apart from the healing power of God in our midst, no one can explain a healing of memories and the magnitude of the change in our hearts that can come with it. In simply obeying God and in saying, "I forgive you, Daddy, for dying," I opened the way for Christ to enter into all the ways that I, even as an infant, had responded to the grief and to the drastically altered circumstances of my life at this early stage.

Instantly, as I forgave my father and these accompanying circumstances, I was set free from emotional bonds I'd not hitherto perceived. At this same time, there was also set into me (or freed, I don't know which) a new ministry. It involved special insight into the healing of men. Before I had mostly prayed with women. The connection here, as I later realized, was not only one of churchly custom (women praying only with women), but of an unconscious and even denied fear and distrust of men. All of this was related to the early psychological injury—the traumatic sense of rejection in the sudden loss of my father.

I was like Edie in that, if I'd known my own heart, I would have said: "Daddy, if you had loved me, you would not have left me." My pain and trauma was not nearly so deep or life-threatening as hers. With an alcoholic mother, Edie experienced gaping deficits of the kind of nurturing love that fills and gives an infant a solid sense of being. Unlike me, she was left empty, starving for another's touch and strong, protecting embrace. But she and I would be healed in precisely the same way. It would be through forgiving and then exchanging our old hurt and sense of rejection for the life and light God longs to flood into all the darkened spaces of our souls.

Every traumatic rejection untouched by the vital kind of forgiveness the cross has won for us, whether at a conscious or unconscious level, will be acted out in some negative fashion. We may reject others—before the feared rejection can come our way. I was, in a sense, rejecting men by failing to pray with them. This was never very strong with me and probably represents what most women in this age of unfathered men and women feel, but even so, it subtly shaped the way I ministered. Too, until the healing, I could not receive from men as I needed to. I was now freed to help men as well as women, and—as I grew in understanding—I no longer feared their rejections or transferences. In the process, I began to receive from men the needed masculine input. It awakened great tracts of my spirit and soul, complemented and balanced the highly developed responsive qualities of my own feminine identity.

This healing then paved the way for yet another. It was the removal of a writer's block, and I wrote of that in *The Broken Image,* the "Appendix: Listening to Our Dreams." This healing involved the recognition that there was a part of me that I had never accepted. After a painful period of being "pregnant" with my first book and unable to write it, I realized I needed prayer for enablement to accept that part of me who is a writer—a part of "who I am" vital to fulfilling the work God has assigned me to do.

In a series of six dreams, I came face to face with the writer in me, though I did not at first recognize her. In these dreams, she came right up out of the depths of my deep mind and presented herself to my astonished conscious attention. She first appeared as a feminine figure unprepared, but contemplating a leap over a swollen stream where a bridge had once been but had long ago washed away. Against all odds, she jumped and was gravely, perhaps even fatally, injured in the leap.

This dream and another revealed the inner fears and feelings in which the writer's block was rooted. In the dream the bridge over the stream of life was washed out, and the girl injured in trying to leap across. My father had been that bridge, and the flood of death had taken him away. But the loss of my father formed no part of this or the other dreams. Rather, they consistently revealed the *fear of exposure* along with the concomitant *deep feelings of inadequacy and inferiority* as the direct consequence of being fatherless. And the little girl within me who felt all this was inextricably combined with the writer within.

In another dream, she appeared as a figure prepared to cross a dangerous river, but fearful of exposure. In another, she appeared as an acrobatic dancer skilled, yet fearful of exposure. And finally, she appeared as an acrobatic high-wire artist, performing with skill and precision, exposed but no longer minding exposure. Dreams are terribly frank, and my fear of exposure was symbolized by being scantily clothed—something not unusual in the acrobatic dance or in high-wire artistry. With the last figure, the writer who necessarily exposes herself and I came together. This understanding, along with prayer, brought quite an incredible healing.

The dreams, so briefly alluded to above, revealed that the fear of exposure was rooted in the consequences my family had suffered through the loss of my father. Please note that it was the consequences, and not the loss itself, which had already been touched by God. At the time of his death and thereafter, we were thrown out upon the world, dependent on others for the shelter we needed. The first healing, that of memories, located and touched my sense of rejection; this healing dealt with the mechanisms I had adopted as a way of coping with the loss of love and security. In attempts to overcome the loss, I, like any good stoic, simply denied it. I steadfastly and consistently denied throughout my life the little girl in me who would admit her fear of rejection and exposure, inadequacy and inferiority, in the absence of a father. I successfully denied that valid part of myself. And it was this figure, the stoic in me, who attempted to leap over the swollen river, rather than admit the missing bridge made it impossible.

Therefore, I had to confess pride and receive forgiveness for it. Feelings of inadequacy and inferiority (like those of presumption and superiority), no matter from what psychological injury they stem, are ultimately rooted in pride. I believe that behind every writer's block, indeed, at the bottom of every need for psychological healing, one will find it necessary to confess, "Lord, there is a part of me that has never confessed its need and pride, and therefore that part of me is still trying to be adequate apart from You; it is still fearful and unable to wholly depend upon You."

When my dreams revealed this condition in me, it would have been easy to go on denying these fears (as I had done all my life) rather than to confess them to God. In fact, if I had not written the insights into my prayer journal immediately, they would have slipped back into the unconscious, just as lost to me as if they had never surfaced to consciousness.

I think my healing is fairly representative of what we most often see in these healings. There is the initial instantaneous healing of memories that has to do with forgiving and receiving forgiveness. I can never say what all was done as I forgave my father for dying. It is clearly beyond our merely human powers of knowing or telling. We can never (nor should we) analyze and categorize it too finely. We are all so different, some so ready to receive more, while others less. But the healing of memories, vital in cases of early and unconscious trauma, is the root healing that forms a basis for any later healing needed.

This further healing requires time and process, such as getting in touch with deeply wounded and split-off emotions and feelings—those that surface in separation anxiety and in abandonment depression. One must also deal with the failure to accept oneself and its unconsciously held negative feelings and attitudes resulting from early trauma.

This distinction between the instantaneous and the process is necessary because we in the healing ministry are often criticized for speaking of the quick accomplishment of these profound initial healings. In observing these healings over the years, I find that we more often understate than overstate the magnitude of what God does. At the same time, we recognize the key part these initial healings play in those that come later. Some require agonizing periods of experiencing and working through emotions that have long been repressed as well as sometimes difficult and painstaking attitudinal changes in relating to God, to others, and to the self. For example, I might still be dealing with writer's block had I not learned to listen to God, had I not searched out other wise souls who understood the symbolic nature of dreams and prayerfully helped me read them aright. Also, in this regard, good writing—that which is in line with the way things really are—is hard work and requires sacrifice. I could have been unwilling to discipline myself, and then insisted on calling that failure to pay the price a "writer's block." That too is a facet of human nature that needs prayer help. But my basic message to all and sundry is: "Hope thou in God." "Trust fully in Him." There are answers, there is healing. Keep searching for it.

Prayer for Groups of Christians Seeking Wholeness

In our Pastoral Care Ministry Schools we always conduct a "prayer workshop" in which we pray for healing of memories for the group. This is not something we recommend that others do, but we've been led to do it, and the results are truly amazing. It would be difficult to overestimate the benefit of these prayer sessions and to exaggerate what we see God do when He puts forth His hand to heal His wounded ones. We see healings of prenatal memories, trauma of birth healings,[7] as well as those traumas suffered in earliest infancy and childhood. Deeply repressed memories come up to be dealt with.[8] In these sessions, persons suffering from all manner of emotional problems are ministered to by the Spirit of God.

Even one such need is overwhelming, humanly speaking, and in our meetings there are sometimes several hundred or more people with these deep needs. We know that if God does not come and heal His people, no amount of teaching and preaching about the need will avail. Here is where the understanding of how to collaborate with the Spirit of God comes in. The usual way to approach healing of memories is through counseling and prayer, addressing the need of one person at a time. However, we approach healing of memories from the standpoint of the *charisms of healing in operation within the context of God's gathered community*. Christian mental health professionals and pastoral counselors are amazed and deeply gratified at what they see the Lord do in these healing sessions. The principles of prayer they see demonstrated often revolutionize their practice. They know so well how formidable are the needs that we see the Spirit of God sovereignly deal with. But most will continue primarily as therapists dealing with one person at a time. I say this to stress the fact that not everyone is called to do what we do. But the principles are the same. We pray, "Come, Holy Spirit, come!" And then we invite the needy one into the Healing Presence of God.

When God is in charge, we are never "gift-oriented" or "gift-centered." If we are thinking about operating in this or that gift, we are in trouble and apt to intrude in fleshly ways into what God desires to do. We are always to be "Presence-oriented." If God doesn't do it, it won't be done. Memories, therefore, are not forced up prematurely. Just as important, coping mechanisms necessary to the person's psychological survival are not prematurely removed. In short, there is no manipulation on our part. We collaborate with the Spirit of God as we lift high the cross of Christ with its full message of good news to all who suffer, and as we invite Him to enter into the memories of those ready to forgive and receive healing. This is a ministry that we grow with. In the beginning we did not see full-blown homosexual neuroses healed or repressed memories surfacing. We did begin, however, with the knowledge that behind someone's agonized statement, "I can't love," or "I should never have been born," was a painful set of memories that God wanted to heal, and somehow we could learn to pray to that end.

Infantile Needs

Most people are by now familiar with the "threat-to-life" experiments done by scientists several decades ago. With their fine instruments, the scientists measured the reactions of plant life to hostile acts. The researchers then were amazed to find that plants reacted as well to hostile threats. How much more does the infant in the womb and the young child in our arms. The thoughts, feelings, words we send out bring life or death. We are either channels of God's love, or—in failure to love and accept others—we destroy.

We've come through a long, dark period when there has been little understanding of what constitutes trauma for the embryo, the infant, or the young developing child. The practice of placing an infant with one nursemaid after another, disturbing its capacity to bond with any significant mother figure, is not only a vice of the wealthy or the unavoidable plight of the poor today. Many Christian women holding their babies to their breasts feel as if they are wasting time, that they should be working in some more meaningful or lucrative capacity. Too, we are paying a price for grievously shortsighted and mistaken medical practices that left the newborn uncomforted and separated from its mother immediately after birth. We've not understood the deep rejection that adopted children have experienced in the loss of their birth parents or what happens when a girl is born to parents who want a boy, or vice versa. We've not understood the profound effects of a mother's emotional trauma on her unborn infant, much less how to pray for healing of these later.

My friend, missionary Ingrid Trobisch, loves to tell of a certain African tribe that is dear to her heart. The chief and all his tribe knew that the most important person among them was the pregnant woman. The tribe's future depended upon her giving birth to children who were strong psychologically and physically. The expectant mother was, therefore, given special protection and a place of honor within the tribe.

I'm deeply concerned that Christian parents lack the basic understanding that their infants grow strong psychologically and become enabled to take the crucial developmental steps by identifying and bonding with their parents. The data we now have on these psychological and physical developments, facts that would enable us to avoid some serious errors with our children, seem slow to filter down to the majority of Christian parents. Our misbegotten notions about how the infant and the young child are "spoiled," for example, can lead us into misinterpreting and ignoring their real needs. The time-worn practice of leaving an infant to cry in isolation, even when it goes against the keenest intuitions of the mother, reveals a tragic ignorance of the way that isolation threatens identity in the infant. Writing on the psychological verity that the baby experiences life by identification with the mother, Dr. Frank Lake states:

So long as the mother is present, and satisfactorily so, the baby experiences its being and well-being in identification with her. It cannot conceive of life going on without her, except for short times when her coming is delayed. So dependent is the baby on her presence that, if she fails to return, the power of being-by-relatedness-to-her is depleted to dangerous levels of hopelessness. Lively expectation gives way to despair and mounting separation-anxiety.[9]

Those of us with long experience in pastoral care know only too well the truth of Dr. Lake's further comment:

> Even though at this point of maximal tolerable panic the mother returns and the experience is split off and repressed, it remains as an indelible aspect of personal identity.[10]

It is no small thing in prayer for healing of memories to have the person bring up infantile memories of this isolation and agonize as they tap into the cauldron of fear and panic that has heretofore been split off and repressed—yet active in ever so deadly a way in the unconscious.

I have had the most wonderful opportunity to watch a young mother, active along with her pastor husband in the life of a growing church, as she relates to her little newborns and then as they grow—one right after another until now there are three. By any standards, she is a busy woman.

I've been astonished, knowing how tired she must be, to see her pick up her infant even when it is not hungry and not crying, when her other children are tugging at her. She just "wools" them around, as the old saying goes. She breast-feeds her babies and is always tenderly caring for them. She knows what weariness is. Bone-deep weariness. But she has the best babies. They hardly cry at all. They laugh and love. She didn't "spoil" them. She gave them the kind of start infants need. She knows intuitively, even as the Indian mother who straps her baby to her back, that the infant's alarm signals mean something and that it needs loving contact in order to grow.

And she will have lots of rest later when mothers who've had less time for their little ones in infancy are spending sleepless nights over their children's difficulties in adjusting and learning and in relating to others.

Christians who misapply the Scripture's warning about "sparing the rod and spoiling the child" can unknowingly create another source of trauma for their children. How easily parents err in this way if they do not understand the rudimentary developmental steps a child takes, or if they attribute evil to the child when no evil was intended. I remember my dismay when one tot, large for her two years, came running toward me. In the process, she ran right over her baby brother sitting in the middle of the floor. Her perception of space was not yet fully developed, and true to her age, all she could see was the goal. Her little brother simply happened to be in the direct path of it. Her mother quickly grabbed and soundly spanked her. Probably even more damaging, the mother verbally interpreted the behavior as stemming from jealousy. I can still see the confusion and bewilderment on the child's face, and I grieve over the knowledge that this child's character will later reflect these types of misjudgment. These parents were not open to exhortation, for they were very strong on not "sparing the rod and spoiling the child." The difficulty was that they were wrongly applying this verse to a very young child and were ignorant of basic developmental stages. Tragically, they had no understanding of the effect their actions had on their children.

These kinds of mistakes, made by well-meaning Christian parents, could be remedied through giving preparation courses in our churches. The stakes are very high. The mental health of our children, not to mention the exercise of simple justice, could easily enough be the fruit. Then our children would be able to receive and benefit by the necessary disciplining we all as parents must undertake.

Our long, dark period may be coming to a close in some ways, for example, in terms of better scientific and medical procedures with the infant. But in other ways it is getting darker still. More and more women are cut off from their true feminine gender identity and are unable to nurture their young. If too many Christian women feel that they are wasting time in the important nurturing process, we will lose not only our healthy children but our capacity to lead in matters of the home, the church, and the state. More truly than we know, it is "the hand that rocks the cradle" that determines finally the fate of a neighborhood, a clan, a nation, or even the world.

CHAPTER 8

Prolonged Healing of Memories: Abandonment Issues and the Repression of Painful Emotions

As we learn more about the processes of healing within the soul, we often find that the power to feel the pain is itself a vital part of the healing. The sufferer has repressed this heretofore and denied it precisely because it was so painful. But now he has to get it up and out. He needs to understand that, if he will stand in the cross and hurt, there is a place for it to go, an end to the pain. This seemingly endless pain is the way he gets in touch with and names the heretofore repressed grief, fear, anger, and shame underlying his depression. In order to come out of certain types of depression, one must feel the most appalling pain and grief. It often seems that death would be easier. But repressed grief and sorrow and loss remain to afflict us in other ways until we grieve them out.[1]

*I*n some of us, our healing requires the pain of getting in touch with soul-shaking grief and loss. The pain, we are stunned to find out, is a vital part of the healing. When we are in the midst of reliving and experiencing the feelings that caused an infantile shutdown of the capacity to receive love from others or of the power to feel at all, even the initial root healing of memories can seem to stretch out interminably. The pain one experiences in such a case is beyond the powers of most to even imagine. At any one time, I will have on my desk letters that express this kind of pain. I'll quote one in full because it illustrates much of what we need to touch on in prayer for such a sufferer. Except for the minor changes that protect this young woman's identity, I am reproducing the letter as she wrote it. Since, however, she mistakenly uses the term "codependency," I will substitute the correct term "emotional dependency" in brackets.

Dear Leanne,

I need your help if you can give it. I have gotten myself into such a mess, and don't know how to get out of it. I've been in law school this past year, suffering more than I ever thought God would let me suffer again in my life. It is hard to write this letter. I am so full of pain, but another part of me says it's my fault, it must be my problem, so quit being melodramatic and self-pitying. I don't know which view is the truth, Leanne. I suspect some of each, but I just pray that the Holy Spirit will give you insight to see and hear the Truth, even where I don't write it right.

I don't know where to begin. . . . I went to the [place name] PCM before going to law school to try to clear up any important remaining "stuff" about my coming out of lesbianism 2$^1/_4$ years before that. *Nothing* traumatic came up. I felt that the prayer time showed me my real task was the self-acceptance step. So, I began practicing that. But, as I look back, I see things were going a little haywire even before I got to school. I got pretty hooked into a new massage therapist I'd recently met. And I don't know how to describe this, but after this year, I see I did with her what I've done with various "special" women all my life. I needed her. I needed her special beingness to stoke my fires of beingness. To feel alive. It's not that I don't know how, on some level, to separate myself and get back into my separateness; it's that my separateness has no aliveness to it.

Leanne, I have lived through hell this past year. I thought I was following God: many things had worked out divinely, including a housing situation with several other Christian women who love the Lord. But from the beginning, I watched myself slide into a more and more hateful, loathsome place.

I became [emotionally dependent] on one of my roommates: I didn't even want to; I kept doing the things that I knew worked [i.e., to avoid the pitfall of emotional dependency], except they didn't work. Oh, there was one thing I couldn't do which I usually did when troubled with [emotionally dependent] attraction: I couldn't go away. Usually in such a situation, I would/could go away until the [emotionally dependent] attraction, the "craving" stopped. But I couldn't. So I crossed over the line. And it was messy. And Lila [her housemate] was angry and not good about dealing with my "gut-level" processing. . . . I was shamed to see my deepest, most embarrassing, un-okay yearning coming out. We got separate, but through another series of events, I just invested and transferred that energy over to another roomie. Again, it seemed to start out good; when I began to recognize the feelings of craving and longing again, I prayed and resolved even more firmly not to descend into an [emotionally dependent] hell. By choosing like this in the past, I had stayed okay! But no matter. I crossed over the line again. We had to have it out, and I had to just get separate again. This amidst the nonstop pressure of law school, spending by far the most of my waking moments on studies, course, I probably overdid it. I probably should have lightened up. But I couldn't. Studying less was more stressful, not less [because] then I was just behind and lost in classes [as well].

I got sick over Christmas vacation. Came back and didn't get well. Nothing really wrong, just a virus. But something, way deep inside me, was so very tired. I started getting pretty nuts—for me anyway. I started going back to AA meetings, just looking for some kind of support group. I started seeing a Christian counselor who works with an ex-gay ministry. I'd just cry. And cry. There was no relief. When I was so depressed and tired I couldn't get out of bed to come downstairs for my birthday dinner, Janice insisted on having everyone come up and pray for me. I could only sob and say, "I don't know what's wrong. I just don't feel good."

Finally, the diagnosis [of the virus]. . . . On to a regimented, incredibly expensive diet. No sugar, no honey, no coffee, no processed foods. . . . I'd cry when I'd eat a piece of fruit: seems that's the only sweetness in my life. . . .

The depression lifts a bit on the diet. I'm not quite so tired. I finish school amazingly, but hell, hell, hell. Right after, I go home for three weeks. I'm so tired. So pent up with all I've been through. But my home church speaks to me. I'm feeling decidedly better by the time I come back—I even feel some lightness in my heart for the first time in months and months and months— but in three days of working full time, I am in unbearable turmoil again. Depressed, tired, screaming to God in my frustration and pain and despair; sobbing, sobbing, sobbing; I can't take it. I want to be well. I hate my life. Finally, I give in. I can't do it. I just can't finish law school. I just can't live like this. If God won't provide the healing and the changes in my life that are so necessary, then I just cannot do law school. I didn't want to be a secretary all my life. I didn't even want to be a massage therapist all my life, but maybe that is all I can really handle, emotionally. That's life.

Sometime after that, (the next morning?), I find I am consumed with a desire to be held, to be loved by a woman. Nothing new about that. I have been living with the almost nonstop craving to be held all year. I cannot look at Michelle or Susan without desiring, wanting, needing to be held. But what is different this morning is that what has not been an option for $3^1/_2$ years— sex with a woman—is suddenly an option. I cannot help it. How frightening. Now all I can really think about is going back to [her home state] to the first woman I ever really "loved," who likes to take care of people. I want to be taken care of so badly. To be held, loved, kissed, caressed. . . . Or I think about crawling into Michelle's arms, nestling amongst her breasts, putting my lips to them. . . . I have this thing about women's breasts. They evoke in me some- thing so deep. A hunger. A longing so strong. Leanne, isn't there a remedy to this terrible, gnawing hunger for—for a woman's breast— or whatever it is? I cannot live with this hunger, unfed, forever. Leanne, I have been a model, a prize "ex-gay" person these past $3^1/_2$ years. I truly have. I have not focused on women sexually, my thoughts have been pure, I have not entertained fantasies. Up to this year, Jesus has been enough. But this onslaught I cannot abide. I must have some relief.

God has spoken to me repeatedly in the past that "breasts are but a symbol of the true nurturance I have for you." At times I thought I was receiving that, but these desires have never gone away. They've been muted, even inconsequential at times, but always, always, always there is another snag. Another time of heart-rending pain surrounding it where it feels like I could die, I hurt so badly.

But I have been unable to really feel Jesus' nurturance since last fall sometime. I am resistant now again to male figures. . . . (That's one of the things that seems to make this "my fault"—i.e., if I weren't so stubborn, I'd receive the nurturance I need from Jesus.) It feels like, despite how "well" some part of my mind is, something is bad wrong inside.

Leanne, I realize that on some important level, I have never had an emotional relationship with Jesus. I feel unable to. When Lila and Michelle both were angry about how they felt I was asking something from them that only God could give me—I understood what they meant, but it feels like a cruel joke, because I can't seem to get that from God. I get it from women who are in strong connection with God, but not from God Himself. This seems another area where one could accuse me of just not being diligent enough in my relationship with the Lord. Therefore it's just my fault. My lack of commitment. But I don't think I'm making excuses when I say I can't. When I'm in a good place, then I can have fairly contactful times with the Lord, it seems. But when I get into that hard place, there's just no connection. I can pray for infilling all I want; I just don't feel a thing.

Leanne, I see that my whole life has been spent in finding emotional meaning and aliveness in other women—even after coming to Jesus. Law school was/is an attempt to chart my own course, utilize my own talent, follow my own dream, be alive inside myself. But I'm dying. Physically, I'm sick, emotionally, I am chronically depressed; spiritually, I am despairing and ripe for a fall *which I know shall never fulfill me anyway.*

I beg of you, if it's true, tell me that Jesus can deliver me from this hell. I can't. Leanne, I can't "wrestle this away in prayer." Every time I think I can, I just get knocked down by a flood again.

Isn't it possible that something is still buried in my unconscious that could make this all *livable* at least? Fill up that longing? Make Jesus accessible to me emotionally/spiritually, and not just [through] His women? Or am I just looking for the easy way out? You know, the do-no-work-just-deliver-me approach. I tell you, if it's up to me at this point I am doomed. I just don't have the energy or strength or willingness, hardly.

I cry when I read *The Broken Image* passages of touch deprivation and failing to come to an adequate sense of being. Could that be me? I know of a situation in my infancy that could be the origin. I developed a staph infection at three days and was put in isolation for a week before my mom took me home and kept me in isolation there. Of course she also had to stop breast-feeding me, but just knowing of it has not healed me. Please write and tell me you'll pray for me/with me. If my problem is not something that can get really, miraculously handled in prayer, then I am lost. Write me, please. God only knows what continent you're on; you are probably deluged with mail, but please write me fast . . . Please help. God, please help.

Sincerely, (signed) Linda

P.S. I confess that I don't want "healing" so much as I want to be *filled up*. I can't explain that; it just seems that "healing" means the feelings will be taken away, but I will still be left empty. Is that the way it's supposed to be?

Linda is one whose infantile memories hold an intolerable amount of emo-tional pain due to what for her was an interminable period of abandonment. You may have noticed that it was not until the last of her letter that she got to the real problem—a prolonged infantile isolation from her mother. After having been an embryo nurtured by her mother's womb and heartbeat, then being nursed and loved as a newborn, on day three of her life she was suddenly placed in an utterly lonely, sterile place due to staph infection. That she mentions it as a last resort, even after having read my books and attended a PCM where we deal with these matters, fits in with the way painful emotions arising out of infantile trauma are repressed and denied. Repression and denial, now in the midst of breaking apart, were the coping mechanisms by which she had survived.

Dr. Frank Lake, English psychiatrist-theologian, describes and explains as well anyone can the pain that this young woman was experiencing:

The roots of all the psychoneuroses lie in infantile experiences of mental pain of such an intolerable severity as to require splitting off from consciousness at about the time they occurred. These have remained buried by repression. The actual cause of the panic may be a time of separation-anxiety endured during the the early months of life, when to be separated from the sight and sensory perception of the source of "being," in mother or her substitute, is tantamount to a slow strangling of the spirit and its impending death. The var-ious patterns of the psychoneuroses comprise and indicate a variety of defences against this separation.[2]

Denial and Repression as Coping Mechanisms

There was strong evidence in Linda's application to the PCM conference she attended, now a year and half ago, that she was dealing with abandonment issues. She was directed, therefore, to see a team member who would under-stand her plight. On seeing her, this prayer counselor discerned that Linda's mechanisms for coping with her pain were still so strong that she could speak only of "co-dependency," insisting that her problem was in that area. She had a serious problem, indeed, with emotional dependency, a term that would have accurately described a large part of her dilemma, but she could hardly yet even admit to that. The prayer counselor immediately understood that Linda was intensely fearful of facing the deep-seated feelings that were so utterly opaque to her.

As stated in an earlier chapter, it is the Lord's work to gently open a person's memories, and His timing is perfect. Our part is to pray in such a way that the heart of the needy one is opened, thereby giving God the opportunity to heal. It is true that we do not hold back important insight. For example, we did say to Linda, "Your main difficulty is likely to be found within the first months of your life." There was resistance to hearing that, however, and when that happens, we do not overrule—either by force of will or by powerful prayer in the Spirit.

In answer to corporate prayers said over the group, our Lord enters in and gives the insight needed as the individual soul is ready to face it. We can therefore rest in God's timing, knowing His faithfulness. We do not forcibly remove a person's mental, logical coping mechanisms before there's a readiness to face the unbearable, that which was a kind of death to them, that which they cannot remember. This can sometimes be difficult for us, especially when we realize, as in Linda's case, that the feelings, though unconscious and repressed, are still driving the person mercilessly and compulsively, shaping the life and robbing it of freedom.

Professionals in the fields of psychology and counseling are very careful with these repressions. After releasing the prayer of faith—a powerful prayer but one that does not forcibly remove the coping mechanisms—for the healing of someone like Linda, one of the first things we do is to recommend therapeutic counseling and to pray fervently with them to find the right physician. If we can work in tandem with a well-qualified psychologist or psychiatrist, all the better. The professional and the sufferer will need the prayer help and the understanding of the Body of Christ. Likewise, we need the special expertise of those able to provide needed medication and to guard the person through the depressions inherent within an acute deprivation or abandonment neurosis.

In the past, we have not always been able to locate the professionals gifted in this area. Especially when the difficulties have resulted in defense mechanisms associated with male homosexual or lesbian behavior, the things that can go seriously wrong in the professional's office—even the "Christian" professional's office—these days are many and varied. Sadly, at times we have to deal with the wreckage a professional has left, perhaps of one who has forced the irrational belief upon those suffering with lesbian or homosexual neurosis that they are to accept their "sexual orientation," i.e., their defense mechanisms. When these persons have severe gender confusion, and especially when they are breaking, as Linda's letter clearly reveals herself to be, they have little defense against powerful arguments coming from those deemed to be experts who are supposed to be helping them.

Besides these kinds of difficulties, we find on occasion the desperate soul whose mechanisms for coping have been removed prematurely, and the therapist working with the person has had nothing of value with which to replace them—the most notable omission being the gospel of truth with its gift of the grace to forgive and its power to heal. There are also the professionals who disregard early infantile injuries. Still others, even though they do understand them, are fearful of dealing with such repressions at all, and simply prefer to tranquilize and sedate persons. It is no small thing to deal with needs such as these. It requires true wisdom (an empathic and intuitive understanding of another soul) as well as sacrificial giving by the caring, responsible professional and by those who pray and provide pastoral care. At this point in time, we have more and more Christian professionals to whom we can turn. Like the late doctors Frank Lake and Karl Stern, these professionals hold to a thoroughly *incarnational view of man and of reality* and are therefore open to God's healing power coming through prayer and the Word of God. They understand Christ's work on the cross and apply it to the deepest needs of the wounded soul. They know that our best efforts and strictly human sympathy cannot accomplish the full healing, but that divine love can, using us as very human, loving instruments.

In prayer for a group healing of memories, I always ask the Lord to guard such memories until the sufferers are ready to face them and until one of our counselors, well able to deal with this kind of emotional pain, is close. And it is perfectly amazing to see how God always and faithfully hears and answers these prayers. Nothing seemingly is "too large" to come up, but it comes at the appropriate time, place, and with the person needed to assist.

Grief

Linda's healing will involve intense grieving. Her need, then, though it requires healing of memories, is better understood as calling for a *healing of emotions*. In a healing of one's memories, there is always, of course, a healing of emotions going on as well. But in the case of someone such as Linda, the painful facing and working through of repressed emotions is by far the greater part of the task. This involves getting in touch with infantile feelings of grief that were unbearable then—and are now. Linda is ready now, however. Her denial barriers are forever fallen. She can no longer stave off the pain. A year and a half ago she wasn't ready to face the grief. Now she has no alternative.

In the first paragraph of the letter, Linda swings between wondering that God allows her suffering to continue and the fear that she is being self-pitying and melodramatic. In the PCM schools, it is easy for someone like Linda to misapply the teaching on "the bent position" and even on "emotional dependency." These are things Linda was grappling with—with all her might. But her main difficulty lay in the fact that the initial and most important attachment of her life had been traumatically interrupted. The ongoing, trusting relationship with mother that provides the basis for a strong personal sense of selfhood, of *being* itself, was cut off in such a way that she passed a crucial threshold of pain. That left her with a terrible deficit, and there was no bridge back across that threshold into a secure sense of well-being. Until healed, she is left to cry:

> It is always the same, if I am waiting in helpless dependence on someone else to come and pay attention to me, they never come, and the agony of waiting will drive me mad.[3]

Linda, in her heart of hearts, believed herself to be abandoned. She suffered with separation anxiety, and until her primary unmet developmental need was addressed, she would continue to harbor within herself the infantile feelings of abandonment. There would have to be, through prayer and, in her case, special counseling therapy, the healing of these early memories. In such a healing, a kind of trust (not easily achieved) is established with the therapist or the one who prays. This trust allows the sufferer, *as the scene is being replayed in the memories*, to compensate for the original loss—experience, as it were, an "initial" attachment with a trusted "other." Undue fear of being bent toward another could jeopardize the healing.

Note the above emphasis on "as the scene is being replayed in the memories," for it is when the unbearable infantile feelings charge forward that we minister to the suffering inner child. This is what ties all of this in with healing of memories, even though the healing is prolonged. Sufferers are at these times of depression *back in the experience of abandonment* with its associated feelings.

In telling about Edie, the adopted girl, I said that had I understood prayer for healing of memories, I could have thrown my arms about her and held her tight as she forgave her parents. Why the emphasis on holding her tight? Because the tiny infant within her was still crying out for her mother's arms. God could have used me in this way as "substitute" mother in the healing of memories.

This brings us to two important points. First, God takes the loving actions we do in His name and multiplies their effects, even as He did the loaves and fishes to the hungry multitude. It never ceases to amaze me the way He uses such small and seemingly insignificant gestures—in relation to a lifetime of deprivation—to bring about so much healing. The miracle He performed in feeding the multitudes has its absolute counterpart in the healing of hungry and unfulfilled emotional beings.

The second point brings us into the area of what the psychologists call "transference"—the way that we helpers momentarily and at crucial points in a person's recovery *become*, as it were, the parent. In a transference situation, we attract the feelings, both negative and positive, that the sufferer feels toward the parent. This differs significantly from "re-parenting," a practice some people get into, but one that is, strictly speaking, not possible. In a healing of memories where the Spirit of the Lord is mightily moving, the person is so deeply ministered to, both on the human and the divine plane, that an embrace by a "substitute" mother can assuage a lifetime of deprivation and become the channel by which the Holy Spirit heals the deprivation and loss.

Though the capacity for self-pity is a live option with all of us and is for some a chief vice, the feelings Linda suffered from were not of that stripe. Her problem stemmed from the deep inner belief that she was abandoned, and this belief could only be reinforced by thinking she should be able to look only to Jesus and not to persons. Relating to others in the right way was, after all, one of the chief things to be set right. Due to her woundedness, she could not relate intimately with others without her unmet need coming into play. How can we achieve friendship and married love before we've achieved the initial relationship that gives us a secure sense of the self, that the self is in fact there, a self from which we can relate to others? That sense of the self brings with it a feeling of well-being, indeed, of being itself. Dr. Frank Lake speaks of this as the "I-my-self."

> Many of us were fortunate enough to be given the security of our mother's and then our father's continual presence to support our being until it became so much a part of us that we could say I-my-self in such a way that we could carry our mother's spirit and our father's strength about in us. We can always enjoy this tripartite 'I-my-self' nature. Much has been given to us, and there is nothing lacking to our essential humanity that we have not received.
>
> This is not so with hysterical personalities. Faith in one's basic spiritual relationship, in the 'self' which should have been mother, has been shattered. It can be represented only by 'I-my-?' or indeed by 'I-nothing-nothing.' This is what we mean by depersonalization, a sense of the complete unreality of the self when it cannot rely by faith on the other necessary elements of its spiritual totality.[4]

Linda knew only the "I." Due to infantile trauma much of the "my-self"— found in a safe start with mother—was lost in the splitting off of the unbearable feelings. Therefore, friendships were always muddied due to attempts to find the "my-self" in another woman. Linda knew nothing, therefore, of a healthy interdependency upon and with others. She had to swing from the extreme of neurotic attachment (the bentness toward another that sought to make up for the loss of the needed initial attachment) to the other extreme whereby she feared and eschewed all attachment.

Linda experienced the kind of early trauma that leaves one with a sense of being that is either extremely tenuous or missing altogether. There is, even as she describes, an identification with nonbeing itself. Can God heal people like this? Yes, indeed. But we have to understand what it is we are praying for here and how important it is that we learn how to pray aright.

We can see by now why she felt "no aliveness when separate," precisely what the tiny infant in isolation felt. One who did not know herself even to be separate from her mother and who had continuously received her messages of love and warmth, whether within or without the womb, was now unaccountably bereft—dead apart from that "other" whose special beingness told her she was alive.

Linda's letter reflected a need so strong to "connect" with mother (or a mother figure) that there was no room for grieving. She could only endlessly strive toward making the vital connection, that miraculous bridge with woman she missed in infancy. In a sense, therefore, she lived in unresolved grief all the time.

There is often, as Drs. Hemfelt, Minirth, and Meier have noted in their book *Love is a Choice,* a repeating pattern in certain cases. Persons like Linda are often drawn toward those who will abandon them—even as the infant "believes" the parent did. They hope to resolve the original situation by reenacting the abandonment scenario repeatedly until they finally are not abandoned. In these situations, of course, when helpers do not know how to put up the right kind of boundaries, they can get so entangled and then, finally, so discouraged that they have no recourse other than to give up. When we understand neither the problem nor what to do to help, it is better that we "give up" quickly in that we acknowledge we are in over our heads. We then can look and pray diligently for those who can give the needed help. But the point is—it is not difficult for these sufferers to find themselves finally shoved aside—even by the most loving of Christians.

The Breakdown of Rational Coping Mechanisms and the Emergence of Neurotic Desires

Linda speaks of her power to *choose* in the past and thereby flee emotional dependency. This was her swing into no intimacy in relationship to others in order to avoid the overdependency. Her cognitive defenses were very strong— and needful. But when these finally failed, she was reduced to the "sobbing, sobbing, sobbing" and the "hell, hell, hell." When she finally broke and gave in, her awful striving ceased. What happened then? The neurotic compulsions returned full force. All her abandonment issues raced to the fore—the craving for touch, to be held, to nurse. All the unmet infantile desires were then a hunger so strong that she could think of nothing more than attempts to get this gnawing, never-ceasing hunger fed. Just as the young lad who can't accept himself as a man after puberty continues to hurt and seeks this affirmation in various (even neurotic) ways, so she sought to make up this greatest of deficits—a truly awful one. Her lesbian neurosis was little more than a symbolic confusion, a defense against the terrible inner emptiness—the fact that apart from strong, nurturing women, she had no "aliveness," no hope of something to blot out her dread feelings of "nothingness." Frank Lake speaks of this as the "reaction into lust":

An alternative defensive reaction to rage is to substitute for the real mother and her breast a mere fantasy of them as if they were back in possession. This substitution of a real loved object by an imaginary one is termed *libidinal fantasy*. In the Anglo-Saxon sense of the word, this is "lust," an absolute desire for that without which one cannot exist. In the first days of infancy the mind instinctively has a picture of the desired object, the nipple or breast, and a vaguely conceived picture of a desired person's face. In the painful absence of the real person or an acceptable substitute, fantasy "recreates" the longed-for person, or a part of them, or an item of their clothing as a memento, in a mental image. Libidinal fantasy occurs independently of the reaction towards rage.[5]

Anxiety

The anxiety Linda is suffering now is part of a defense mechanism against her split-off feelings—those inherent in an abandonment depression. It is, in effect, the defensive wall in her soul she (and we) can see and that she is painfully experiencing. On the other side of the wall—behind or underneath it—are those things she cannot as yet see—those things she most dreads and fears.

This back side of the defensive wall of anxiety holds back truths people cannot bear to look at, such as those they hold about an idealized mother or father, or fears of annihilation, or repressed memories of traumatic incidents. In Linda's case, the realities of repressed grief, anger, and fear of nonbeing appear to be as yet unfathomed and unnamed. In the economy of the soul, it is better to suffer and deal with terrible and even chronic anxiety than to have to look at something the heart deeply and unconsciously feels is worse.

As this wall of anxiety starts to crumble, the autonomous nervous system kicks into high gear. The body and the deep mind (unconscious level of the soul) are anxious, for they know what the person does not yet know. Some of the severe physical reactions that occur when the break comes include trembling and chattering of teeth, bodies drawn up into contorted positions as muscles respond to the deep inner tension, sweating, and tachycardia (abnormally fast heartbeat). Because the feelings are those of the panic-stricken baby, there will be a heightened adrenalin flow and, therefore, rapid respiration and pulse.

The time may come when we who pray with others are asked to pray for someone whose wall of anxiety is beginning to crack. We will find ourselves attempting to comfort the person as the fear takes hold, and perhaps his or her body will start to shake violently. This state of panic and anxiety can go on for a very long time, even hours.

If when we invoke the Presence of the Lord and lift our voices to Him in prayer, the sufferer can then say, "I can look at this now because God is with me and those I trust are holding me, praying for me," the defensive wall will begin to crumble. If, in other words, the sufferer is enabled to trust that the resources are there with which to face the dreaded infantile memories with all their inherent panic and grief, then healing can come. But when the sufferer cannot in the natural flow of prayer reach this point, we need the help of a gifted physician/psychologist who will, among other things he deems necessary, administer medication as it is needed. This medication will not tranquilize the person to the point of never being able to deal with his grief, but it will grant the merciful reprieve needed so that the sufferer can go on with the dreaded work of facing the inner deprivation and loss.

When we see our fellow Christians suffer in this way, it is terribly difficult to realize that with all our crying out to God there has been little or no relief for the sufferer. Our distress is heightened when we have no understanding of the psychological dynamics—what is going on in the sufferer or what has yet to happen. There can be no relief until the acute anxiety lifts, and then, when it finally does, we are further distressed to see the one we love and want to help plunge immediately into clinical depression. But it is here that the person will begin to relive the infantile memories and thus will get in touch with the split-off feelings. This process can and often does go on for months. What we need to know and what we need to assure the sufferer is that there *is* an end to this suffering. There is light at the end of the dark tunnel. The hurt and pain, unbearable as it is and inescapable as it is, turns out to be a vital part of the healing. It signals that the repression is lifted and that the split-off feelings are coming to consciousness where they can be dealt with. If we know how to pray for healing of memories and help the depressed person to face the worst with Christ, he will in the end be spared a great deal. Healing will not only come, but it will come much faster.

At this point in ministry to the sufferer, relief comes to him as we who pray remember to speak not to the hurting adult before us, but to the suffering infant within reliving the trauma. The ministry the person receives at this time requires the utmost sensitivity and skill on the part of the professional therapist, and for those of us who pray, it requires the same. Our "skill" will differ from the doctor's, but it consists in humility before God in the face of such suffering and in seeking God's guidance, wisdom, and knowledge in every step we take. And He is so faithful, so willing to give it. Above all, our "skill" mainly consists in trust in Him. This trust grows as we see the Lindas, time after time, and in spite of the long, delicate process, set free to enter into joy and into healthy relationships with others.

When the pain is at its worst, though still ministering to the suffering infant, I use the imagery of standing in the cross and hurting. For example, I may pray something like this, "Lord, I stand here at Your cross with this tiny one, and these feelings of panic and fear are so terrible we cannot bear it. But You died to take these feelings into Yourself, and we take our place in Your dying just now. We die with You to the sins and shortcomings of anyone or any circumstance that contributed to it. We forgive them, Lord. We forgive the very circumstances of our lives, Lord. Lord, with You I feel this pain, and now I know it cannot destroy me. In Your perfect being and sacrifice, it has a place to go, and I'm yielding it up to You. Thank You, Lord. Strengthen me to feel in Your good time the other split-off feelings that have to come up, and I will again take my place in your death and dying. Lord, I will stand and hurt in You and then receive Your healing and life in return."

Time

Time is different for the newborn. Minutes are hours, hours are eternities. When persons like Linda relive these early memories, it is as if time itself almost grinds to a halt. The present moment, even as it was then, seems endless, and the pain too great to bear.

In the midst of abandonment depression, there is a loss (as we see in Linda's letter) of the power to function. Linda was crying out to God, but she was unable to feel His Presence ("up to this year Jesus has been enough") or His nurturance. Though she is not yet in touch with the memories, at a deep level she is feeling her mother's absence and the loss of *beingness* she suffered as an infant. She had cried out for mother, and mother didn't come. Now she could cry out for God to come, but she could not, as it were, *be* in His Presence. *Beingness* itself was at risk within her, and so the painful thinking, thinking, thinking and striving, striving, striving. Once this emotional activism peaked, she plummeted down into passivity and depression and then faced the fearful work of getting in touch with what was in her deep mind and heart.

When Kierkegaard cried out that we have forgotten how to exist, to be, and that we can only *think about* being, he was describing Linda's condition. It is evident that he suffered a grief like Linda's—and found no relief for it. He was, therefore, keenly aware of this pathology as it now spreads itself over the church and the Western world.

Our parents in their functioning symbolize God to us, and for Linda there was no nurturing symbolization here. By the time her staph infection was cleared up, she had a far more serious difficulty. She was too wounded to accept in trust the love her mother had to give her. Her reactions now to others would not arise out of a serene sense of having been loved and protected. She could not feel her mother's love and protection; therefore, she could not feel God's help and protection even when it was being given. She never stopped knowing by faith that He was there, but her need to rest in a restored sense of being and to feel safe in the love of God and of others was now overcoming her strong rational defenses.

Touch

Here within the adult person, we see the suffering infant, and for it, as we've noted, time virtually stands still. Its physical sight differs. As these person go into these memories, they sometimes describe difficulty in seeing (hazy or blurred vision), but even so are able to tell us what is happening—or what is failing to happen. Loving human words addressed to the suffering baby and *touch* are what sink deeply into the soul of the inner hurting infant—the very missing ingredients from long ago. Therefore, we comfort the baby within. And the baby responds to touch.

When their worst feelings charge to the surface, they are not relieved by our audible prayer to God but by the comfort given the inner child. (Even in the "Standing in the Cross Prayer" and others that we are led to pray aloud, we are at the same time comforting and relieving the child.) These dear ones find relief as we speak to the tiny abandoned infant and to God for them. We are, in a manner of speaking, back in time—we are ministering to the infant as it was in its initial suffering and wounding. Therefore, we do what we would have done had we been there and understood what was going on. We assure the baby it is safe, that it is no longer alone.

Although our prayer at this time is immensely effective, it is not something the suffering one can yet "think" or "feel." We have ourselves become a prayer—God's love together with ours links the sufferer ever more securely to Himself and to His healing love. When a person is experiencing the hitherto repressed feelings of an infantile trauma and/or emotional shutdown, we are, as it were, holding the inner suffering infant and speaking words of assurance and comfort to it as a mother would. This is where the sufferer can make the vital start—the beginning of trust that *another* is indeed there.

The healings that can take place at this point are nothing short of miraculous. They do not happen, however, apart from our taking great care in the way we minister and pray. The therapist or counselor continues to be important, even pivotal, as the healing proceeds. He or she is the one with whom a vital transference is taking place. But it is good, even ideal, when others (especially family members) can also be involved. The therapist is not always there when the feelings hit. Abandonment depression is intermittent: it comes and goes as the waves of grief come forward. When someone in the family knows how to pray and is also trusted by the sufferer, the whole process can be speeded up. In fact, the major part of a healing can take place with that person.

A husband or a wife, for example, when mature in Christ and trusted by the sufferer, can comfort the inner child when these terrible feelings charge forward. A spouse will need the wisdom and the objectivity at these times never to confuse the situation by introducing conjugal love—a mistake married persons could easily make, but which would be counterproductive at such a time.

Through our prayerful and wise touch, the vital connection missed in those first months of life can be made up for. Some would even say *made*. This much I know, a bridge is built, a new selfhood begins to be experienced in identification and in a truer and healthier interdependence with others.

Transference

First [still using the feminine for both sexes], the hysteric must be able to posit her insecure selfhood in some Christian person, or better still, a family or group of accepting Christians. Here she can recapitulate with another set of parents and brothers and sisters something of what was lost in the vicissitudes of her own unfortunate babyhood. We must interpret this transference activity as a necessary kind of bridge-making bringing her from distrustful isolation (however concealed) back to the reality of the social family. This way she replaces her own neurotic bridge, with the force of forbidden impulse and retributive punishment surging back and forth over it, and substitutes a new and as yet untried bridge of actual trust of a real person outside herself. Only when she has tested the bridge to see if it can carry her weight can she begin to respond in mutual trust again. She has to ensure the new relationship can stand the weight both of the ingratiating attractive side of her personality as well as the unattractive fears and rages and paroxysms of envy and hate that are inalienably part of her tortuous self.[6]

As those who pray, we do not set the stage for a transference. We learn to recognize it when it is occurring. When one who suffers separation anxiety relives memories of perceived abandonment, we who pray with or counsel them are parental figures. We minister into the woundedness. If we've been close to the needy one and they've been looking to us for help, we've likely experienced the ambivalence inherent in a transference situation. Both love and hate can come our way; in other words, we draw toward ourselves both the hysterical and the schizoid reactions in our attempts to minister. Setting appropriate boundaries and knowing the importance of timing and touch are some of the ways we avoid the difficulties.

Bonding

In regard to abandonment depression and deprivation neuroses, I hesitate to use the term *bonding* except to describe what happens between mother and child. That term, it seems to me, carries with it the strong and appropriate image that rightly defines what occurs with good mothering. Used in the context of the healing of someone like Linda, however, it implies that she found something equal to what she lost when the bonding with her mother was interrupted. Therefore, we are in danger of being led astray in several important ways if we use that term in the context of the healing of adult sufferers. Their loss will always be a loss. No one person or ministry can ever take the place of the missing mother or mother substitute. Nothing can replace her love and sensitivity that enables the attachment to her (as well as the healthy detachment later on) as one comes into a sense of being and selfhood. But I know the inestimable value of the healing of memories as one relives in the presence of a trusted soul the trauma one early on faced in absolute aloneness. By placing the trusted one in the parental position as the sufferer relives the past, God makes of him or her a unique instrument of healing and wholeness. And it is a "kind" of bonding, an attachment on the human level that enables God to multiply within that heart and mind the infilling of *storge* (nurturing, familial) love it missed as an infant.

What happens in these instances is truly miraculous. But it is different from what happens in the natural process, and we err if we try to duplicate it.

There is another reason for my hesitation to use—other than very carefully—the term bonding. When helpers take this process too literally, as in the concept of re-parenting, they tend to make cripples of the sufferers. It is too easy to develop emotional dependency on the mother figure. This is especially true when the sufferer tends toward the clinging (*hysterical*) position.[7] The likelihood of emotional entanglement is far less a threat to the counselor when the sufferer tends to fear attachment (the *schizoid* position).[8] Therefore, the counselor may feel that re-parenting is working. But this "attachment" to the parental figure will not necessarily help the person to true interdependency with others nor to overcome his fear of intimacy. It may even inhibit full healing.

This is where the negative aspects of transference take place. In a transference situation, all the delayed hopes for a mother instantaneously rush in. (This could be termed an "instantaneous transference" and should be differentiated from the natural bonding that occurs normally between mother and child, beginning even in the womb.) The miracle of trusting a mother figure is for the first time not only a possibility, but is experienced, and the sufferer feels safe. This is not bonding, though it possibly feels like it. It is the priceless place of safety that allows all the sufferer's memories and feelings of rejection, anger, and abandonment to surface. It is also the place where real trust can take root in the sufferer's heart and a bridge of intimacy be built—one that prepares the way for a healthy normal attachment to occur and then from there interdependence with others to grow. But here the counselor's part grows more crucial.

For this the counselor has been waiting—the emergence of the diseased, repressed feelings. This is not only the critical place of healing for the needy one, but it is the place where the helper needs the most wisdom. Such a sufferer will invariably (from this place of safety) perceive rejection and abandonment on the helper's part because he or she is reliving (at the deepest emotional level) the failed relationship with mother. The woman counselor, as a mother figure, will then be the object of the person's worst fears.

It is for this reason that attempts to re-parent, strictly speaking, lead in the wrong direction. Re-parenting (something the sufferer desperately wants) doesn't work. Though the helper has given the gift of a place of trust and safety where there can be the kind of transference that abreacts these wounds (allows them to surface) and their accompanying fears and feelings, the helper's job at this point is not to be the mother the person never had or a savior from pain. Counselors are not and cannot be either.

Women counselors can, however, especially as Christian women, be serene symbols, icons as it were, of the best and the truest in womanhood. They are indeed sacramental channels of a blessed feminine giftedness into the lives of those bereft of such. They can even be empowered by God in special ways to respond to the wounded. But they cannot be all this to hurting people if they draw toward themselves these persons' fear of rejection and abandonment instead of objectively deflecting these fears into Christ crucified.

They are called to pray and then in the wisdom God liberally gives, they deflect the feelings of deepest dereliction from themselves up to God, who is Mother-Father-Savior. They do this by helping the sufferers to acknowledge before God all these dread feelings, heretofore repressed, and by helping these persons to forgive their parents and the very circumstances of their lives.

This does not happen if the helper has presented herself as the ideal mother, in which case the sufferer will either be bent toward her or demand that various therapists do what the helper has seemed to promise. In the initial stages, the counselor was "the only trusted one." But if the helper does not understand what the later stages hold and how always to call the sufferer to the truth (I am not your mother; you cannot find your identity or sense of being in or through me), the helper will experience the down side of the transference mechanism. Then she will think she has failed and will (apart from some fortunate circumstance) constellate an irrational and hysterical acting out on the part of the sufferer. Even more serious, if the counselor becomes the desired feminine object to the brokenhearted, she then will be an idol, a dead icon that ceases to point to reality.

Some books on deprivation neurosis present re-parenting in such a way that the helper is bound to burn out (perhaps even become codependent or give up on healing prayer in the process), and the sufferers—with their irrational needs either to cling or to flee—will be tempted to stop short of finding their true identity as responsible adults. In focusing too exclusively on the inner suffering child, some have neglected to minister to the responsible adult the person now is. They have over-identified with the "problem" to be healed and under-identified with the true self, the full person who is to be called forward to become all he was created to be in God. In effect, they have lost sight of the person's true identity. It is the adult (albeit one who is suffering greatly due to infantile memories) that we encourage and strengthen to come present to his or her worst memories and see them healed. It is the adult who is to be helped to see and repent of immature or sinful responses, and who is to be led in confession of sin and in prayer for the forgiveness of others.

It's a wonderful thing to watch these adults learn to grieve out their wounded feelings, while at the same time they grow as responsible adults in the midst of their suffering. I've seen the most courageous stability here as they maintain these objective stances, knowing themselves as responsible adults even as they experience feelings of dereliction that few can imagine who've not been afflicted with such depression.

This, I think, is a marvel—but it is part of the grace God gives those who trust in Him. Christian counselors or therapists can get in the way of this grace, however, when they forget the prime identity of the suffering one before them. Some sufferers, of course, those mature in Christ, would never regress and remain in the "wounded child." It would make little difference if we as counselors were unclear in our approach. But there are many more who would continue to live from the center of the wounded inner child rather than from their true center, if they mistakenly focused on their suffering. It is from that true center alone that they as adults take their place in Christ's suffering and in His cross. That is where they die with Him to the pain, releasing it all into Him, and then go on to grow up into the most astounding maturity in Him.

Some of the most balanced and powerful ministers I know have come through these very woundings. My files are full of their joyous letters—letters that proclaim the truth that God turns our worst hurts into healing power for others. Several of these are deeply loved and valued PCM team members. They preach the cross, lifting it high as few others do, for they know its awesome efficacy.

Healing is a delicate process in all these souls, and we who pray for this healing must keep our hearts closely attuned to what God is doing and saying. It is only with the greatest of humility and sensitivity that we can either discern what is going on in the mind and heart of sufferers or continue to simply trust in God with and for them as those inner needs are hidden from us. As we do this, something new and wonderful replaces what was lost in the early trauma, and a new sense of selfhood, of identity-in-relationship comes to the sufferer.

More on Timing and Touch

In prayer for healing that involves deep abandonment issues, I need to emphasize again the vital importance of human touch appropriate to the need, and also timing, that dance-like harmony and rhythm we achieve as we learn to collaborate with God in His healing work.

Inappropriate and lustful feelings associated with touch deprivation often surface in prayers with those suffering separation anxiety, especially when their defense mechanisms have resulted in gender confusion and sexual neurosis. As these feelings occur, we are to help the person note them objectively and then yield them (like all other diseased feelings) up to the Lord. We assure the sufferer he is to feel no shame, but he is to admit rather than deny and repress these feelings, and he is to name them before the Lord as they surface. These feelings are usually related to symbolic confusion, and we need to look at them in that light, thus helping the sufferer to resymbolize the feelings. Often their bodies are stimulated in this process in ways that embarrass and even alarm them. Here too we ask these dear ones to be patient with and speak peace to their physical bodies, which (like the soul) also manifest anxiety and symbolic confusion. It is amazing what can be accomplished in a short time when we help others to this objective stance. We are not ordinarily to eschew touch out of fear of inappropriate responses. Rather we are called to understand the responses, thereby apply the antiseptic of reason, and then ask God to replace unhealthy responses with healthy ones. Prayer, together with honoring the need for human touch, works miracles.

Linda suffered greatly from touch deprivation. After receiving her letter, we put her with one of our prayer counselors. As the counselor prayed for her and held her in the midst of her depression, Linda noted nervously that she experienced erotic sensations. The counselor assured her she was to feel no shame, that they were most likely a leftover association from her former homosexual experiences. When the feelings came up, they acknowledged them together before God and lifted them up to Him. Linda wrote later:

> The fact that [the counselor] did not cringe when I told her nor flinch from touching me thereafter made me know, like nothing else could, that it was o.k. to receive her touch. I was able to receive her touch for the unadulterated nurturance it was and let go of the sexual nuance.

One of the results of this time with the counselor was that touch was resymbolized for Linda.

One can readily see why Linda was so "into" massage and massage therapy. Godly massage therapists who understand all these things can have amazing ministries. Of course, they will not allow others to "bend in to them," but will be pointing those they help always toward identity in Christ. These therapists know their own boundaries and do not allow others to transgress them. Thus they help the sufferers to gain the kind of boundaries *they* need. Those boundaries eventually will form the strong circumference of the "city" of their own unique soul, their own selfhood.

Again it is a continuing marvel to see what God can do with one godly, well-timed, prayerful embrace. Just as Christ multiplied the loaves and the fishes so that all were fed, so He can take the small loving things we do and multiply the healing effects beyond all knowing.

I sometimes have sufferers such as these focus on me so strongly that I cannot minister to them. One young man with a need like this came from a distant country for help. He was bent toward me so strongly, however, that I had become everything. In God we live and move and have our being, but he was far from being able even to imagine this reality. He was centered on me with an enormous compulsion to, as it were, crawl into my sphere of being and disappear into me. Throughout the week of lectures and ministry, his eyes never left my face. There was no way I could minister to him apart from God's bringing him out of this fixation, one that had to do with severe separation anxiety and his lack of personal identity. I sent him to others for prayer, but to no avail. At the very last meeting in the midst of the consecration service, I saw him break. He had lost hope I would minister to him, and this had (together with God's answers to our prayer for him) brought him out of the fixation. I immediately prayed with him, and the Lord seemed to rush in to meet this man's need. It was an extremely powerful moment, and it would have been missed if I had yielded to the powerful hysterical need in him to bend into me. This man, a young physician from a troubled European nation, then told me he had planned his suicide for right after these meetings if he did not get help. As it is, he perseveres in the Lord even in the midst of a torn and tumultuous country.

I share this to emphasize our need to fully depend upon God. In our zeal to help others we can get in the way of what God wants to do. On the other hand, it is through the most commonplace gestures of human love and touch that God often finds a pathway through to the sufferer. Through these small things the power of Christ's love and the full efficacy of His work on the cross issue forth to save the derelict soul, the one suffering the "hell, hell, hell" of which Linda speaks.

Christians gifted in prayer for healing are to pray for the wisdom, the knowledge, and the balance needed here. They must themselves be mature and always maturing in Christ, and their full trust and dependence is upon Him. We know and praise His faithfulness, His lovingkindness. Otherwise, we are in danger of moving unwisely to try to help the needy one escape the pain, the pain that is in these cases part of the healing. We move too quickly to try to meet on the human plane what can only be met on the divine. We thereby find ourselves not the channels of healing, but the objects of idolatry. When we know the work is not ours, but God's, then the person's relief and healing does not hinge upon us. We can celebrate our own inadequacy and smallness, all the while knowing that as we continue to pray, God's will is being done. We learn to collaborate with Him according to His timetable and His knowledge of the soul that is suffering.

With all this in mind, we see how easily touch can be misused. Here we see that a mere touch that seems so insignificant in terms of a person's having had a lifetime of need for it, is used by God to heal touch deprivation. But we also see that there are times when our touch would work against such a person's healing, as in the case of the young physician.

Many, especially those coming out of sexual neurosis, are fearful of touch, as many in the church are. Touch is a volatile thing, and we are careful never to misuse it. But touch is important in healing, and God uses it to a phenomenal extent when and as it is appropriate. It is an exciting thing to follow God's leading in the healing of emotional hurts. On the one hand, we cannot let a soul bend toward us in the wrong way, as Linda would have done had we not helped her with boundaries. On the other hand, we see how God uses so incredibly our human expressions of love and touch. How wonderfully God uses our humanness, how incarnational a thing this matter of healing turns out to be.

The hard thing for many Christians who pray with others to realize is that we cannot always (much less immediately) relieve or even appreciably diminish people's suffering. We cannot get in there and "fix things," not even with an instant powerful prayer (although sometimes we do in fact see God do it!). If we try, taking the initiative out of God's hands, we will fail. We may end up reinforcing neurotic defenses as surely as the physician does who over-sedates. To try to "fix things" or to try to shore-up and defend God's reputation as a loving, healing God allows our own misplaced sympathy and empathy to get in the way of the healing. We cannot magically take away their suffering. No matter how hard we try, we cannot take away their feelings of abandonment. Before healing can take place, their task, hard as it may be, is to face the inner loneliness. It is the same task we all have, only it is excruciatingly difficult for them.[9] Thanks be to God, He knows and understands all this, and He is the righteous judge, too loving to remove the necessary task that precedes healing. As Dr. Lake, writing of the full-blown hysterical personality, says:

> The demands for sympathy and care which the hysterical woman [using the feminine for both sexes] makes are her misunderstanding of the problem. She thinks she needs company; what she actually needs is courage to face aloneness. That can only come when experience of attentive caring has enabled her to possess for herself the reverberating circuits of information within the cortex which enable the normal person to feel, 'I am never alone.' She thinks she needs just a little attention here and a little there. The basic therapeutic task is being evaded so long as she declines to face the depths of her inner solitariness, the infant in utter panic and near dereliction. If these could be repressed again, we might be content, but that is not a very adequate ideal of therapy, for it leaves the personality always on the defensive. Our experience and our confidence is this, that when the infantile separation-anxiety is openly declared, then, in the power of the Holy Spirit's abiding presence, there is an entirely new ability to come to terms with separation-anxiety.[10]

That too is our experience. Over and over again we see these persons not only come through the darkness of abandonment depression into the Light that is always waiting for them at the end of the dark tunnel, but—as they mature within the Body of Christ—we see their wounds turned into the most incredible healing power for others. Their joy, wisdom, and depth of insight are invaluable gifts to the rest of us who've never known the failure to find early on, even in the first months of our lives, a sense of being and of well-being in a mother's love.

When Schizoid Elements Are Strong

The root *schizo* derives from the Greek verb "to split." In this condition there has been a radical split in the ego, in fact in the total person. This took place earlier, and goes deeper than it does in hysterical splitting or depressive splitting. As a result of this overwhelming infantile trauma, the ego, which was beginning to develop a relationship of trust in persons in its environment, is split from top to bottom. Only a semblance of trust remains. A part of the ego splits off and becomes regressive, seeking the intra-uterine security from which it has been ejected. Another part of the ego, forced into continued contact with the "terrible mother," is split off and is identified with a longing for death and annihilation. This ego-splitting experience may be due to "biological pain," such as crushing or distress in the birth passages during a difficult delivery, or to "ontological pain," such as the post-natal suffering of the too-prolonged absence of the mother who is the necessary personal source of being.[11]

Because Linda's letter reflects the hysterical elements and the striving to attach rather than fear (even panic) at the thought of attachment, we have illustrated the hysterical condition more fully than the condition in which the schizoid reaction is more apparent.

I would hope that this chapter will encourage all pastoral counselors to read Dr. Lake's book *Clinical Theology*, prepared specifically for them. It is now out in an abridgement of his original 1200-plus-page book. In it he writes of the hysterical, the schizoid, the paranoid, and the depressed as they are in the extreme—the full-blown conditions or personalities—and of the anxiety and related defensive reactions and so on. That is not how I write. I describe persons in whom these elements are to be seen. Linda is not a full-blown hysteric. She is in many ways a mature Christian who is suffering abandonment depression, one with strong hysterical elements that indicate her failure to make the initial attachment. She could easily, however, have fallen finally into the full-blown hysterical position apart from help from the Body of Christ. And in the same way we write of the other elements (such as the schizoid), hoping to help those who pray to understand more about what is going on.

The "Internalized Bad Mother"
Sometimes in our healing meetings, persons suffering in these ways begin to, as we term it, "throw up the mother." Long before I ever heard the term "the internalized bad mother," I knew what it was. We on the PCM team find ourselves holding people as they quite literally gag and spit "her" up and out. We've learned how to spot this as it starts to happen and how to pray for these persons.

The internalized bad mother is the result of emotional and/or physical incest. In cases where the child is forced to meet the emotional needs of the mother, it has had to abdicate any need of its own. The mother has so forced herself on the child that the child has, in a manner of speaking, "swallowed" the mother. Sometimes the internalized critical voice of a mother (or a father, in which case we have the "internalized bad father") is so loud that the personality of the child is crippled or even displaced. There is then the need to get this up and out so that one can hear God. (See case example on pages 136-37.) A great release and healing comes when God enables people to empty themselves of this evil. It was good, therefore, to see in Dr. Lake's book his reference to this phenomenon:

In deep therapy paranoid patients may spend hours feeling identified with a most "distasteful" experience, as if the mouth were full of a substance so insipid, mawkish or tasteless, and so useless as the food they hoped it was to be, that they will spend hours in abreaction as if spitting out some cloying stuff. This "disgusting" truth compels consciousness to tell a lie and deny that one could ever have been identified with such an insipid and offensive source.[12]

I remember well one young man in one of the services who began to vomit up the internalized "bad mother" in this way. His mother, the most disgusting of sexual deviates, had been his only companion in growing up. He had been hospitalized on several occasions with depression and had made progress. He eventually married, but then all his schizoid feelings in relation to woman rushed to the fore. One cannot imagine the pain his bride must have endured as she began to receive all his transferences and became the object of his enormous fear of being swallowed up by the female and of his disgust. His spiritual advisors were utterly baffled by the tragic turn his marriage took and could make no headway until they realized what they were dealing with.

Such a person needs expert therapy right away. He is fearful of attachment to woman, and his irrational reactions to her along with his paranoia will only grow until he gets help. If he is thoroughly trapped, say for example, as one whose religious convictions will not allow him to desert her, his sickness in relation to others may worsen. He may begin to irrationally hate and blame other women. Men who are deeply and dangerously misogynous can be formed out of circumstances such as these. It is one thing to "vomit up one's mother," and it is quite another to deal in depth with the dereliction and fearful associations that underlie the fear of attachment, all that must arise when such a one marries.

This young man's need showed up in his face and in his actions. But some whose suffering exhibits the schizoid and paranoid elements can more easily hide their need, appearing quite well integrated, strong, and efficient. Not everyone's face or life on the surface reveals early infantile abuse and abandonment. Probably this is especially the case when the power to feel (the feeling being itself) has been paralyzed. Then, if they have survived the ordeal at all, their cognitive, rational powers are highly honed. Their mental defenses and mechanisms for survival are especially clever and strong. From my perspective and experience, it is more difficult for those of us who pray to recognize what is going on in these cases. We can more easily misunderstand and even find ourselves stricken by their reactions. For example, these persons can be almost uncannily secretive. And even if we've been close to them, we may not realize the difficulties, much less the extent of their needs. These have been too well hidden. Then when the breakdown occurs, we who are close to them will not be the trusted ones. We may even (quite irrationally) be mistrusted.

Unless we recognize what is going on—and that there has to be someone outside what has been the Christian fellowship for this secretive, suffering one—we may feel not only rejected but betrayed by the sufferer. We will be the objects of mistrust. We will be getting the "projections" or the downside of the transference. As mother or father figures who are not trusted, we will be wounded and dismayed if we do not understand the dynamics here.

Regression

I am ministering to a young man, gifted in many ways and not the least in a healing ministry. He ministers to others coming out of severe abandonment depression, even as he himself is still coming out of it. This means he often has the burden of knowing what his needs are, as the inner split-off feelings erupt into consciousness, and of knowing that he could give the help to others while at the same time he is frustrated in attempts to get this help himself.

As anxiety hits, Jason has learned not to run from it. He waits in the Presence of God, there facing the inner loneliness with Him until the feelings come to consciousness and he can do the necessary grieving. He has learned to listen to God. He is strong in the Lord, knowing the Word of God, and His commitment to God is absolute.

However, along with the anxiety and panic, he has often been shamed by the fact that in the presence of his pastor, he nearly always regresses to the hurting little boy. A misunderstood movement or word on the part of his pastor calls forth his most inordinate feelings of rejection, disappointment, and just plain need to be loved and touched by a father. It also calls forth his worst compulsions to somehow get from this man what he was unable to receive through his own father and mother.

This pastor is a "mothering" father figure to him and, therefore, is the object of his transferences. The pastor has the unique power to affirm and even bring him through abandonment depression, but also he is the object of his worst and most paranoid transferences. In order to help him and to straighten out their pastor-parishioner relationship, the pastor needs to understand both Jason's regression in his presence and how to set up the proper boundaries with him.

Jason's compulsions were much more powerful than he realized, and so he was often in danger of depleting his pastor's tolerance and patience. In his constant demands for prayer with his pastor, he was demanding more than anyone has to give. Lest this seem to contradict what we've already said, this situation merely points strongly again to both the timing and the grace of God (His love, not ours) operative in healing prayer.

We then talked again about what Jason already knew—that the pastor, just in existing, had the power with one word or the lack of it to plunge him into joy or despair. He knew this was immature; he knew also that despite his best efforts to rationally control the feelings, in the presence of this man his heart always desired something from him. Wanting "more and more" from his pastor, he would ask for prayer—something he needed but could never be quite satisfied with. He was looking to the pastor for both the healing of abandonment he had suffered with his mother and the protection and affirmation his father had never been able to give. The pastor, with many other responsibilities, was naturally growing weary of this constant demand and draining.

I asked Jason to stop requesting prayer from the pastor and to lift up all his anxiety and feelings of need to God, listening to Him for directions as to what to do next. I told him that when his demands stopped, the pastor would be free, as led by the Spirit, to minister to him effectively. And that is exactly what happened.

Pastors need to understand this regression mechanism and how to put up the needed boundaries to avoid playing into it. Then when they are not at the mercy of the sufferer's neurotic desires and compulsions, they are able to minister the healing with all its needed affirmation as they are led.

In these matters, we see once again how prayer and touch heal when they are appropriate, rightly timed, and come at the leading of God. That healing then prepares the way for the next appropriate prayer and touch. The prayer that attempts to meet neurotic need only works against the true healing. This exemplifies again the fact there is the adult, and there is the inner wounded infant and child. We neglect neither. We minister to the person as he or she is now, seeing him or her as a responsible adult. Even further, in seeing the person through Christ's eyes, we see the full, mature man or woman as he or she shall soon be. It has been necessary to minister to the wounded inner child as memories and feelings have surfaced, but we never forget or neglect to relate aright and with appropriate expectation to the responsible adult before us.

Jason is now largely free from these compulsions. His pastor has ministered deeply into his life, affirming him as a man and in his full personhood. He has helped him through his humiliating regression, an immaturity Jason was rationally so aware of but unable to control or conceal emotionally. Better yet, he helped Jason receive his Heavenly Father's greater affirmation and the manly maturity that goes with his inheritance in Christ.

Fantasy Bond

In prayer for healing of these deepest hurts in the memories, those things that inhibited the crucial attachment to mother, a most incredible window is opened into the emotional life of the infant. Along with the feelings of abandonment, for example, one may relive crucial and traumatic moments when one's emotional life (or the life of the mother) is threatened, or the very moments when the emotional-feeling being shut down. And on occasion, there is the matter of a fantasy bond to deal with.

It seems that if the natural bonding is interrupted, we do in fact bond to something. I've prayed with some who have bonded to the bed, or to the pillow, to some very unlikely object, or even to a shadowy fantasy.

In the first chapter of this book I said I would tell of two other significant healings in Clay McLean's life. One involved getting in touch with the fantasy bond. In the failure to bond with his mother, he had bonded with the dark. This startling knowledge came to light as the team and I prayed with him in response to his fearful bout with temptation and self-hatred. At this time, much healing had already been securely set into his life, but he was still fearful to travel or be alone, especially at night. It was extraordinarily difficult for him to leave home alone, which he often had to do in the ministry.

As we were in prayer for him, I "saw" this fantasy bond and knew instantly what it was. In my spirit I saw it as a black disc and knew (as one can only know by the Holy Spirit) that Clay was yet one with it. Immediately, I cried: "Clay, you bonded with the darkness!" This was surprising to us, for we had not anticipated such a thing, but instantly as I named it, Clay saw the same black disc. He also knew he'd bonded with it. This was a powerful breakthrough for Clay, for we were then able to deal with his failure to come to a sense of being in those first months of life, something he had been in denial about up to this time. To say it was a major healing in his life is an understatement.

From that time forward, he has been able to travel everywhere—and alone. Only a few days after this prayer session, he phoned from his hotel room in a city where he was holding services. He was literally exulting in the fact that he was not only happy alone, but cherished the quiet and the time for reading and prayer. This healing then paved the way for another major one that integrated him with the feminine. It occurred about one year later. Since that time, nothing much has slowed this young man down. From the various parts of the world where he's ministering, I get phone messages such as, "I'm the most blessed man in the world," and so on. He writes songs, extraordinary music and lyrics that exult in the Christian's emerging from darkness into light.

Mira Rothenberg tells of a very troubled little boy who as an infant bonded with the lights in his incubator, and of his uncanny fascination with all light, as well as the remarkable way she helped him get in touch with this fantasy bond.[13] Stories such as hers, of successful therapy carried out in a controlled situation, accurately reported, and proved by its healing results would strain the credulity of many—but not of us who minister in healing prayer to persons with deep abandonment issues.

All his life Clay had had a fascination with the dark. He states that he learned to cope with fear and darkness by becoming fascinated with it. At his birth, there was stress and darkness in his home. His earliest infantile memories reveal intense fear for his mother, a feeling that he needed somehow to protect her but was helpless to do so. These feelings remained with him throughout his childhood and apparently got in the way of his ability to bond with her. Later, as a small child he would make his way through the dark rooms of the house to his mother's bedroom, fearful of the night yet more fearful that his mother had not survived it. Once there he would touch her face—to make sure she was breathing. He played this out, time and again, as attempts to keep her alive. Though afraid of the darkness, he loved and searched out dark, enclosed womblike places. From early on, he had unlimited access to television, and, in his words, "I put faces with my darkness, the faces from old horror movies." He states that he felt a "dark numinous presence" come to him through those dark faces, and a fantasy world grew up around them. His fear of death became a fascination with death. He recalls that "old late night horror movies flooded my mind with concepts, ideas, personalities, and the faces which fleshed out my night specters and filled my inner void. Here again, names like Dracula and Frankenstein had a numinous effect on me. Fascination with these figures would hold my eyes captive to the screen until the screen went black; then the fascination would give way to mute terror as I made my way from the TV set to my bed."

Clay had not achieved a secure attachment to his mother, a woman unprotected and far from being at rest; therefore, his own identification with the true feminine and his own sense of well-being did not develop. The parental inversion came extremely early for him. Rather than the feeling of being nurtured and kept safe in his mother's arms, he was overwhelmed with feelings of dread and the need to protect her. His love and loyalty to his mother prohibited his coming out of denial about the extent of his earliest injuries and what had never been achieved in relationship to his mother. He, like everyone who gets help in these areas, had to come out of denial.

A last illustration of how fascination with certain objects comes as a result of a fantasy bond involves the healing of a *cross-dresser*. We use this term for the heterosexual male who wears women's clothing. The homosexual male who cross-dresses we term a *transvestite*.[14]

The cross-dresser suffers from separation-anxiety and gender confusion related to his failure to make a secure attachment to his mother and thereby gain a strong sense of being or of well-being. This loss has led to a most grievous symbolic confusion in him. The related coping mechanisms (cross-dressing) leave him in the throes of a dread-ridden shame and compulsive behavior.

The cross-dresser, then, is a man obsessed with the idea of putting on a woman's clothing and is either doing it or is experiencing compulsions to do it. Unlike the transvestite who is fixated on his own sex and attempts to bond homosexually with a man, the cross-dresser is not afflicted with homosexual desires, but is fixated on woman. He is obsessed with literal woman and her symbolic representations. He is usually married or desperately desires to be. The Christian men of this type I've seen genuinely love and value their wives and homes, though they are emotionally afflicted and confused and are aware of neurotic aspects in their way of relating to their wives. Unlike the *transsexual* man who cross-dresses and who believes himself to be a woman trapped in a man's body, the cross-dresser knows that he is not a woman. Even so he often desperately yearns to be.[15]

In both the cross-dresser and the transvestite, there is a calming effect in putting on woman's clothes, but only in the cross-dresser is there sexual arousal as well. (See qualifying footnote 14.) He is eroticized in donning feminine attire as well as temporarily comforted, and therefore cross-dressing in him is a fetish.

We should distinguish the cross-dresser from the transsexual at this point. There are no female cross-dressers or transvestites, but there are female transsexuals, those who believe themselves to be men trapped in a woman's body, and they cross-dress. The transsexual male, on the other hand, believes himself to be a woman trapped in a male body.[16] Both male and female transsexuals attempt to live as the other sex while despising their body's sexual features. At times they even try with the help of medicine and surgery to obliterate their sexual organs. Until there is healing, these persons suffer depression, usually with thoughts of suicide, and sometimes there are suicide attempts.

Mary Pomrenning, who is on the PCM team, is one who suffered the transsexual neurosis. From actually thinking herself to be a man, Mary has blossomed into a most effective minister of healing, and having fully integrated with her feminine gender identity, she is a lovely woman as well. (The story of her healing is available on audio tape. Write to Pastoral Care Ministries, P.O. Box 1313, Wheaton, IL 60189 or Church of the Resurrection of Illinois in Wheaton.)

Symbolic confusion in cross-dressers is deep. To have the neurosis at all indicates failure in initial efforts to meaningfully relate to their mothers, but some of these sufferers will perhaps seem all too bonded to her. Even so, they suffer intense separation anxiety in relation to her. Together with that, they have never gotten their gender identities, confused as they are, separate from hers. This is the reason why there are no female cross-dressers, for their sexuality and gender are the same as their mothers'.

The immediate need for all these persons is for strengthening of the true self in Christ, their oneness with Him, and then prayer for a sense of being. They always have much shame, and we can help them deal with it as they forgive their mothers and all others who've contributed to their difficulties. (This presupposes the fact that these persons have made a full confession to Christ, repenting in depth and fully for the ways they've sinfully acted out their compulsions.) Some will have no idea that they need to forgive their mothers and will not recognize her part in their painful dilemma.

The following is a classic example of a Christian suffering this neurosis. This case illustrates the need both to recognize and deal aright with a fantasy bond and its later expression in an eroticized fascination with feminine objects. This example illustrates as well the way the cross-dresser's eroticism (fetishism) is connected to separation anxiety, which in the young infant is experienced as tension in the genital area.

For one Christian man whose battle with this horrible neurosis had been particularly severe, the fantasy was of a woman's hair, and he had bonded with that. His mother, herself unable to warmly relate to her children, apparently wished he had been born a girl. A number of memories from his very early life revealed unusual treatment by his mother, but the root trauma changed his life. He was about three and his mother had furtively dressed him in an item of girl's clothing when his father surprised them by arriving home early.

He was badly alarmed, sensing her shame and guilt as she quickly pulled from him the feminine clothing. He remembers feeling acutely ashamed, feelings that never left him after that for long. But it was what had happened just before his father appeared that shaped his whole life into a battle against a compulsion to cross-dress, until these memories were addressed and healed. The feelings he remembered, just before this guilty action of his mother's, were of desperately wanting to please her—wanting to be someone she could love. In a moment that seemed to seal her rejection of him as a male, she tied a woman's scarf about his head and then wondered aloud what he would look like if he had hair like a girl's. This was the root memory to be healed, and the fantasy bond came out of this moment. His attachment to his mother interrupted, he bonded with this fantasy image of himself. It was such a strong moment of rejection for him as a male child, and coming as it did so strongly upon a child still striving to bond with its mother, it left an indelible, even technicolor image of himself with women's hair. If she had crammed down upon his head a girl's wig which for some evil reason could never be removed, she could not have done him more damage. He bonded with that fantasy of a woman's hair, and from that time on, it served as both fetish and bond. It critically shaped and determined the way his personality was formed. He was thereafter compulsively fascinated with woman's clothing and especially woman's hair. His heart was never free of anxiety, guilt, and overpowering compulsions to dress as a woman.

I'll never forget when this dear man received his first healings. They started with his reading of *The Broken Image,* and as he said to me later, "Just having my compulsions named as the symbolic confusion they were gave me power over them and a way to cope with them." He had, of course, repented in depth and fully for the sinful way he had acted out his compulsions in the past. Filled with joy and hope, he wrote me right away, and I invited him to a PCM where he received a great deal more healing. He and his wife were ecstatic, for he was free from his irrational yet compelling desire to be a woman and could cope with occasional compulsions to cross-dress by understanding what was going on. Moreover, as he grew in the Lord, his masculinity was being greatly affirmed.

However, he was still troubled with the symbol (inner and outer image) of woman's hair. The image of himself with long hair would compulsively arise every time he was due for a haircut. He would begin to experience anxiety, and he would have to battle a compelling desire for hair like a woman's. Then, to his utter dismay and sense of having failed God, he would find himself eroticized. There would then be even more guilt over the pleasure involved in the sexual arousal.

When he shared this with me, I sensed we were dealing with a fantasy bond and asked God to reveal it. That is when the specific memory and image of the scarf on his head came to the fore. So much healing had already occurred in him, and he was making great strides forward in his sense of himself as a man affirmed in his masculine identity in God. However, it was not until we dealt with this memory of his mother's acceptance of him only when he had a girl's hair and scarf and we realized that he had bonded to this fantasy image of himself, that the stage was set for his final deliverance from the intense anxiety rooted in his emotional abandonment by his mother. We then understood as well why the symbol of woman's hair held such a fascination for him and why it stubbornly refused to go away with the plethora of other symbolic confusions and fetishes that had plagued him.

Another thing to note in the matter of fetishes is the way great pain can be strangely turned into pleasure for such a sufferer. He has forgiven his mother and even come out of denial about the fact that he didn't love her very much. But for many years before he received healing, he could only wish she had dressed him fully as a girl. The very thought caused a pleasurable eroticism in him. He could not for the life of him feel the need to forgive her; he could only wish she had continued to cross-dress him. (Later, some of these men do attempt to involve their wives in this activity.) But here again, we see the great value of prayer for healing of memories. As he relived the moment the little boy was about to have a girl's scarf put on his head, *he realized the little boy did not want to be a little girl.* He realized that this condition was set into him only after he bonded with the fantasy of himself with a girl's hair. His anxiety over being unable to bond with his mother was then transmuted in a most distressing way to a pleasure in being erotically aroused. This is symbolic confusion, and it is always operating in the person with gender neurosis.

For all those coming out of compulsions to cross-dress, the strengthening of their true gender identity is key. This man's great strides came, even before the uncovering of the fantasy bond, as his true masculinity was affirmed and strengthened, something that always happens when we come into a place of truly trusting and obeying God. For Mary, so critically wounded as the one with a transsexual neurosis is, her true femininity was evident in an amazingly short time as she made her will one with God's. To see gender identity restored is a beautiful thing, and it is necessary if one is to see the full restoration of a person's soul.

A Quick Healing Akin to Miracle

Only a few weeks ago I saw the most wonderful healing of a very great need. I've written this chapter to help Christians realize the long and painful process some have to move through in order to get in touch with repressed feelings, but this story illustrates how quickly a very deep deprivation neurosis can be ministered into by the Spirit of God. This healing came to a lovely, young Korean named K——. She, like Linda, had fantasies of a woman's breast (fear of touching one and being rejected and so on), but with her there was not the complication of lesbian responses. A Christian, she had long suffered with depression and longed to die. She was in a college course I taught, and on the first day in class, I saw the pain in her face.

She was a victim of the type of misogyny (hatred of woman) prevalent in the Far East that prohibits many parents from valuing girl babies, especially as firstborns. These little girls are born to women who due to the longstanding virulence of these misogynous attitudes in their culture are unable to accept themselves as women or to value their feminine giftedness. All of this woundedness within K—— quickly came to the fore, even in the first classes. Her face alternately reflected fear and depression. After several days, I received the following note from her, and I quote it exactly, preserving the fact that English is not her first language:

This is K——. My growth group leader encouraged me to see you, Leanne. I sometimes have thoughts of death, and Hopeless, I can find hope only in Christ. I don't have excitement for life, life is so hard & tuff. (but my real life is not hard or tuff). When you prayed for me for self-being, I believe God wants to do something, but I don't know.

Through your lecture, I start to see darkness which I never seen before in my life. Could you help me? Thanks, a lot.

K——

I put off seeing K—— because so much illumination and healing was coming to her through the class sessions, and her need was being addressed and ministered to at many levels. Her main and root healing came after two weeks of the classes as we prayed for the group for healing of memories. When we came to those first months of life and prayed for the Lord to set in a secure sense of being and for healing for failures to make the initial attachment to mother, her healing commenced and went on for an hour or so. After several days, she wrote it out:

When Leanne start to speak about "self-being, infant experience" [prayer for sense of being], some kind of pain start to heat my heart with oppression. I start to sob. The pain continually hurt my heart. At that time I start to remember something I didn't think about long time which is my mother had some problem in her brest when I was born, so she need to stay in bed and even she couldn't hold me until she recover from her operation. And she couldn't feed me through my babyhood with her brest, either.

I felt grief is comming out from my heart. I start to cry, and the pain of my heart was getting worse and worse. I start to feel phisical pain in my heart, too. I asked God to help me from this pain, Holy Spirit touched my heart, and I start a little bit relaxed.

At that time Leanne asked Esther [a student but also one of the school counselors] to come over to me for holding. Esther came over and hold me. When she hold me, I felt something touched my heart. Grief start to comming out more, after that, I start to see pictures in front of my eyes.

I see a baby who is in mother's arm nearby mother's brest. I recognize I am the baby, and *mother also is father.* My face is leaning on her brest, and then the baby start to suck mother's nipple. When the baby suck continually I felt something start to fill it up from bottom of my heart and some solid thing start to form inside of my heart. After that, I felt full and relaxed. While I was relaxing in mother's arm, from bottom of my heart "smile" rise up and come to my mouth, and changed my sad-looking lips to smiling lips. Until then my mother was holding me in her left arm close to her left brest. But next moment scene changed. My mother was holding me with her right arm close to her right brest. I suck a little bit more, and rub my face on her brest. [While this healing was going on, she was acting out the motions, and there were long sucking periods.] I wanted to know that she is there. I could feel the nipple. I felt safe and secure. A little bit later I rubbed my face again on her brest and her nipple, I would feel her brest and nipple on my face. I rubbed again, and felt her. I felt so good, safe, and satisfied.

Next scene I saw, I look like between 1 & 1.5 years old. My mother is holding me in her arm close to her brest. I rubbed my face to her brest, and got up from my mother's bosom, and play a little bit, and run toward my mother's bosom. She hold me again, I rubbed my face to her brest, I could feel her nipple.

I felt safe and secure. I rested a little bit in her bosom, and run out to play, and then I come back to her, I did something [this] several times. When every time I came back to my mother's bosom, my time for staying with her was getting shorter and shorter. The last time I came back to my mother, I touched her brest with my hand, and I felt that now I know she is there for me. I felt safe, secure & loved. I run out to play, and I know that I don't need to come back again. This is what God showed to me in front of my eyes. When this picture disappeared, I knew that God did wonderful thing in me. He brought healing, joy, security, life, and freedom from dead-wish. This is more than miracle. Hallelujah! (italics mine)

K— then drew a smile on her note to me, something that until "from bottom of my heart smile rise up in me" she could not have done. I had noticed her frozen emotions, that only with the greatest effort could she attempt a smile. In the two weeks, the attempt never quite made it. The corners of her mouth, try as they may, could turn up only slightly, and then never enough to make the smile. Neither in person nor on paper could she make a smile. In contrast, after this healing, her face was absolutely radiant. For the next week that I was there, it wore an exquisite smile, one that could only belong to a beautiful oriental woman. I'm sure it's still there, and the capacity for it will remain.

Here we see not only a healing of memories, but the way our Heavenly Father moves at times to heal deprivation neurosis. There was no "re-writing of the past," no changing, as it were, of K—'s past history with her mother. There *was* a divine and miraculous move to heal her of deep deprivation. If we can be released from fantasy bonds into the reality of a healing of the failure to make the initial and crucial attachment to mother, how much more can God use a divinely orchestrated fantasy (which is not really a fantasy but only the way our heart pictures what He is doing) to heal us of deprivation neurosis! Here is the P.S. to K—'s note:

I wrote what happened on Thursday morning. Thank you for your obedience to our loving Father. Oh, Leanne, when I saw picture in front of my eyes, I saw mother, *and also she is father.* I asked God what is it. I felt that because I didn't have any close experience with my mother, *heavenly Father became my mother and ministered to me.* Oh, it is wonderful, isn't it? (Italics added)

From being held by Esther, she went right into the arms of God, and He became both mother and father. These are the kinds of healings we see, whether they require time and process or happen immediately as in K—'s case. With K— we say, "Yes, truly, it is more than miracle." These healings do not occur apart from the Healing Presence of God, a Presence that is always with us to heal as we forgive others and the very circumstances of our lives. And the divine Presence does not despise the very human need to suckle. As K— was being healed, we watched her sucking motions as she was, as it were, nursing in the arms of the Lord. Yes, K—, "Heavenly Father" became your mother and healed you.

K— will never, even remotely, be the same. This is not to say she will not have pain as she grows out of many attitudes she has had toward herself as woman and perhaps as she relates to her family. But I've seen enough of these healings to recognize not only their miraculous nature, but their lasting effects. As K— walks in obedience to Christ and learns to listen to Him with her fellow Christians, the next healings will come, and they will come quickly. But abandonment depression and the effects of deprivation neurosis she will no longer have to face.

Physical Movements in Certain Healings

We've referred to K—'s sucking movements, something we've seen often enough to know it is important not to interrupt them. In *The Healing Presence*, page 107, I speak of people who come to us for prayer and then begin to behave in distorted ways—in an attempt to receive from God. They are perhaps trying to reproduce body movements that may have at one time been part of a valid religious experience. These movements are now merely part of a ritualized "liturgy" of behavior or sensory responses. There is no divine action, just reproduced behavior. We on the PCM team can spot this quickly and always stop it in order to help the person receive what God is wanting to do in the present.

Having said this, I want to mention some valid bodily responses that sometimes occur in response to certain kinds of healing. (These do not occur on a large scale, and I hesitate even to write about them for fear someone might try to imitate them. However, to help those who pray with others discern in these matters, I include these responses.) For example, sometimes the person receiving prayer begins to shake or even jerk, almost rhythmically, for long periods of time. As I was writing this section, a colleague, John Fawcett reminded me that this phenomenon occurs in the one whose *true self is emerging*. He said, "It is important that this shaking not become an issue and that it not be seen as demonic. We are to allow the person to feel what he or she is feeling, and we are not to stop the shaking prematurely as the feelings of repression and suppression are being shaken off along with the bodily movements." It is, he says, as if "the true self begins to fill the whole body."

Mario Bergner, a long-time minister with PCM, cautions that this phenomenon should not be tied solely to abandonment issues: "I see these particular movements occur in connection with any severe *suppression* of the real self." He lists some of the most common examples he sees.

The first example involves a suppression of the real self related to sin. Mario then reminded me of the prayer for a priest, one who had purposely repressed the truth in his life and ministry. In his case, the true masculine identity, both as man and as priest, had been denied and suppressed by his failure to obey God and by his continuing in sexual sin. In prayer, as this priest repented and as Mario ministered to him, he began to shake violently. He shook for hours as the true self came forward, and after that prayer, he started to obey God. This man's entire personal life and ministry have changed radically since this prayer.

Mario's second example was that of a woman he and I prayed for who, as a member of a oppressive discipleship movement, had seriously repressed her real self. As we prayed for her, she started convulsing, and she shook for ever so long. Frightened, she looked to me for comfort, and I said to her, "That's o.k, honey, it's just your real self coming forward and shaking off its fetters." As Mario pointed out (and on the front lines in PCM conferences he and John often see this played out), this was not a case involving deep abandonment issues, but one of a deliberate and long-term severe repression of the self in the name of the submission of woman.

A third "category" is one unlike the above. But it has to do with the suppression of the real self through severe practices of introspection, and usually it goes hand in hand with abandonment issues and the failure to come to a secure sense of being. The intermittent shaking can go on for weeks, as the real self comes out from under the control of the conscious analytical mind. In this case, all the intense cognitive thinking, thinking, thinking has all but annihilated the real self. As one emerges out of such suppression of the true self, this shaking goes on.

The person doing the shaking can control it. But to control it amiss is to stop the shaking off of the false and in many cases to prevent the surfacing of the split-off feelings that the one suffering abandonment depression needs to bring to consciousness. The simple truth is that the body works with us!

Earlier on, I wrote of "throwing up the internalized bad mother," and I used an extreme example. But there are more subtle ways in which an infant can be overpowered by a mother, and these are just as serious. Persons affected in this way also at times shake violently as they receive prayer and the true self is coming forward.

One young man, a classic example of the above, received quite a healing as he forgave his mother and "threw up" his internalized version of her. This mother had learned to cope with existence by means of a neurotic perfectionism and a super control of persons and events within her sphere. The pictures we received as we were praying with him reflected this control and revealed that it had affected him from the moment of birth. We "saw" the strongest controlling "tendrils," dreadfully ugly root systems, running throughout his body, and these were stubbornly rooted deep into his male organs. There had been erotic overtones in his mother's behavior toward him, though probably unconscious on her part. These—combined with her general responses to him—had resulted not only in an intense emotional revulsion toward her, but in a thorough repression of his sexuality and masculine gender identity. Through prayer, we called up and out of him this internalized emotional junk, seeing with our hearts these stubborn and deep-rooted tendrils lose their hold. We prayed until the last root came up and out and was yielded up to Christ, and then we prayed into those darkened spaces God's healing light, freedom, and love. This was a major healing, and after this he was able to deal with his fear of his mother and with many other needs in his life.

In this healing, there was not the shaking and jerking movements as mentioned above, but a year or so later—as he was in prayer with a Christian brother, the following healing word from the Lord came. It illustrates not only the more subtle ways an infant is overpowered and his own being repressed, but also again the incredible accuracy of the pictures and words that come from God as He moves to heal and call forth the real self.

As J— was praying for me, and for the strengthening of the true masculine within me, he received this word, and it spoke directly to my abandonment depression and the suppression of myself as a man.

It is as though your head was surrounded by a pillow that would suffocate you. Jesus removes that pillow. It is as though you inhaled your mother's exhalation, the stale air of her own lungs. Jesus is giving you the crisp fresh air of His Presence . . . and a new chest . . . the chest of a man.

I see the cross of Christ, and it extends from the top of your head deep down into your body, and its cross beam fills your chest horizontally. This is your true identity. Over the cross is a purple robe of manly dignity, the mantle of the true masculine, humble yet strong.

As this healing word was ministered, the violent shaking started, and this young man's true self together with his true masculinity made giant strides forward.

This ministry paved the way for the Lord to speak into the next need that was to be addressed. He was yet seriously alienated from woman and had a deep-set sense of gender inferiority that had affected his whole life. This led him to overreact, sometimes with intense fear, to women he perceived as in any way controlling, and irrationally to any who expressed the least hint of a romantic interest in him. A day or two after receiving the word that had so deeply spoken into his entire being and need and left him shaking violently, he was in prayer and in a day vision the Lord moved to correct this inability to relate to woman aright:

I was standing before the throne of God, and He made me keenly aware that His hands had shaped me and formed me. As I was accepting myself as His good creation, He brought woman to me and asked me if I would receive her as a worthy companion, in much the same way He had brought Eve to Adam. This was not an automatically easy response, since my fear of woman had been so great. In the Lord's presence, though, I knew that He was doing a great healing. So of course I accepted His gift to me. We stood hand in hand together before the throne when I became aware of another man standing next to me. As I looked to the Lord, the woman turned from me and took the hand of the man standing next to me and went off with him. I cried out to the Lord that it hurt me to lose again. Since my mother had emotionally abandoned me, this picture in my heart clearly named my worst fear in relation to trusting woman—that I would love and then lose. The Lord then said to me, "Am I not sufficient security for you? Wait upon me, and I will bring you the friendships and the life-long companion you need in my own time. Do not fear to face the loss of love, for I will never leave you or forsake you."

Once God starts to heal the soul, He does not stop until the full work is done—and this is the fruit of remaining in His Presence. As a last bit of understanding we have to share on this matter of bodily movements and how they are related to the true self coming forward, Jason (see pages 126-27) would shake when receiving touch. Although he of course had often been touched, it was only as he was being healed that he was enabled to *receive* the touch. The touch, now divorced from separation anxiety with its erotic sensory responses, went deeply into him, connecting him in a most wonderful and healthy way with his peers and others.

Discernment in Bodily Manifestations

Discernment is truly crucial in all these cases. Sometimes in our meetings before we can get to a person manifesting in a certain way, someone nearby starts "ministering" to him or her in the belief that the activity is the work of demons. We have to quickly speak to this error. There are of course physical reactions to the expulsion of demons, but with the Holy Spirit's gift of discerning of spirits, these are easily differentiated from the body's reactions to emotional healings and from the ways the body wonderfully works together with the whole of man in receiving God's healing.

Bodily Movements in Misogyny Healings

Those who attend PCM schools see what we've come to term misogyny healings. The related bodily movements as well as the words coming up out of the woman can be frightening to anyone who does not understand what is going on. In these healings, the effects of misogyny (stress, self-hatred, rage toward men as well as women, etc.), often coming down through the generations, are as it were coming up and out of the woman. Often the body reacts violently as the woman spits out, screams out, breathes and prays out the long tendrils of that awful "presence" that is not demonic, but is in effect the expulsion of the hatred toward woman that has taken on almost a presence or identity within her. There are often words such as "I hate you," said with such venom, and these are words stored up in the woman's being, words she has long experienced directed toward herself as woman, and these words are internalized, even as the internalized bad mother or bad father. They are even the words she constantly directs toward herself, hating herself because she has been hated.

Sometimes weeks or months *after* these strong, valid bodily reactions—which must be allowed if the woman is to yield to the healing going on in her entire being—she may experience an awful shaking and think she is going back into a misogyny healing. But that is not what this shaking is all about. It indicates a *weak center,* that is, a very weak sense of identity and of being. Such a one needs to be strengthened in her true identity in order to utterly throw off the misogynous attitudes of a lifetime and in order to know that she is stronger than the emotions that threaten to overwhelm her. Shaking related to a weak center is to be stopped, and the true self is to be ministered to in order that there may be the glorious coming forward of the true woman.

It's a glorious thing to see the true self come forward and fill the human vessel and how wonderfully, as C. S. Lewis says, the body also prays. It is a wondrous creation, and itself receives healing as it works with us to the healing of our souls.

This entire chapter, meant only as an introduction to these subjects, is written to encourage those who pray for others and to help them recognize abandonment issues. I hope as well that it will help many to appreciate the ways God would have those who pray work together with those who are medically and professionally trained. The possibilities here are endless, the rewards so very great.

All the healing here is predicated on the cross of Christ. In fact, such healings are not seen apart from God's intervention, which is available to us because of Christ's Passion. As Dr. Frank Lake so wonderfully puts it:

> There is nothing in the hystero-schizoid makeup of the androcentric man or woman which limits the action of God upon the soul. Rather, since infinite attachment and infinite detachment are already present in such souls, they have, even on the human level, a premonition of the dimensions of the abyss over which Christ was stretched upon the Cross.[17]

CHAPTER 9

Third Great Barrier to Wholeness in Christ: Failure to Receive Forgiveness

But because of his great love for us, God, who is rich in mercy, made us alive with Christ even when we were dead in transgressions—it is by grace you have been saved.

(Ephesians 2:4-5)

*I*f by God's grace we have been forgiven, why is it sometimes hard to *receive* that forgiveness? How do we *administer* forgiveness to others?

It is often harder for us to *receive* forgiveness from God than to forgive even our worst enemies. Have you ever confessed the same sin twice, three times? We can go to God directly, but we do not always obtain the forgiveness Christ died for and freely gives. We can know so well that "if we confess our sins, He is faithful and just and will forgive us our sins and purify us from all unrighteousness" (1 John 1:9)—*but fail to receive it when He hands it to us.*

How do we know when failure to receive forgiveness is the real block? In this failure, a good many things can be involved. The following root causes I find the most common.

Remaining Under Law

"Christ is the end [fulfillment] of the law so that there may be righteousness for everyone who believes" (Romans 10:4). The man "under the law" will always feel guilty. He does not receive forgiveness because he is still trying to be "good enough" on his own merit; he strives to be perfect on his own.

The law, as someone has said, is a fence to make us be good. In Christ, the fence has been removed. The walk in the Spirit replaces the fence. In listening-obedience to Christ and His Word, we are trusting always in His righteousness and doing what we hear Him say. In this way, we do indeed fulfill (not just the letter but) the spirit of the law.

The following is perhaps a helpful way to picture the difference. Under the law a priest wore a breastplate on his robe, and this was anointed. I heard one Jewish rabbi say that when the robe was off, the anointing was off. Since Christ came, we who are His wear the breastplate of righteousness—we have "put on Christ." It is a practice of the Presence.

As ministers, we help others to recognize and put off the "old man" (see *The Healing Presence*, pages 94-95). We watch with them as they confess their sins and put to death all the diseased forms of love: fornication (actual or in the imagination), uncleanness (homosexuality and all other forms of sexual perversion), inordinate affection which is a neurotic dependence or love, evil concupiscence (depraved desire, lust, etc.), covetousness, and all idolatry (all bentness toward the creature). We watch with them as they "put off" anger, wrath, malice, filthy communication, and lying. Then, after proclaiming God's forgiveness for all they have duly confessed, we help them "put on Christ," the New Man. We teach them to practice His Presence, their righteousness, and they are thereby freed from their striving to get "good enough" and from the wrong kind of fear of God. Then, and this is ever so important to get straight in their minds, we assure them on the best Scriptural grounds that they no longer have to practice the presence of the "old man"! "So then, my brothers, there is no necessity for us to obey our unspiritual selves or to live unspiritual lives" (Romans 8:12, *Jerusalem Bible*).

In ministry to others, we need to quickly discern in whose righteousness the sufferer is trusting—his own or the Lord's. Jesus prayed that we might be able in a future Day to stand before the Son of Man (Luke 21:36) and taught us that we do not stand before Him in any righteousness we have earned. We stand in His righteousness, a fact that keeps us always practicing His Presence. Satan, as the accuser, constantly attempts to make us look to our own righteousness. But we have "by the blood of the Lamb" and "the word of [our] testimony" (Revelation 12:11) overcome the accuser of our souls.

Martin Luther is as good an example as we can find here. Until he understood Incarnational Reality, God's righteousness within, he could not receive forgiveness, and he certainly could not accept himself. In the terms of today, he very much needed inner healing. Our counseling rooms are full of people who have this problem. They may not be crawling bare-kneed on sharp stones, wearing hair shirts, or flagellating themselves with whips, but they are doing the psychological equivalent.

Later after his healing, Luther said of the Christian that "he stands at one and the same time a sinner and a justified man." Before Luther understood this, he had been afraid of God. The "righteousness of God" that Paul spoke of in Romans terrified him. He thought of it as the justice of God that judges sinners—as Luther knew himself and all people to be.

Some of the hardest folk to see healed and gotten through to a godly self-acceptance are those who compulsively strive to be perfect. They in effect are denying the necessity of an incarnation of grace, of God's righteousness, and are trying to gain it on their own by their good works and their attention to the letter of the law. Hence, their perspective is askew. Rather than fixing their eyes on God and glorying in the ability He gives us to walk (dance!) before Him in freedom, their eyes are fixed on the "law," wanting to satisfy its demands, something Christ has already done.

Luther was in this terrible place until he came to understand that "the righteousness of God" that Paul spoke of, rather than being a wrathful, legalistic thing, was indeed something we "put on" by faith, that, even more importantly, it is something *in us*—God's life within. When he finally understood this, he cried out: "Faith has the incomparable grace of uniting the soul to Christ as bride to husband, so that the soul possesses whatever Christ Himself possesses." He was thenceforth freed from incredible fear—the fear of always trying to win God's love, of never being quite able to keep the law.

Apart from the need to rightly understand God's grace, there is common to fallen people a terrible passion to be perfect on their own. We need to recognize this for the pride that it is and help men and women confess and come free from it. People prize their autonomy and think of it as freedom. Men, as a rule, have more difficulty than do women at this point. The feminine capacity to worship God and thereby submit and respond fully to Him is an ability a woman often needs to help her brothers in Christ get in touch with.

In addition, there are many "compulsive perfectionists," as they are labeled today. These persons often are the victims of an early training in which love and affirmation was withheld from them apart from good performance. Since a person's performance, no matter how gifted he is, can rarely be perfect, these persons have suffered a deep injury to their souls and have been trained in "the passion to be perfect." Along with helping them "put off the old man," we have to help them replace the law of their parents, a law that still (as a broken record) plays on and on in their minds.

The Need to Acknowledge the "Bad Guy" Within

If Luther could see only his own unrighteousness, the "bad guy" within, before his healing, there are others who deny him altogether. Some people have even been taught this denial, either through inference or bad theology. They genuinely do not understand that Christians, once regenerated (born again of the Spirit) and converted (their wills made one with Christ's), yet need to set apart certain times when they once again kneel as sinners before God and ask Him to show them their sins, conscious and unconscious, that they might confess and be forgiven. Difficult as it may be for many Christian counselors to believe, especially those from the more sacramental traditions, numberless Christians have never been taught to do this on a regular basis.

These Christians, then, denying that the bad guy is there and that they have in fact "practiced his presence," whether consciously or unconsciously, can go through life feeling guiltier and guiltier. They can get on their knees and feel their lives a dreadful mess, but have little insight into what is wrong. They have denied rather than confessed the existence of the "old man," the sinner. So they go about unforgiven. Others, in this same situation, rather than feeling guilty, become prideful and cause other Christians a lot of misery. The Pharisee in them becomes quite strong. Practicing the presence of the old man, they become legalistic and judgmental of others while never seeing their own darkness.

The most dangerous Christians we can ever meet are those who do not know about the bad guy within. More frightening still are the Christians who have a superspiritual religious spirit, deluding them into thinking themselves better Christians than everyone else. I have seen a few of these in my time, and it is wonderful to see them healed. They are not the ones who ordinarily seek help, but cause everybody else who gets involved with them to run for help. There are, of course, different degrees of this problem, but religious tyrants, great and small, come out of this stance. They will always be found slandering other Christians, especially Christian leaders. While accusing others of being demonized, they will often themselves be demonized and will have to be dealt with as such in order to find freedom.

The bad guy in each one of us puts self rather than Christ at the center. The Christian is fully capable of doing this. When he does, he is not living from the center where Christ dwells, but from another center, that of the old man or the bad guy within. As Christians, we can wake up any day of the week and descend into that center. Hence, we will be found practicing the presence of the bad guy. This is why C. S. Lewis can say that if being Christian does not make a man a lot better, it can make him a lot worse.

> For the Supernatural, entering a human soul, opens to it new possibilities both of good and evil. From that point the road branches: one way to sanctity, humility, the other to spiritual pride, self-righteousness, persecuting zeal. And no way back to the mere humdrum virtues of the unawakened soul. If the Divine call does not make us better, it will make us very much worse. Of all bad men, religious bad men are the worst.[1]

That the line between good and evil lies in every human heart was a discovery Alexander Solzhenitsyn made while lying on rotting straw in a Communist prison camp, still a Communist himself, awaiting an operation for cancer. Shortly after this, Solzhenitsyn found Christ.

> Gradually it was disclosed to me that the line separating good and evil passes not through states, nor between classes, not between political parties either— but right through every human heart—and through all human hearts. This line shifts. Inside us, it oscillates with the years. And even within hearts over-

whelmed with evil, one small bridgehead of good is retained. And even in the best of all hearts there remains . . . an unuprooted small corner of evil.[2]

Is it any wonder that the key to healing is repentance and forgiveness?

We must know and acknowledge our two identities—that of sinner and saint. Our prime identity, of course, is that of saint. We are children of God, children of the resurrection. But the rhythm of repentance and reception of forgiveness must be woven into every life. We are always to rise up from confession in our prime identity, having received forgiveness.

When I minister to people whose difficulties are in this area, I lead them in a prayer of confession of specific sin and then help them to receive God's forgiveness. After this initial ministry, I recommend to them ways of setting into their devotional and spiritual practices a regular time for allowing God to search their hearts, a regular time, in other words, to kneel as sinners before Him.

> Who can discern his lapses and errors?
> Clear me from hidden [and unconscious] faults.
> Keep back Your servant also from presumptuous sins;
> let them not have dominion over me!
>
> (Psalm 19:12-13a, *The Amplified Bible*)

> Search me, O God, and know my heart;
> Test me and know my anxious thoughts.
> See if there is any offensive way in me,
> and lead me in the way everlasting.
>
> (Psalm 139: 23-24)

I instruct people always, after confession of sin, whether at home, at church, or wherever, to *receive that forgiveness*. This is an act of faith, a conscious and deliberate reception of God's grace. For many people, the best ongoing way to incorporate this into their lives is in connection with Holy Communion. Before going, they can kneel as sinners before God and listen to Him as He shows them their hearts. They can then take this confession to the Eucharist. There they kneel, having confessed their sins, and as they receive, they take their place once again in Christ's death, dying to their sins and to the world. As they receive the Body and the Blood, they receive forgiveness. They have knelt as sinners. They rise as saints. And they rise prepared to live from that center where God's righteousness abides.

Many ministers of the gospel are today "burned out" because they do not recognize their need for the confessional, their need to receive absolution and laying-on-of-hands by others who love and serve the Lord, their need for regularly acknowledging that there is a bad guy in them.

It is when I have just completed the most successful missions and seen God do the most remarkable things for His people that I need to take several days (rather than hours) to simply wait on God, asking Him to search my heart and soul. We must leave all ministry to others while we are doing this, for we cannot minister to others while in a posture of repentance. This does not mean we cease living from our true center, knowing who we are in Him. It simply means that we acknowledge that we do carry about with us the "old man," the capacity to be the bad guy; we have in very truth sinned and come short of the mark.

Praying, but Not to God

"Prayer was made without ceasing of the church unto God for him" (Acts 12:5, KJV). As R. A. Torrey points out, "The first thing to notice in this verse is the brief expression *unto God*. The prayer that has power is the prayer that is offered unto God."[3] C. S. Lewis expresses it this way: "May it be the real 'I' who speaks, the real 'Thou' I speak to."[4]

Quickly we see that this category of difficulty is related to the disease of introspection (See *The Healing Presence*, chapter 12). In this introspective age, we easily substitute our subjective feelings about ourselves for the objective gift of God's forgiveness. If we are on our knees, hating ourselves, we are not likely to look up and receive forgiveness. We have sunk into an inculcated, emotional state of feeling toward the self, an emotional view we've had so long we hardly notice it. And this is not prayer. It is a common and a serious barrier to receiving the forgiving grace of God.

Lack of Awareness of the Need for Forgiveness

Just as we can be so out of touch with our hearts and feelings that we do not realize the need to forgive another, so it is in the matter of receiving forgiveness. We can be so "heady" that we rise from our knees after confession of a sin we are quite conscious of having committed and fail to notice that we still feel guilty. We do not know the joy of forgiveness, nor do we move from a position of authority and wholeness. We are simply too out of touch with our hearts and feelings to notice. In lieu of having received forgiveness, we become more and more restlessly "active" until the time comes we can no longer control and repress the feeling being.

Inability to Name the Sin

In this category, a person will have a conscious sense of guilt, but it stems from sin at unconscious levels of the heart. It is closely related to what we've already considered—the fact that Christians are both sinners and saints and that there will be those hidden and unconscious faults that they are to ask God to search out on a regular basis. It may or may not also be related in a given person to the fact that "sin consists, not only in the positive transgression of the law of God, but in the want of conformity to His Will."[5] The old Anglican prayer is at once so comforting and so needful: "We have done the things that we ought not, we have left undone those things that we ought to have done." This two-pronged fork is, as Dr. Meyer has said, needful. But most often what we are dealing with here is related to the depth of sin in the human heart and is therefore apropos to all that is considered in this book.

The Christian theologian and historian Richard Lovelace chronicles not only our loss of the understanding of sin, but of its depth within the human heart:

> During the late nineteenth century, while the church's understanding of the unconscious motivation behind surface actions was vanishing, Sigmund Freud rediscovered this factor and recast it in an elaborate and profound secular mythology. One of the consequences of this remarkable shift is that in the twentieth century, pastors have often been reduced to the status of legalistic moralists, while the deeper aspects of the cure of souls are generally relegated to psychotherapy, even among Evangelical Christians.
>
> [T]he structure of sin in the human personality is something far more complicated than the isolated acts and thoughts of deliberate disobedience commonly designated by the word. In its biblical definition, sin cannot be limited to isolated instances or patterns of wrongdoing; it is something much more akin to the psychological term complex: an organic network of compulsive attitudes, beliefs, and behavior deeply rooted in our alienation from God. Sin originated in the darkening of the human mind and heart as man turned from the truth about God to embrace a lie about him and consequently a whole universe of lies about his creation. Sinful thoughts, words, and deeds flow forth from this darkened heart automatically and compulsively, as water from a polluted fountain. "The Lord saw that the wickedness of man was great in the earth, and that every imagination of the thoughts of his heart was only evil continually" (Genesis 6:5). This is echoed in Jesus' words: "Either make the tree good, and its fruit good; or make the tree bad, and its fruit bad; for the tree is known by its fruit. You brood of vipers! how can you speak good, when you are evil? For out of the abundance of the heart the mouth speaks. The good man out of his good treasure brings forth good, and the evil man out of his evil treasure brings forth evil" (Matthew 12:33-35).

The human heart is now a reservoir of unconscious disordered motivation and response, of which unrenewed persons are unaware if left to themselves, for "the heart is deceitful above all things, and desperately corrupt; who can understand it?" (Jeremiah 17:9). It is as if they were without mirrors and suffering from tunnel vision: they can see neither themselves clearly nor the great peripheral area around their immediate experience (God and supernatural reality). At the two most crucial loci of their understanding, their awareness of God and of themselves, they are almost in total darkness, although they may attempt to remedy this by framing false images of themselves and God. Paul describes this darkness of the unregenerate mind: "Now this I affirm and testify in the Lord, that you must no longer live as the Gentiles do, in the futility of their minds; they are darkened in their understanding, alienated from the life of God because of the ignorance that is in them, due to their hardness of heart" (Ephesians 4:17-18). The mechanism by which this unconscious reservoir of darkness is formed is identified in Romans 1:18-23 as repression of traumatic material, chiefly the truth about God and our condition, which the unregenerate constantly and dynamically "hold down." Their darkness is always a voluntary darkness, though they are unaware that they are repressing the truth.[6]

When Christians suffer with an ongoing sense of guilt, they need first of all to ascertain whether it is false or real. In prayer for healing of memories, we can often get to the roots of these matters quickly, and then, as ministers, we help those who are suffering discern the false guilt from the real. The real is taken care of through confessing sin and receiving forgiveness. False guilt is taken care of when we help the sufferer to distinguish between violation of an authentic standard as opposed to an irrational or an inauthentic one.

The person who has internalized the "law" of controlling and/or legalistic or perfectionistic parents, authority figures, or communities often needs help to be released from false guilt. The person whose mother died in giving him birth, or the twin who survived at birth when his brother or sister did not, are examples of those who sometimes suffer a deep, unconscious sense of false guilt.

The following story exemplifies how easy it is for us in childhood to misconstrue what we hear and so to pick up false guilt. A woman came up to me after I had been speaking on this topic and blurted out with some desperation that she always felt guilty and had never known why. "I soak up guilt," she cried. Others could do something amiss and she, not they, would feel guilty. I had hardly started to pray, inviting the Lord into any root memory that would shed light on all this, when the knowledge of where it all began came to the fore. On the night she was born, her father had rushed her mother to the hospital, and in all the excitement, he had forgotten to turn off the stove. The house burned down. All her life she had heard, "Oh, the night you were born, the house burned down!" And her heart interpreted this to mean, "It's *your* fault the house burned down." She dissolved in laughter at this knowledge, wondering that she had never seen it before. We then prayed about the false guilt patterns that had formed in her, and she understood that as soon as she was aware of guilt feelings, she was always to place them before the Lord. She was to give them to Him and receive, through listening prayer, the true and right pattern of thinking and feeling in exchange.

There are those who go about for most of their lives with a vague, gray cloud of guilt over their heads. This is not necessary. Real sin is programmed into the memories, and we can usually get to it rather quickly as we learn to pray, asking the Lord to show us any specific sin or complex of sin that we might confess it to Him and receive His pardon. In cases where nothing is revealed, we can confess the "unknown" sin that is behind the sense of guilt. If the guilt is real, it will lift. Usually, it is not long before insight comes and we get in touch with the memory or with the pattern of sinful behavior for which we are feeling guilty.

Failure to Settle the Sin Question

Sometimes we simply have not settled the sin question. While confessing our sin, we may feel, "Oh well, I'll just do it again." In this case we not only fail to receive forgiveness, but we do not like ourselves very well. It is a healthy thing, then, that we experience real guilt, that we get depressed over our sin. It is this despair over what we are and what we have made of our lives that brings us to the end of ourselves and causes us to throw ourselves upon the mercy of God, the "righteousness of God."

There are many, many "unforgiven" folk about who fit into this very category, and one reason is that the organized church itself is full of compromise. Such a church does no better with its prophets than Ahab and Jezebel did; it simply cannot tolerate the true prophet who majors on the grace of God and, therefore, at the same time can preach an uncompromising gospel. Prophets such as these can call the people of God to a radical obedience (radical for the day in which we live) because they know the grace available to those who will walk in the Spirit.

Chapter 14 of *The Healing Presence,* which deals with the renunciation of sexual sin, illustrates the incredible way God's healing power is released when people renounce their idols and take a sure stand against sin. These people gain as well the power to overcome temptation when they truly settle the sin question.

From time to time, I encounter persons who have conscious sin at the top of their conscience, and they have no intention of turning from it. Even so, they will come for prayer, hoping to be healed. I remember one such man about to be hospitalized for emotional problems, who on arriving told me he did not know what lay behind his depression. Realizing that he was too near the breaking point to communicate on the conscious level, I simply laid hands on him and asked the Lord to go to the root problem, the memory where the problem lay. Not one thing emerged. I was led to ask quietly, "What unconfessed sin lies at the top of your conscious mind?" He then told me he was sexually involved with another man's wife. I asked him if he was willing to repent of his adultery and turn from it, and he said no. I then told him it would do no good to pray for him, that he was probably depressed over that and other sin in his life that he had failed to "put to death." I asked him to leave and make a decision about this matter and then return for prayer only if he decided to repent. I have seen him and others, just hours away from hospitalization, healed as soon as they decided to repent. To pray for such people apart from repentance is to waste precious spiritual energy and power. It merely singes them with the flames of God rather than allowing His holy fire to burn away all their impurities. Their hearts are left even more hardened than before.

There are many whose consciences are so seared they no longer feel guilt. They too can receive forgiveness as they *will* to confess their sins, knowing that besides the fact that their consciences have been seared, their feeling being is also out of order. God can restore consciences and the capacity to feel compunction as they confess and deliberately turn from sin.

Conclusion of the Failure to Receive Forgiveness

These "categories" overlap and intermingle, of course, and often we find ourselves ministering to someone whose difficulties fall into several of them at once. We ascertain when failure to receive forgiveness is the block; we provide the needed illumination; we minister the forgiveness with laying-on-of-hands.

In ministering God's forgiveness, as in all prayer with others, we need to be very careful about the person's physical comfort. If we (or an entire group) lay heavy hands on such a one, he may forget his need for forgiveness and be able to think only about how to get his next breath. I nearly always lift the penitent's face up to God, making sure he can get great draughts of fresh air into his lungs. Often, I even ask him to breathe in deeply several times. In this way, he relaxes his body, often breathing out tension and releasing his muscles, and he is thereby all the more ready to receive. Too, I make sure there is room for the person to lift his arms to God when the moment comes for him to receive the forgiveness. The whole person, after all, is interacting with what God is doing. I personally have to remove my large ring since occasionally I have a bit of a heavy touch. The impress of the ring on a person's forehead could distract him during the prayer and inhibit him from receiving the forgiveness.

It used to be that when praying with a woman, I was especially sensitive to her coiffure. Now, having learned more along the way, I am careful with *both* men and women. Often, just before speaking to a group, my prayer team will pray for me. They know not to lay a dozen hands on my head. If I'm worried about how I'm going to look with hair all askew, I won't be able to receive the fullest benefit of their prayers. The same seems to go for most of us.

If there is a crucifix available, I ask the person to look up to it before closing his eyes in prayer. This helps many, for quite a few moderns have imaginations utterly bereft of Christian images and symbols. The person also may be thinking about and perhaps even trying not to picture the thing for which he has heretofore been unable to receive forgiveness. In this way he lifts his eyes from the problem to that which symbolizes God's forgiveness.[7] In a recent PCM, many seasoned church leaders were quite amazed to see how God uses the crucifix not only in deliverance but in healing prayer. The healing ministry can never be understood apart from the cross, apart from the Atonement. Out of the Atonement flows our full salvation: justification, sanctification, the indwelling Holy Spirit, authority in spiritual conflict.[8] The crucifix, rightly used, symbolizes all that is in the Atonement.

The person who has failed to receive forgiveness has most likely confessed the same sin over and over. Even so, I ask such a one to confess the sin once again, this time while "seeing" Jesus, dying on the cross to take that sin upon and into Himself. After the person has confessed it, then I proclaim forgiveness in a way that the penitent can receive it.

In ministering forgiveness, I anoint with oil, making the sign of the cross on the forehead. Then I lay one hand on the forehead and the other at the back of the head. Then, with their confession, I proclaim forgiveness, saying: "Receive God's forgiveness, receive it into the very depths of your being." And it is as if the forgiveness they have never been able to receive before comes right through my hand and into their forehead, and from there, it flows down into the depths of their being: spirit, soul, and body.

At times I have realized that the human spirit is somehow timid and shy, that it is having a hard time opening up to receive the forgiveness. In this case, I then pray very gently that the spirit of this person can open as a lovely bud or flower to receive the forgiveness Christ is sending. And it does.

CHAPTER 10

Conclusion to Healing of Memories

*E*very time we forgive another, or confess a sin and receive forgiveness, we experience a healing of memories and a cleansing of our hearts and consciences. But there are times when our own "self-searching and prayers" or our "grievous reactions to the sins of others" leave us powerless on our own. It is then we need to pay close attention to words such as we find in "An exhortation for one preparing for Holy Communion" from the *Book of Common Prayer.*

> If there be any of you who by this means [the means of self-examination, repentance, reparation] cannot quiet his own conscience herein, but requireth further comfort or counsel, let him come to me, or to some other Minister of God's Word, and open his grief. . . .

"Surely he took our infirmities and carried our sorrows" (Isaiah 53:4), but sometimes we need the help of one another in order to be enabled to yield up that grief or sorrow. Christ, speaking of Himself said: "But so that you may know that the Son of Man has authority on earth to forgive sins" (Matthew 9:6), and this enraged the religious leaders of the day. But the fact is, He has given us this same power. When we know ourselves as what we truly are, sacramental channels of His healing, His forgiving word, and His Presence, this ministry flows through us.

"I tell you the truth, whatever you bind on earth will be bound in heaven, and whatever you loose on earth will be loosed in heaven" (Matthew 18:18). In the Scriptures, the matter of binding and loosing has to do with loosing people from their sins and from the effects of the sins of others against them. Unfortunately, there is a misunderstanding abroad in sections of the church, especially in the renewal movement, regarding binding and loosing. These Scriptural passages have been taught erroneously as having to do with binding Satan and demons, elemental spirits, principalities and powers, and so on. We do not "bind" and "loose" demons, principalities and powers, etc. In Christ's name we command them to leave, knowing that Christ's death and resurrection have already bound them and that they have no power over us. As long, however, as sin is unremitted in a life, the demons and other dark forces have power in that life. It is the sins and the effects of those sins in the lives that we, the ministers and servants of Christ, are to "bind and loose," that is, lift from the souls of those who truly turn to Christ, repentant and ready to forgive those who have sinned against them.

In the ministry of binding and loosing from sin, we may (even as Christ did) incur the wrath of Christians who misunderstand the priestly role of all Christians as the priesthood of believers. We are to hear confessions of sin and proclaim forgiveness and release to those confessing them (either their own sins or those of others against them). Hostility to the idea of the believers' priestly role is the root of a great deal of the criticism leveled against prayer for the healing of emotional problems, and hence some of the terrible assaults on prayer for emotional and psychological healing. This kind of theological blindness and ignorance catches us up into spiritual warfare, for the accuser of our souls opposes in every way the true ministry of the confessional.

The truth is, Jesus has commissioned us to do His works:

Again Jesus said, "Peace be with you! As the Father has sent me, I am sending you." And with that he breathed on them and said, "Receive the Holy Spirit. If you forgive anyone his sins, they are forgiven; if you do not forgive them, they are not forgiven." (John 20:21-23)

I never get over my awe at the power of the ministry of healing of memories, that is, of the forgiveness of sin. It is the power of the cross, of the love of the Son of God who made Himself utterly vulnerable, even to the point of crucifixion, to free us from sin.

This ministry of prayer for the healing of the soul is not merely related to the sacrament or ordinance of baptism; it is a vital part of the work of baptism.[1] In baptism we are "buried with Him" and are "raised to life with Him," and this is the crucial imagery in the releasing of the soul from sin and in the calling forth of the true self:

We were therefore buried with him through baptism into death in order that, just as Christ was raised from the dead through the glory of the Father, we too may live a new life. If we have been united with him like this in his death, we will certainly also be united with him in his resurrection. For we know that our old self was crucified with him so that the body of sin might be done away with, that we should no longer be slaves to sin—because anyone who has died has been freed from sin. (Romans 6:4-7)

Victory over sin in our lives—which is what the healing of memories is all about—is the extension of the work of baptism. It is essential that we who minister in prayer for the healing of the soul not only realize this, but continue to image this healing aright. In that way, the healing of the soul will never be separated from the central doctrine of the forgiveness of sin. The imagery of Christ's death and resurrection and of Christian baptism is absolutely vital to the retaining of a Christian symbolic system,[2] and it is vital in the comprehension of all Christian prayer and healing.

The Interview Preceding Prayer for Healing of Memories

INVOCATION OF THE PRESENCE OF CHRIST
At the very first, before starting the interview with the person desiring healing, we pray, "Come, Lord Jesus, come," asking the Lord to bring up from the person's heart and memories that which needs to come up. We petition God for ears to hear what the person is *really* saying.

GIFTS OF THE HOLY SPIRIT
Effective listening and "listening prayer" are related to the gifts of the Holy Spirit[3] and are key in the ministry of healing. To learn to listen to God and collaborate with Him in healing prayer is to experience the gifts of the Holy Spirit in action. These gifts of wisdom, knowledge, discernment, and so on are not guesswork, but are the fruit of getting the mind of God on the matter.

We who train others in the work of healing prayer are alert for the misguided person who, rather than getting the mind of God on another's need, is still so involved in what God has done in his own life that he wrongly sees his own needs and problems in the lives of others. The counterpart of this we see also in the professional world where therapists fit others into their own favorite theories or methods, and their clients' main difficulties remain unperceived. Every soul is so unique, and even in the cases where needs are similar, the Lord often moves in very diverse ways to heal different persons with like problems.

Here as always, our model is the Lord Himself. The prophet Isaiah spoke beforehand of the power that would rest upon Christ and of the way He would move in it:

> The Spirit of the Lord will rest on him—
> the Spirit of wisdom and of understanding,
> the Spirit of counsel and of power,
> the Spirit of knowledge and of the fear of the Lord—
> and he will delight in the fear of the Lord.
> *He will not judge by what he sees with his eyes,*
> *or decide by what he hears with his ears;*
> but with righteousness he will judge the needy,
> with justice he will give decisions for the poor of the earth.

(11:2-4a, italics mine)

With Christ as our supreme example, we learn to stop speaking our own unaided wisdom and instead seek and find the mind of God.

THE ROOT OR MAIN CAUSE

Although there are nearly always multiple factors and "causes" to deal with (failing to understand this can be a problem), in the interview we often get to the root cause of the difficulty right away. But when we don't, there is no need to pray through the person's entire chronology. Agnes Sanford's method here can hardly be improved upon. She asked the simple question, "Were you happy as a child?" If so, she knew the difficulty did not lie there. The next question was, "Then when did you begin to be unhappy?" As the person told where the unhappiness started, then she knew where to start.

THE DISEASE OF INTROSPECTION

We are alert to recognize this prevalent twentieth-century emotional problem and deal with it right away. Otherwise, the person will continue to tear apart and fragment himself and his thoughts through over-analyzation, destroying the healing work even as it is being accomplished.[4]

THE OLD SELF

We learn to avoid helping someone practice the presence of the "old man" through endless dialogue with "it." We learn to speak to the real person, calling him or her forward, and to teach that one how to shake off the old man or the false self. The old self can talk endlessly and is often today allowed to do so, even though all concerned know that truth is not being spoken. This misplaced empathy and sympathy is not the kind of love that heals.

BENTNESS

We do not allow others to bend toward us, but point them straight up to God. The mark of a great Christian helper or leader is that he is able by the power and assistance of the Holy Spirit to inspire those he helps to be all God called them to be. This means we never draw disciples to ourselves, but help others into full discipleship with Christ. To be a disciple of a disciple is to be a pale Christian, and we help those who have "bent into others" to straighten up into Christ and into their full identity in Him.

THE WILL

We note when special prayer for the will is needed. We remember that sin kills the will.[5]

SIN IS TO BE JUDGED

It is important that we care enough to confront the soul that is hesitant in putting sin to death. We judge not the brother or sister, but the sin that is killing him or her.[6]

THE CRUCIFIX

Many of us need to be reminded that a crucifix is more than a valid symbol for today; it is and always has been a central one. Only as we keep that Christian symbol can we fully retain the equally valid one of *Christus Victor,* the risen Savior. (See chapter 11.)

CHILDHOOD VOWS

We are alert for childhood vows that need be renounced.[7]

TRANSFERENCE AND AMBIVALENCE

We are alert to detect transferences and to name same-sex and other-sex ambivalence as they are revealed either in the interview or in the time of prayer.

For example, if I am praying with a mother who has problems in relating to her son and I know that she experienced rejection by her father, I will ask her, "Could your problems with your son have to do with your unresolved difficulties with your father?" And she will nearly always instantly know if this is a valid insight. In prayer for healing of memories, we get at the root rejections and hurts and the ways that inner negative or idealized feelings and attitudes are irrationally projected onto others.

These come to light as a matter of course because in seeking forgiveness of sin, relationships with others are necessarily coming into the light of the Lord. We do not look for these "projections" or "transferences," but when we discern them, we present them humbly to the person's attention.

TIMING

As in all important matters of the soul, in our zeal to see someone healed we are careful not to move ahead of the Lord or to lag behind. We are quick to acknowledge when we need to bring in wiser, more experienced heads and when special medical and psychological help is called for.

Important Things to Remember in the Prayer

As we go to prayer, once again we invoke the Presence of Christ. We remember that as the memories come to the fore, the key element in the prayer is release from sin and its effects, either the sins of the people for whom we pray or the sins of others against them.

Therefore, we do not forget to function in our capacity as one of the priesthood of believers. It is possible to get so thrilled over the way the Lord moves to heal souls that we fail to fully follow through on the matter of the confession of sin and the full proclamation of God's forgiveness in Christ.

Then, as the Lord uncovers things that need to be confessed:

We direct their eyes to the Lord, and they confess specifically their sins to Him.

We proclaim forgiveness of those sins—so dark and burdensome to the souls confessing them—in the authority of Christ and in such a way as the *heart* can receive it.

We discern false guilt that results from the judgments and suggestions of men, and distinguish that from true guilt that results from consciousness of having betrayed an authentic divine standard.

We bind the sins of others that have so wounded the ones for whom we are praying—leading them to forgive. We then seek to loose them from the effects these sins have had on their lives. This is no small prayer, but is incredibly effective. For example, the man who as a child has seen his father shoot his mother and then kill himself has suffered a trauma that only God can heal. This man will go through life seeing himself as a son of a murderer; he will suffer as a motherless, a fatherless child. In our prayer for him, he is to be "released" into seeing himself as God's child, fathered and mothered by God Himself. He is not to go through life ashamed and hurting, but he is to hold his head and shoulders high, knowing who he is in God. As we pray for the release of his soul and body from the the terrible effects of this sin (after having confessed the sins of murder and suicide and whatever else was amiss), we are to pray in such a way as he will know and receive to the depths of his being the mighty truth that he is not determined by his past, but rather, his wounds are to be turned into healing power for the sake of others.

We discern and send away any oppressing or possessing evil spirits. When necessary, we lead people in a renunciation of idols such as Baal or Mammon.

We pray for God to pour in all the holy love that has been missing and to fill every space where sin, rejection, or a demonic presence has been. The parable of sweeping clean and leaving empty is a meaningful one, far beyond the power of most moderns to comprehend. But the simple truth is, we do not help people rid themselves of darkness and evil apart from helping them to fill up with the light and the life of God. God's glory (fullness of being) is to replace and fill in the space left by the removal of even one fear. "Nature abhors a vacuum," and we scarcely comprehend the vacuum within us left by the removal of sin and darkness. For this reason we are careful not to "deliver" people who are demonized apart from their decision to serve Christ. The demon comes back, even as the Scripture says, bringing others even more evil with it to inhabit the emptied but unfilled space in soul or body.

In the prayer for healing of memories, Jesus journeys into what for us is the past (though for Him all times are one), and He heals the past so that it no longer has the power to shape our present or our future.

As those who counsel and pray with others, we have learned to listen to God and to man. We have discerned the situation and have brought as best we can the light of God to bear on it. In the prayer for healing of memories, we are still with all our beings listening both to God and to the one for whom we pray.

The art of listening is key here. As Christian counselors, the Word of God has been hidden away in our hearts, and, in our obedience, it has taken full root there. That Word is there and active, ready to work with any other word the Holy Spirit may be speaking. God never ceases, in fact, to send the healing word; we need only have the ears to receive it. And it can come as the gift of the word of knowledge, the gift of the word of wisdom, the gift of discerning of spirits, etc. We are carefully, quietly, and gently collaborating with the Spirit of God to see this person released into wholeness.

We know that as emissaries of Christ, His anointing rests on us, that "He hath anointed me . . . hath sent me to heal the brokenhearted . . . to set at liberty them that are bruised" (Luke 4:18, KJV). And Christ does it—through us. As ministers of Christ's healing power, we allow Him to touch others—in a most profound and powerful way—through us.

A disciple is one who has been unchained himself—he then unbinds others. That is what we do when we "carry the cross." We carry God's love and forgiveness into the hearts and minds of others. We are, as Henri Nouwen has said, wounded healers: "Those who proclaim liberation are called to make their wounds into a source of healing power."

It is in forgiving our personal injuries that we learn to pass on to others (the broken, wounded, bound) the forgiveness of Christ. We are channels of Another Life. We listen, we collaborate with God. Ruth Pitter, the English poet, says it this way, in one beautiful line of her poetry, and our hearts resound with it:

"Alleluia all my gashes cry."

PART III

SPIRITUAL WARFARE AND THE GIFT OF BATTLE

The reason the Son of God appeared
was to destroy the devil's work.

(1 John 3:8b)

CHAPTER 11

The Use of Holy Water and
Other Powerful Christian Symbols
and Agencies

*Then the Lord said to Moses, "Make a bronze basin, with its bronze stand,
for washing. Place it between the Tent of Meeting and the altar, and put
water in it."*

(Exodus 30:17-18)

*Then he shall take some holy water in a clay jar and put some dust from
the tabernacle floor into the water.*

(Numbers 5:17)

To purify them, do this: Sprinkle the water of cleansing on them. . . .

(Numbers 8:7a)

*Jesus answered, "I tell you the truth, no one can enter the kingdom of God
unless he is born of water and the Spirit."*

(John 3:5)

*"And now what are you waiting for? Get up, be baptized and wash your
sins away, calling on his name."*

(Acts 22:16)

W e read of many different ceremonial washings in the Scriptures, water baptism being the foremost for Christians. From earliest times, both within Judaism and the Christian church, the faithful in obedience to God have been seen calling down the grace of God, the "sweet unction of the Holy Spirit" upon water, oil, bread, and wine, and upon holy things and places such as crucifixes and "tents of meeting." The following liturgy illustrates the way the church has prayed since its beginning to set apart and hallow water for the purposes of purification of persons and things. This of course makes it important to the healing ministry. These prayers are taken from *A Manual for Priests* (Society of Saint John the Evangelist, Cambridge, MA, 1978) and are the ones my pastor presently uses.

THE BLESSING OF WATER

Salt and pure and clean water, being made ready in the Church or Sacristy, the Priest, vested in surplice and violet stole, shall say:

> *Our help is in the Name of the Lord.*
> *Who hath made heaven and earth.*

And immediately he shall begin the Exorcism of the salt.

I adjure thee, O creature of salt, by the living God, by the true God, by the holy God, by God who commanded thee to be cast by the prophet Elisha into the water to heal the barrenness thereof, that thou become salt exorcised for the health of believers: and do thou bring to all who take of thee soundness of soul and body, and let all vain imaginations, wickedness, and subtlety of the wiles of the devil, and every unclean spirit fly and depart from every place where thou shalt be sprinkled, adjured by the Name of Him, who shall come to judge both the quick and the dead, and the world by fire. Amen.

> *Let us pray.*

Almighty and everlasting God, we humbly beseech thy great and boundless mercy, that it may please thee of thy lovingkindness to bless and to hallow this creature of salt, which thou hast given for the use of men, let it be to all them that take of it health of mind and body, and let whatsoever shall be touched or sprinkled therewith be free from all uncleanness, and from all assaults of spiritual wickedness. Through Christ our Lord. Amen.

Exorcism of the water
I adjure thee, O creature of water, by the Name of God the Father Almighty, by the Name of Jesus Christ his Son our Lord, and by the power of the Holy Ghost, that thou become water exorcised for putting to flight all the power of

the enemy; and do thou avail to cast out and send hence that same enemy with all his apostate angels, by the power of the same our Lord Jesus Christ, who shall come to judge the quick and the dead, and the world by fire. Amen.

Let us pray.

O God, who for the salvation of mankind hast ordained that the substance of water should be used in one of thy chiefest Sacraments: favorably regard us who call upon thee, and pour the power of thy benediction upon this element, made ready by careful cleansing; that this thy creature, meet for thy mysteries, may receive the effect of divine grace, and so cast out devils, and put sickness to flight, that whatsoever in the dwellings of thy faithful people shall be sprinkled with this water, may be free from all uncleanness, and delivered from all manner of hurt; there let no spirit of pestilence abide, nor any corrupting air; thence let all the wiles of the hidden enemy depart, and if there be aught that layeth snares against the safety or peace of them that dwell in the house, let it fly before the sprinkling of this water, so that the health which they seek through calling upon thy holy Name may be protected against all things that threaten it. Through Christ our Lord. Amen.

Then the Priest shall cast the salt into the water in the form of a Cross, saying:

Be this salt and water mingled together: in the Name of the Father, and of the Son, and of the Holy Ghost. Amen.

> *The Lord be with you.*
> *And with thy spirit.*

Let us pray.

O God, who art the Author of unconquered might, the King of the Empire that cannot be overthrown, the ever glorious Conqueror: who dost keep under the strength of the dominion that is against thee; who rulest the raging of the fierce enemy; who dost mightily fight against the wickedness of thy foes; with fear and trembling we entreat thee, O Lord, and we beseech thee graciously to behold this creature of salt and water, mercifully shine upon it, hallow it with the dew of thy lovingkindness: that wheresoever it shall be sprinkled, with the invocation of thy holy Name, all haunting of the unclean spirit may be driven away; far thence let the fear of the venomous serpent be cast; and wheresoever it shall be sprinkled, there let the presence of the Holy Ghost be vouchsafed to all of us who shall ask for thy mercy. Through Christ our Lord. Amen.

These are exceedingly powerful prayers, but ones seldom heard in churches across the land. God waits to answer such prayers, and He does so in incredible ways. It is these prayers in conjunction with the charisms of healing that make holy water, when rightly understood and used, a powerful aid to deliverance and healing.

It was out of sheer desperation that I first made use of blessed water, now nearly thirty years ago. The results were at once amazing, and for me personally so overwhelming, that I made sure I was fully prepared before using it again.

The occasion was the need to protect a group of Christian young people from one of their own members who had, in hatred and rebellion toward a minister father, gotten into Satan worship. This emotionally troubled teen had actually begun praying to Satan while on the mission field where her father was ministering.

The situation was such that I could not face it or the youngster directly. A number of rebellious young men outside that Christian group were in league with her, and there was destruction of property, unexplained gunshots, and real danger for the innocent teens under her influence. Had she been faced with the truth, she would have denied it and would have certainly exploited to the fullest the "accusations" against her.

All this was taking place in a summer camp, and the young people were under the immediate authority of intellectually gifted college students. The adults ultimately in charge of the group were far from understanding such spiritual warfare or accepting the workings of the Holy Spirit and would have rejected the Christian who would deal with these dark matters in the only way they can be dealt with. Also, Satan worship, witchcraft, and so on were at that time simply unthinkable for most Americans, except as one might read of it in Haiti, Africa, or some such place. This young girl realized these things and—intensely angry with all in authority—was keenly (even diabolically) clever in manipulating and dominating the situation. Her campmates, many separated from their parents for the first time, were as vulnerable as only adolescents can be. Most had grown up in Christian homes and environments and had been protected from the grosser forms of evil.

Closely associated with this group, I knew that something very dark and mysterious was going on, but could only intercede, asking for God's mercy. I finally found out what was happening when several young people came to me with severe stomachaches and vomiting. The mystery quickly unfolded as their story tumbled out. Jane had stunned them with an aggressive announcement that she prayed to Satan and that he answered her prayers. She had then coerced them by a series of manipulations into "touching their pinkies (fingers) together," and she told them to "pray to Satan for he answers prayers." When they refused, she ridiculed them and accused them of being silly for taking this "game" too seriously or of lacking courage or of being in league with the hated houseparents and so on.

It was just after they succumbed to these pressures that the vomiting began. After having them checked by the physician who could find no cause for the upset, the houseparents sent them to me for prayer and counsel. To say that these young people were terrified is surely an understatement. They had encountered real evil and were in need of deliverance from demonic oppression. They were intensely fearful not only of what was happening to them, but of what would happen should this girl find out they had "told." Before telling me their story, they had secured my promise that I would not go to the authorities, but instead put the whole situation into God's hands. At this point, I reserved the right to share with my trusted prayer partners, including my pastor. They agreed to this after being assured of the confidentiality, even the "seal of the confessional," under which this prayer group operated.

We then went to prayer, and after much repentance and reception of forgiveness, together with laying-on-of hands for the teens, they were much improved. I, however, was then weighed down with the knowledge of what was going on and the urgent need to protect the young people in this camp. My only consolation in being unable to divulge the full truth to the authorities in charge was the knowledge that they would have bungled the situation and that the houseparents of these teens as well as the teens would have suffered the consequences.

I began to pray and intercede, singly and with my prayer partners. Matters only got worse. More property was destroyed; more truly threatening and obscene things were happening. Jane in the meantime was wrapping the authorities around her little finger as they attempted to counsel her in the usual way. She had a way of effectively slandering others in charge, thereby dividing the adults. As in all situations where the demonic goes unchecked, confusion reigned.

Finally, in desperation, I told my prayer partners that I had to do something, but I did not know what. It was then that the pastor suggested the use of holy water, something that utterly amazed me. I was not at all quick to take up the idea but, as he said, "You've tried everything else you know to do. It can't hurt to do this."

After several days and much prayer, in fear and trembling I accompanied the houseparents, whose duty it was to check daily the camp rooms, into this girl's cubicle. Then I sprinkled the holy water, made the sign of the cross over her bed, and commanded any and all demons to come out of her the moment she returned to her room and laid her head on the pillow. The whole procedure took only a few moments.

That very night, legions of demons came out of this young girl. How do I know? I stayed in the camp overnight, and my room was close to hers. These evil things, in this instance all wearing masks, "visited" me on the way out of that place. It was the worst spiritual battle I ever encountered. If God had not opened my eyes to "see" the demons, they might have succeeded in taking my mind.[1] I simply stood my ground, "pleading the blood of Jesus" through what seemed an interminable length of time, and towards morning they had to leave.

It took me several weeks just to recover physically from the battle. The young girl came to Christ immediately, and the terrible things stopped happening.

I had a great deal to learn about this experience, and I remember asking God a multitude of questions about why I was attacked. Foremost, with the use of holy water as in any prayer for deliverance, I should have commanded the demons in Jesus' name to depart the place hurting no one. Perhaps then there would not have been so severe a battle. But after this, I never again questioned the use of holy water in deliverance prayer.

Since this time, I've recommended that this sort of prayer be carried out when, for example, a parent has a youngster whose will is captured by the evil one—perhaps through alcohol, drugs, the occult, or simply through allowing sin and perversion to take deep root in the life. The young girl in the camp situation got to the dangerous place she was in through a deep and abiding hatred of her father, some of which was fueled by an internalization of her mother's resentment of her husband's ministry. To pray in the way I did for her is to gain the gift of time. I don't know how else to say it. For a time, the essential will is freed and the power to choose a better way is given these persons. They then, on hearing the truth as it comes through a parent or minister, can make a better choice. They are freed to accept Christ fully into their lives as they repent and turn from their sinful ways. This prayer, then—once it is understood and administered in wisdom—can yield the highest results. But I always issue a warning in regard to this prayer. I ask the parent or other praying person to use the prayer only after thorough prayer preparation and guidance and not to use it more than once. The reason is that once the demons leave, if sinful and needy persons choose (will) to refuse Christ admittance to their hearts, then as the Scriptures warn, seven times more demons can come in to fill the void in those lives.

Why, you may be asking, have we never heard, much less read, such prayers as those said over blessed water and salt before? In short, it is because, as I've set out at some length in *The Healing Presence,* even Christians today are at bottom rationalists, materialists. We no longer understand the sacraments, much less the use of the sacramentals such as blessed oil and water, or sacramental actions such as the laying-on-of-hands in which we ourselves are the sacramental vessels.

The principle behind sacramental reality is simple yet profound, but as rationalists, we miss it. It has to do with the Presence of God, the "sweet unction of the Holy Spirit," being channeled to us through material means. God does not despise *matter*; He deigns to come to us through the womb of Mary, through baptismal waters, through the Communion cup, through the hands of our brother or sister in Christ who lays them on us and prays in such a way as we are flooded with light and life from above.[2] This understanding of reality is vital to the whole matter of healing prayer. We do not understand the sacraments and the use of sacramentals for the very same reason we have failed to understand and move forward in healing prayer.

The church that omits prayer for healing of the sick in mind and in body is a church that has either become wholly rational or is in danger of becoming so. This state contrasts with being *reasonable*, for the good of reason is preserved in the church only when the windows of our minds and hearts are fully open to God's immediate Healing Presence and Word. When a church is content to remain merely "rational," it inevitably proceeds toward unbelief and apostasy and ironically is eventually given over to the dark supernatural. Pagan superstitions and even the outright occult infiltrate, for they take root in and arise out of the darkness of unbelief. One way we see the pagan and the occult penetrating parts of the church is through the spirituality of C. G. Jung.[3] As John Richards states in his book *But Deliver Us from Evil: An Introduction to the Demonic in Pastoral Care*:

> Jung accomplished more than any other twentieth-century thinker to make occult theorizing respectable, finding his concepts of the "collective unconscious" and "synchronicity" corresponding in many ways with oriental and occult theories. . . . [4]

There are other influences besides Jung, and these will increase until we regain a fully Christian spirituality and by it overcome our rationalism and unbelief as we move to heal the people of God.

Spiritual Warfare in the Modern Christian Institution

Two letters I received from a young seminarian, excerpted below, illustrate the spiritual warfare we get embroiled in when we come under the domination of religious educational institutions that no longer hold the "faith once delivered" but only rationalized and therefore reductionistic versions of it. The loss of freedom to speak the truth in such situations is as insidious a form of tyranny as one could imagine. Sadly, the situations described here are not rare. They point up our need to prepare ourselves to move more effectively in the exorcism of institutions. These letters contain classic illustrations of spiritual bondage—what it looks and feels like, as well as the very real danger it poses to the health of body and soul. This man could have lost his life had he not come out of the bondage. These excerpts also illustrate the effective use of holy water, as well as the struggle that, strangely enough, a man studying for the priesthood had in finding a book containing prayers for use with holy water.

Dear Leanne,

Spring break is here, and . . . I am definitely on the downhill run in school. I got my GOE scores back two weeks ago and did well in all areas. The same week I came through the faculty ordination vote unscathed (not to be taken for granted here with my theology even though I have maintained a low profile). All I have left is a couple more papers and seminary will be behind me.

It is . . . sad to realize that for all the problems this school has in lack of direction, lack of vision for ministry, and misguided emphasis upon the sensate and the "demonstrably rational," it is apparently one of the more solid ones in the [denomination]. Of the survivors in my class (we lost over one-third), only a half dozen or so have their feet firmly planted enough in Jesus to really go out and minister. The others . . . will go out as ordained professionals: social workers, mass priests, administrators, or frustrated theologians who are always answering the questions which no one in their congregation is asking. . . .

It is very difficult to succinctly sum up my experiences here. . . . I have obviously gathered a great deal of information about church history, liturgies, ethics, etc., that is necessary . . . but so much has been neglected . . . even denied—that is part of our heritage and so essential for ministry.

The lack of moral absolutes is one of the most distressing aspects of what is taught. While most of my classmates (we are an almost boringly straight group) are exemplary in their conduct, they have continually had their values undermined to the point that few of them feel the liberty to point their congregations to specific standards of conduct. It is all reduced to a matter of relativity. Last week our pastoral theology professor showed us a pornographic homosexual film—ostensibly to desensitize us to "homosexual love-making" and to create sympathy for homosexual lifestyles. We spend sixteen hours in required Biblical courses so that we can place this information on an equal par with Shakespeare, Kant, Marx, Nietzsche, and Freud as we search for truth. The fact that the church has survived at all must be the most powerful witness there is to God's continued activity in the world—we surely aren't giving Him much help through the institution itself. I am so thankful for the foundation that God had laid in my life through your influence and that of many others before I came here!

This man had come to Christ through our ministry, received a powerful infilling of the Holy Spirit, and then had gone on to become an effective witness to the faith. From the first, his pastoral gifts were evident, and he knew he was to go to seminary. Midway into his school work, however, he became very ill and phoned me. As I listened, I realized his physical condition was directly related to demonic warfare, so after several days of prayer about the matter, I phoned and asked that he get blessed water and oil and receive laying-on-of-hands at once. Even though before going to seminary he had received such ministry and had effectively ministered it to others, the following (written after his graduation) describes the difficulty he had in praying the prayer that would break the bondage. Months of serious illness elapsed before he could do it:

It is difficult to know where to start in regard to the tremendous inertia which [my wife] and I had to overcome in taking authority with the holy water during my second year. Perhaps I need to go back to the very beginning of my first year. Although I felt that I was well prepared as to what to expect at seminary—emphasis on academics, no three-year spiritual retreat, constantly under scrutiny, etc.—nonetheless I did want to be receptive to what was being offered. After all, these were the professionals which the church had selected to train its next generation of priests. Also, I was lulled to sleep somewhat by [and here he describes the gentle, loving spirituality of one of his profs, one who finally proved to be without power and without mental or emotional health]. All during the first year I rationalized to myself and others that there really must be some purpose and overall design in what we were being required to do that made sense in the context of the historic church. On the one hand, we were told at the outset that religious truth and scientific truth dealt with somewhat different questions and therefore could not be in juxtaposition with one another. We also were told that we would be dealing with questions of faith which could be experienced, but not actually proven one way or the other. Yet, we found the only arguments which were acceptable to the faculty were those which were sustainable by a rational approach which could meet with the criteria of the nonbelieving academic world. (This contradiction between the nature of religious and scientific truths and the methods which were permissible to use in searching for or developing religious truth was something I was unable to get my professors to acknowledge in three years of seminary work.)

Although I felt that intellectually I was remaining true to what God had shown to be true and of value in my life, experientially I was becoming more and more a part of the general atmosphere of the school. My spiritual life was rather barren. It was very easy to find someone with which to drink and party, but that first year [my wife] and I did not find anyone with whom we were at ease to really share our experiences of Jesus and with whom we could consistently pray.

[He describes his "internship" program in a hospital.] . . . where the theology very forcefully presented was that God could not intervene to alleviate the suffering that we encountered on the hospital floors each day. To suggest that He (really She or It) could be anything other than an opiate for those who were suffering met with derision and criticism from the chief supervisors in the intensive, large group meetings. The frequent group sessions were at the best dangerous—lots of amateurish probing and prying with no attempt at healing, and they were at the worst brutal. A classmate . . . struggling with cancer (which was largely in remission and which his doctor thought was very stress sensitive) had to leave when his white count shot out of sight.

Finally, about six weeks into the ten-week program, I decided to take control of my life and began to try to stand up to my immediate supervisor. The road back was more difficult than I even dreamed. Within a week I found myself in the emergency room with the life-threatening condition I later wrote you about. My [internship] ended with a standoff in which we sort of agreed to overlook the negative and accent the positive. My problem was not really with the individual people, but rather with the system that denied that which was the foundation upon which my life was based.

On my return to seminary in the fall, I was determined not to succumb to the system and be seduced in the way I had my first year. However, the work load was so heavy that it really was just a matter of survival without much of a chance to work on my spiritual life and personal growth or actual personal healing. Also, my situation was similar to that of many of my classmates. We had left good jobs or professions in which we had seniority, sold homes, uprooted our families, and put the future of our families as well as ourselves on the line. The criterion for evaluation was much too ambiguous to be able to stand up and make too many waves. The faculty could ask you to leave or recommend that you not be ordained without ever giving specific reasons or being individually accountable for how they had voted.

Although we did establish a good relationship with another couple that fall, our year at school had robbed us of the will to fight with the spiritual weapons with which God had previously equipped us. Our spiritual sensitivity was very low, and we had fallen into the trap of looking for scientifically demonstrable reasons for all that we encountered. Even when we discussed the possibility of there being a demonic element to what we were experiencing, somehow there seemed no way to do anything about it.

When you called . . . and urged us to get the holy water and use it to break the bondage, I could think of many reasons why it wouldn't work and see no way that it could. There was no clergy person to whom I felt I could turn. We had not at that time developed a close enough relationship with our prayer partners to risk such a radical suggestion to them. . . . It was as though someone within me was saying, "You have risked too much to try something this crazy and get called before the faculty for such a thing. You know that this could very easily get you canned in a hurry." Besides, my own spiritual impotence was so pronounced at that time that I could not believe that anything would happen anyway (what a far cry from where I had been a few short years ago!). Why take the risk?

In my journal entry on the day you called, I described myself as beleaguered and confused, and yet, very desirous of being true to God's call in my life. As you know, it took us over two months to get a copy of the prayers from the *Priest's Manual* . . . and then to convince ourselves that we had the authority to act without clergy assistance. An amazingly long time for two people who are normally impatient self-starters, much concerned about my physical health if not our spiritual health. In retrospect it was like being in one of those horrible dreams in which one can see disaster coming, but is unable to move at a normal pace so as to avoid it. When one lives in the midst of a lie long enough, it becomes a part of you whether you want to rationally accept it or not.

We finally, with great reluctance and very little expectancy, blessed the water and used it as you suggested. We did so more out of respect for you than any faith that God would really move. As you know, the result affected more than my serious physical state. It was a turning point for us spiritually and emotionally. It was as though in the next few days the clouds parted, and God's light began to show through for the first time in a long time. The situation at school did not change, but our perspective of it did. Dimly at first, but with increasing clarity, we began to see the struggle which raged around us. We could do battle with the real adversary for a change and allow our anger at individuals and the system to abate. We could see that they were as blind to what was going on as we had been. They simply could not see the way out because they had not been set free. Unfortunately, as long as I was in the position of a student, I did not feel that I could do much to help the situation because the intimidation and prejudice against certain theological positions were real and not imagined.

As I write this to you, I am aware that my resolve to loose myself was not enough . . . I had to get to the point that I could see the problem with my spiritual eyes, and I had to fight the battle with spiritual weapons. My will, my good intentions, and my intellect were not enough. I thank God for the experiences I had prior to entering seminary which encouraged me to take the timid, belated steps which finally led to my being set free. I also thank you for your love and concern which caused you to push us to take the necessary steps.

As I looked over my infrequent journal entries from this period, I came across one which perhaps best sums up what this is all about, "If Satan can spiritually castrate and lobotomize us before ordination, he has little to fear from our ministries."

I want to reiterate how subtle and seductive the attack was in the beginning of our battle: "Does God really expect you to do this or believe that? Is it really so important that you adhere so strongly to that point of view? After all, look at all those who feel differently, and they aren't such bad people, are they?" Eventually we all became targets of, as well as agents for, the deception that was being perpetrated. Like Peter, I sold out all too easily—even before I realized it. . . .

We love you and pray for you regularly.

In Christ, _____

Could this seminarian have been prayed for, delivered, and healed without the use of holy water? Yes, but not nearly so easily. This takes us back to the point I made earlier about the inestimable value and power of prayer. When we use holy water, we have the force not only of our own prayers, but those of the Church as well. The *prayer of faith* that makes a pathway for the Spirit of God to heal and set the sick free is to be stressed, never the use of holy water per se. But then, that is precisely what makes holy water, when used appropriately, so extremely effective—the prayers said over it.

Besides the fact that we have the prayers of God's people with us when we use holy water, many demonic spirits are quickly, even instantly, routed by it. Working as I do to see people healed and set free from sexual perversions and neuroses, I often have to send phallic demons (unclean spirits) away. These are extremely subtle and seem better able to hide than most. But the fact is, they cannot stand holy water, and they flee from it. Most who have been to our meetings have seen this firsthand.[5]

The following is taken from Michael Green's book *I Believe in Satan's Downfall*. He is an Anglican pastor and theologian, now teaching at Regent College in Vancouver, BC.

Holy water is another effective symbol, and indeed agency. I discovered its value by mistake, not coming from a churchmanship where the use of holy water was common. One person under the influence of multiple demon possession crowed at me, "Ah, you haven't got any holy water." "I have," I replied, and at once consecrated some water in a glass in the name of the Trinity, and proceeded to sprinkle her. The effect was immediate, electric, and amazing. She jumped as if she had been scalded. The spirit manifested itself powerfully and in due course departed. But I learned a lesson from that. Holy water is a most valuable adjunct to deliverance. The funny thing is that if the person is not possessed, or after they have been delivered, there is no reaction whatever when the water is applied. It becomes a useful thermometer therefore.

It is interesting to reflect on the status of holy water in the church. The Catholic strand of Christendom has retained it, but does not know what to do with it. It had once been dynamic in the days of faith, but became static and fossilized when men no longer believed. The Protestant churches have rejected it as superstition, seeing only its fossilized state and reacting against that. In fact we are fools not to use it both in places and with people who are or may be possessed.[6]

Since my first experience with the young girl who wandered into the unthinkable path of Satan worship, I've used holy water anytime someone is oppressed by evil[7] or invaded by demonic spirits. This was always quietly done—few if any ever questioned it. Many who receive healing prayer expect the anointing with oil that has been hallowed for healing purposes and most likely do not differentiate between it and the holy water. Both the oil and the water are "standard equipment" for most who minister with us in the schools and seminars. I suppose I could fill a book with humorous "holy water" stories, for most Protestants (Catholics too!) simply do not have "holding spaces" in their minds for the kinds of things we see happen with its use.

One man, Pastor John, to give one of the latest examples, a teacher in a Christian Bible school, simply was not going to accept the notion that any good could come of using holy water. He held to this even after experiencing a PCM and seeing its effective use firsthand. But all this changed one day when into his office came a prominent woman who was manifesting demons. Pastor John was beginning to get anxious, for his ministrations seemed to be getting them nowhere. The situation was growing in intensity, along with his alarm.

His secretary, Annie, quietly opened the door and saw immediately what was happening, for it was mirrored in Pastor John's face. Annie could see only the back of the demonized woman, but she knew from the foul words and behavior that demons were manifesting. She had also attended our seminar, and knowing about the use of holy water, she ran to get the bottle she had acquired after the conference. The demonized woman did not hear Annie's quiet reentry, yet she began screaming, "Where's the holy water? Where did it come from?" And her head began spinning around as if it would swing off her neck— all of this under the influence of demons. Needless to say, Pastor John and Annie used the water quite liberally that day, and the woman was set free. Stunned by this, the pastor has since revised his thinking and now has a very large "holding space" in his mind for the use of sacramental helps.

One Jesuit priest, running up to me after a prayer for deliverance from Baal (idols) that had resulted in literally hundreds being set free, said: "I've never seen holy water do that!" We laughed together, for he knew, even as I, that holy water, the crucifix, or anything else can be used perfunctorily and without faith—in which case it is, as Michael Green has stated, merely a fossilized relic. Again, of course, it is never the holy water, per se. It is, first of all, the prayer said over the water—together with the gifts of the Holy Spirit and God's gracious leading in the administration of it—that combine to make the use of sacramental helps such a blessing.

Because of the way holy water is now used in our healing services, its use is apparent and noticed. We realize this is all right and are comforted by the fact that this too is the Lord's doing. It has to do with a vital part of our message— the fact of Incarnational Reality and that God does not despise matter but hallows it. It has to do with healing the rift we moderns suffer between head and heart, reason and faith, and the restoration of both ways of knowing. It also everywhere brings together Protestant and Catholic in ways we'd never envisioned, especially overseas in countries such as Ireland, England, Scotland, and on the continent of Europe where the divisions between these Christians run even deeper than in the United States. Protestants begin to repent of their headiness and their subjective overreactions to what has become for them "Catholic practices"; Catholics receive new understanding and life into the sacramentals they retained, and repent of any perfunctory or superstitious use of them.

Holy Washings

. . . Christ loved the church and gave himself up for her to make her holy, cleansing her by the washing with water through the word, and to present her to himself as a radiant church, without stain or wrinkle or any other blemish, but holy and blameless. (Ephesians 5:25)

Besides the way the Holy Spirit attends the use of holy water in deliverance prayer, we see His power at work in (I don't know what else to call it) "holy washing" prayer. After prayer for healing of memories and for deliverance from false gods, we are often led of the Spirit to ask people to come forward who need the administration of "more holy water." Sometimes this doesn't occur until the last day of a school when we are praying "consecration" prayers with individuals. We know there is yet more cleansing to be done—a cleansing that in a special way ties together all the healings these persons have experienced and enables them to more fully "put on Christ" and to more fully accept the call to minister to others.

The team and I often shed tears as, for example, incest and ritual abuse victims who have received healing of memories cry, "Wash my face, please," or "Wash my hands," or "It's my mind I want fully washed," or simply, "More water, please, more holy water." We then, as led by the Holy Spirit, apply the water, making the sign of the cross over them as we pray. It is as if now not only their memories are touched and flooded with healing light, but the very pores of their bodies and the cells of their minds receive a holy cleansing and release. The skin is washed with that which is holy, and the poisonous effects of having been impurely touched and hated (as only Satan, using another human being, can hate and destroy) are neutralized and lifted.

Those who have misused their bodies sexually have special needs here, and enormous healings occur as those who've been in perverted sexual lifestyles, now set free, come forward crying out for more holy water. As one young man wrote:

> After we renounced Baal and Ashtoreth, I knew that I needed even more cleansing, and when you said to come forward for more of the holy water, I knew the Lord had made the way for this. I asked you to wash my mouth because, in my past sexual activity, my mouth and throat had received the most vile defilement. . . . As soon as you passed the holy water over my mouth, my lips felt so precious and my mouth holy. I felt that there was a word written across the back of my throat which must come out, it was the word *horrible*. For a little while this word stubbornly refused to move, but as you poured more and more holy water over me, this word dislodged and I felt a new word written there. It was my Christian name! Alive with its full meaning!

My files are literally filled with letters chronicling the healings that take place during these holy washings. And they are not just from those who've experienced gross abuse or suffered the ravages inherent in sexual sin, neurosis, and perversion. Many others, when led to come forward, receive additional cleansings, healings and insights. As the following excerpt from a letter reveals, one received a fleeting glimpse of the joy and holiness toward which our cleansing in Christ leads:

> The most amazing thing happened during the washing with holy water. At first, when you announced it, I was in turmoil, as I was thinking of the saying of Jesus, "He who has washed already needs no further washing." Knowing how much washing the Lord has already done in me, my main concern was that I should not dishonor Him in going up. But on the other hand, I was keen not to miss out on any blessing! Finally, I . . . came forward. What happened next was quite extraordinary in its intensity.
>
> You had just finished washing me and tipped my chin up a little. . . . At that moment something clicked in my head and I heard the words, "Washed in the blood of the Lamb." And what I next saw and heard had a split-second quality—it was as if a curtain were momentarily lifted. . . .
>
> I saw people dressed in white with their arms up in the air, praising the Lord, and then I seemed to catch an echo of bells, or singing wafted on the wind . . . the effect it had on me is almost beyond description. I was possessed with a fierce desire, a desperate longing, to get to that Land. The word *Heaven* seems too weak to describe it. The intensity of the experience is almost impossible to convey in words. Indeed I was practically unable to speak of it for months afterwards. Suddenly the rest of my life seemed like a bore— to be got through as quickly as possible. In fact, I have always asked the Lord for a long life, if that is His will, as I want to bear fruit, and I don't want my loved ones to have to grieve me prematurely. And anyway, I enjoy life. So this desire was certainly no kind of death wish. I don't understand why the Lord gave me that experience then, but I do understand why such moments are generally fleeting—we'd none of us be here otherwise!

A year or so ago, after an overseas PCM where we made particularly generous use of holy water, Fr. William Beasley and I were flying home, praising God and talking about the unusual healings we'd seen as God had led in this way, when it became clear to me that we'd had, among other things, a great baptismal service. "William," I said, knowing he did not have a rigid bone in his makeup, but that he nevertheless was a churchman with strong inclinations toward a "proper" baptismal liturgy, "along with all the other washings, it seems to me that we are carrying out the commandment of Christ to go out into all the world, preach the gospel, and baptize. Don't you think some of what was going on in these holy washings were water baptisms in the fullest sense of the word?"

"Yes," he said quietly, "I realized that was happening; in some cases that is exactly what was going on."

Interestingly enough, we got several letters after that conference indicating those who experienced it *knew* as well that this was their water baptism. The young man who received his name (a christening such as occurs in baptism when the Christian name is given) wrote:

> I had once had a "believer's" baptism, but there had been no real repentance. . . . Like a Pharisee, I had gone for the outward show. There had been no change of lifestyle, no bringing forth the fruits that the Lord was looking for. I had worried all week as to whom I could ask to baptize me. After my "holy washing," I couldn't stop laughing. . . . such was the joy. . . . This was my water baptism.

This is in no way to recommend multiple water baptisms. However, this young man's first, deliberately undertaken in unbelief and rebellion, had obviously been farcical. But there can be multiple washings, and God uses the hallowed water in and with the Word to hallow his Bride, the Church.

As Rev. Canon Mark Pearson states:

> God may choose to make use of material objects by which grace, blessing, and healing are conveyed. In Scripture and in Church tradition we read of blessed prayer cloths (Acts 19:11-12) and holy oil (James 5:14). God may also use Holy Communion, holy water, or any number of other objects. The historic term for these things is "sacramentals." One contemporary Pentecostal minister of healing has called them "delivery systems." In addition, the laying-on-of hands is frequently a part of healing and indeed of many different acts of blessing.

And please note the chief reason why this is so: *"The reason for this variation in manner of healing is to keep our focus on God."* Christian healing does not believe God to be capricious. We can confidently offer prayer, administer the various sacramentals, and lay hands on the sick. But since we are never certain how God will heal or the time-frame in which He will accomplish it, our focus is to be kept on God. There is no "technique of healing," no "magic objects."[8]

It is surely the greatest blessing to be able to hear the Lord say:

> [G]o and make disciples of all nations, baptizing them in the name of the Father and of the Son and of the Holy Spirit, and teaching them to obey everything I have commanded you. And surely I am with you always, to the very end of the age. (Matthew 28:19-20)

And what joy it is to see the myriad ways the Spirit of the Lord uses to send His cleansing flood, and then to engender within the fallen creature His new and uncreated Life. May it be so, we cry, "Come, Holy Spirit, wash us anew. Maranatha! Even so, come Lord Jesus!"

The Use of a Blessed Crucifix

In addition to Scripture there are other aids we can use. The cross of Christ is of course the great sign of demonic defeat, and I find that few things so provoke the demon to manifest itself and to leave as using a cross to hold before the eyes of the patient. They will often shut their eyes to exclude the sight. Marking the cross upon the patient's person is equally certain to provide a reaction if they are in fact possessed.[9]

In *The Healing Presence,* I have said a great deal about symbols and imagery, that they bind up reality for us, and that we as twentieth-century Christians have lost our Judeo-Christian symbolic system. Christian reality is diminished for us because it has been reduced to an abstraction. Our hearts and minds are bereft of the great Christian symbols and images ("pictures" that mediate a transcendent reality) and contain instead the images and thought patterns of a materialistic or pagan worldview. We've abstracted away the great Christian realities, and we are now at the mercy of alien symbolic systems such as those that form the framework of Freemasonry, the occult, and the various Eastern, pagan, pantheistic, and Gnostic (feminist, Jungian, New Age) systems.

To further compound this loss, many Christians are not only in denial of their intuitive, imaginative faculties, but are taught to be afraid of them by those in extreme reaction to the New Age and related paganisms. As a result, many churchgoers sit in the pews these days, their imaginations furnished with alien images, yet they have learned to hate and deny their own intuitive, imaginative capacities and no longer think in the terms that symbolize the incomparably great Judeo-Christian reality. They may even fear and eschew the crucifix as that which symbolizes Christ's death and resurrection, and ours in and with His—all that pertains to salvation, redemption, justification, sanctification, and spiritual authority over evil.

Interestingly enough, however, the Devil and his demons have not lost the Judeo-Christian symbolic system. They are just in the business of tempting us to lose ours. They cannot stand the crucifix, that which symbolizes our full redemption, the fact that Christ took upon Himself the wrath of God against evil and paid for us the price of His blood.

I'll never forget the deliverance of one grievously possessed young man brought to us. His sexual compulsions were of the worst, and he was, by his own admission, close to murdering his sex victims. Especially memorable were his tormented, blue eyes—eyes that yet retained a beauty Satan had been unable to entirely obliterate and a promise of the true man within who was about to come forward in the Healing Presence of God. He was terrified lest he should hurt me or the ones standing with me, for in other deliverance attempts the demons had caused him to flail about with the strength of many men. He was indeed the sort that would have knocked out the walls of the place we were in had we gone about it in the more popular way of today—with loud speaking and binding of demons, and with no use of crucifix or holy water. But we had a good supply of holy water and a very large crucifix, one we took down from over the altar in the chapel we were in.

As I placed that huge crucifix in his hands, his fingers curled round it in a death grip. Though he remained seated with his hands fixed to the very large upright cross, his head plunged to the floor and he was frothing at the mouth and in agony of the demons. As we prayed and poured the holy water on him, he was gradually able to honor my request that he look up into my face. The crucifix was between him and me, facing him, and as he looked up to me, it was through the face of Christ crucified. It was then I looked into his pain-stricken eyes and called forth the real man, the man who was anxious *to work with me* toward his deliverance. In Jesus' name, we then commanded the demons to leave and to harm no one as they left. Demon after demon tore out of his body as we continued to pour on the water and call forth the true man. Within forty-five minutes this man was delivered. The next day we had extensive prayer for healing of his memories, and we made arrangements for him to have Christian fellowship. Several weeks later, a Christian psychiatrist helped him deal with the serious dysfunctions in his family that had led to such a critically eroticized self-identity. I am happy to report that this man is not only whole today, but he is a leader in the Body of Christ.

What could have taken days took a short time because a ministry team did not focus on demons or darkness, but rather on seeing the true man and calling him forth into the Presence of a Holy God. This, together with the fact that demons cannot stand that which is holy and signifies Christ's death for us, made what would have taken hours and even days into the work of less than an hour.

By reason of the way God put it together, our PCM team is evenly divided between Catholics and Protestants. Patsy Casey, one of our music leaders, is thoroughly Irish and Catholic in background and is, at the same time, gifted in evangelism—ordinarily considered to be more the purview of Protestant evangelicals today. She does not express her special evangelistic gift with some variation of: "Are you ready to make a decision for Christ?" but in a more immediate and colorful way, crying out, "Kiss the cross, brother," and she thrusts out the crucifix.

In our first full London PCM conference, we were in an absolutely packed auditorium. We were about evenly divided between church leaders and truly needy persons. There came a healing moment in the meetings when God was dealing with the most seriously needy, and a good number were being delivered of demons. Patsy was up in the balcony ministering at this moment, and, instantly discerning the demonic, she drew forth her crucifix. One young man, obviously needy and wanting help, began to manifest demons, and she went toward him. The demons within him caused him to hit at her crucifix, knocking it across the balcony. All eyes were on her as she retrieved it and turned to me on the platform, speaking loudly enough for all to hear. In an incredulous voice, as if such a thing were uncommon, she cried out to me: "This man doesn't know Jesus!" She then marched straight back toward him, crucifix in hand thrust toward his lips, saying, "Kiss the cross, brother!" And with no small struggle, that is exactly what he did. He received Christ and was delivered. We saw many, many healings and deliverances that day, but this young man's healing birthed yet another—and it has continued to bear the finest of fruit—that of a vital healing between Protestant and Catholic.

We often see God bless in a signal way the use of a blessed crucifix. It at once images and symbolizes Christ's death for us, the price He paid to deliver all who are oppressed and under Satan's foul heel. Hell and all its minions hate it, for it images the one reality they most fear. For the demon, the Judeo-Christian symbols are clear—and for them, they spell eternal damnation.

Satan's Temptation in Regard to Sacramental Actions and the Use of Sacramentals

The tempting of the Christian in regard to the use of holy water and a blessed crucifix is the same as it is in regard to all things that are true and useful. When we are committed to Christ, our temptations from the evil one are usually the more subtle ones. As Oswald Chambers states, Satan

> does not come on the line of tempting us to sin, but on the line of shifting the point of view, and only the Spirit of God can detect this as a temptation of the devil.[10]

He does succeed in shifting the point of view of some, for example, from the true imagination with its intuitions of the real, including the mind of Christ—to *merely* the picture-making faculty of the mind itself and its power to visualize. For another example, Satan seeks to shift our point of view from the prayers made over the hallowed water and the true principles behind sacramental reality to the water itself and either magical notions about it or the opposite error of seeing it merely as water used by those who are superstitious or in error. As a final example, the enemy would tempt us to shift our point of view from focus on Christ, crucified and risen again for our full salvation as symbolized in a crucifix, to the crucifix itself. *Prayer, the focus on Christ and communion with God, is the reality.* Here again, Oswald Chambers states it succinctly and powerfully, summing it up: "Prayer is the battle," and "Prayer does not fit us for the greater works; prayer *is* the greater work."[11]

We must learn to pray in such a way as to see individuals as well as organizations and programs delivered from the demonic. And when we listen carefully to God, we may find (as our forebears have, generation after generation rediscovering the fact) that sacramental actions, signs and symbols, such as the use of holy water and a blessed crucifix with those needing deliverance, may play a greater part than we would have dared think before the battle grew so grave and we were startled out of our rationalism. The use of what has been hallowed and set apart unto a holy God constitutes one of the ways by which the unhallowed, all that is foul and profane and hates God and His creation, is put to flight.

This chapter is not intended to be a full explication of the use of holy water and other Christian symbols and agencies in spiritual battle. Moreover, it is not an attempt to put forward or push the use of these things. It is, however, a plea for the understanding of symbol and *unction* and explains the unchanging principles behind their use. Both are vitally related to sacramental actions in prayer for the sick. Finally, this chapter underscores the important principle of focusing on God rather than upon demons in deliverance prayer. It is in focusing on Him that the charism of discerning of spirits operates.

As Christian history reveals, the knowledge of how to pray for healing is often lost to the church. It is only in times of the church's renewing that we regain it. This knowledge of healing prayer is one of the first things to be obscured in times of backsliding and the resulting loss of a full understanding of Christian Incarnational Reality.

In the ministry of healing prayer, we often find ourselves trying to reinvent the wheel, so to speak. It is comforting to find information from past ages that confirms, along with the Spirit of God, what we've learned. There have been several such finds in my life, and one of them is a large section on healing prayer from *Liturgy and Worship: A Companion to the Prayer Books of the Anglican Communion*.[12] Dr. Charles Harris wrote the section, and I know of no finer historical overview of healing prayer and the use of the sacramentals in the church. It is well researched and scholarly, yet readable, and retains the good of reason as well as full faith in a God who heals His people through those who pray. Though out of print, this important book can be obtained through libraries.

I found it only a year or so ago, and in reading through the entire section on healing prayer, I was impressed over and over again with the way the Holy Spirit teaches us not only the same truths, but the same ways of following through on these truths. I was especially delighted to find Dr. Harris's report that on occasion instantaneous healings of those with sexual perversions and illnesses occur. Our reports of the instant healings we see in our ministry are at times criticized by some within the church.

Our God is good, and His power is beyond telling. He has always used the small and despised things, such as blessed water and simple faith in Him, to confound the wisdom of this world.

CHAPTER 12

The Gift of Battle

We are not sent to battle for God, but to be used by God in His battlings.[1]

(Oswald Chambers)

Finally, be strong in the Lord and in his mighty power. Put on the full armor of God so that you can take your stand against the devil's schemes. For our struggle is not against flesh and blood, but against the rulers, against the authorities, against the powers of this dark world and against the spiritual forces of evil in the heavenly realms. Therefore put on the full armor of God, so that when the day of evil comes, you may be able to stand your ground, and after you have done everything, to stand. Stand firm then, with the belt of truth buckled around your waist, with the breastplate of righteousness in place, and with your feet fitted with the readiness that comes from the gospel of peace. In addition to all this, take up the shield of faith, with which you can extinguish all the flaming arrows of the evil one. Take the helmet of salvation and the sword of the Spirit, which is the word of God. And pray in the Spirit on all occasions with all kinds of prayers and requests. With this in mind, be alert and always keep on praying for all the saints.

(Ephesians 6:10-18)

Be on your guard; stand firm in the faith; be men of courage; be strong. Do everything in love.

(St. Paul, 1 Corinthians 16:13-14)

*J*esus said, "But I tell you, Do not resist an evil person. If someone strikes you on the right cheek, turn to him the other also" (Matthew 5:39). Such a "hard" saying of our Lord's chases many of us time and again to a full study of the Sermon on the Mount. In that discourse, Jesus makes a number of statements like this one, and in doing so, contradicts and overturns the best Jewish wisdom of the day. A study of these words reveals, as Oswald Chambers says,

> the humiliation of being a Christian. Naturally, if a man does not hit back, it is because he is a coward; but spiritually if a man does not hit back, it is a manifestation of the Son of God in him. When you are insulted, you must not only not resent it, but make it an occasion to exhibit the Son of God. You cannot imitate the disposition of Jesus; it is either there or it is not. To the saint personal insult becomes the occasion of revealing the incredible sweetness of the Lord Jesus.[2]

Our Lord's words can never be understood or lived out in the natural. They have to do with the Paschal mystery and with Incarnational Reality, the fact that Another, the One crucified for sin, lives in us and that He is Love. We are to listen for a higher wisdom and collaborate with it. If we are to overcome in spiritual conflict, we must move forward in the knowledge of Christ's Presence with us and in the gifts of the Holy Spirit as these operate through listening prayer. In doing this, more often than not we are sent scurrying back to our Lord's words in this discourse. To experience real spiritual battle is to know what real enemies are. (Many think they are in a spiritual battle when they are merely beset due to lack of knowledge and wisdom as to how to deal with matters.) Nothing will send us back to Christ's words about loving our enemies more quickly than a skirmish with those who truly hate the word of truth (Christ and His gospel) and therefore hate and malign us. We soon find out if we are battling partly in our own strength, and we cry out for mercy to battle only in His.

In *Crumbling Foundations,* Dr. Donald Bloesch writes of our need to pray for the "gift of battle." In a section entitled "Rediscovering the Spiritual Gifts," he reminds us that "Christians can only live out their vocation by discovering and exercising the gifts of the Holy Spirit," and he writes of this additional gift which he says is alluded to in both Testaments. As a theologian and a keen observer of the times, he believes this gift of battle has a crucial significance for our day:

> Christians who are under the cross of persecution need to pray for the gift of battle, the ability to endure under trial, the boldness to challenge immorality and heresy in high places. The gift of battle is properly included in the gift of might or power (Isaiah 11:2). It is the power to enter into conflict and the stamina not to grow weary. It must be accompanied by and fulfilled in the gift of love, since we cannot wage war against sin successfully unless we love the sinner. We must speak the truth, but we must speak the truth in love.[3]

Speaking the truth in a love born of God is, it seems to me, the greater part of the gift of battle. There is nothing weak about this love, for truth—full orbed and aptly spoken—is incredibly powerful.

A first principle in spiritual warfare is the knowledge that we cannot function in the gift of battle without *agape,* the gift of divine love coming from God's life within and issuing forth through us. In such a stance, our trust will be wholly in Him. We will be looking to no other power, no other intervention—but His. This looking straight to God and receiving His battle plan keeps us on a safe ground in another very important matter—we know that we are to hate sin, but we are not to hate our enemy.

The following, a prayer from a Greek Orthodox liturgy, has a permanent and prominent place in my prayer journal. It helps me pray aright for my enemy when the battle is at its height and I am least able to muster up my own words for such a prayer. An absolutely wonderful one, it has within it the true spirit of Christ's Sermon on the Mount.

Save, O Lord, and have mercy upon those that envy and affront me and do me mischief, and let them not perish through me, a sinner.

Prayer such as this is what loving our enemy is all about.

A second principle is that we cannot function in the gift of battle apart from mature prayer partners. They are the foot soldiers who trudge alongside us, persevering in the same battle:

Christians who enter the battle against the powers of darkness cannot persevere without a life-support system, without a supportive fellowship that continually holds up its members in intercession to the living God.[4]

Those of us who have these "life-support" systems are deeply grateful for them, but those who do not must pray earnestly for them. The intercessions of the saints who gather together in Christ's name to pray for us are absolutely vital in the Christian walk, and most assuredly so in spiritual warfare. God's gift to us of precious souls that not only intercede for us, but hear and pass on the word that God is speaking when we are sore besieged and fainting is true wealth. All through the years when God would move me from one locale to another, the first thing I besought God for was trusted prayer partners. I often had to train Christians in prayer, but God always sent them, maybe only one for a while. Then another or so would be added. My prayer partners are among my greatest spiritual treasures. To watch God at work in their souls and ministries is an amazing reward in itself, only one of many, many that these "masterpieces" of God's love, these servants of His, bring. I am confounded and amazed to see how rare it is that pastors and leaders have prayer partners such as these. Often they fear to share with others, and there will be no corporate listening for God's voice or intercession for others that is worthy of the name. No one can stand long in battle under these conditions or win the prize of pressing through to victory in the vocations we've been assigned.

I recently prayed with a precious, strong leader in the Body of Christ. She was undergoing the worst spiritual warfare that the archenemy of our souls can muster, and the fierce battle had brought her excruciating suffering. This pain enabled her for the first time to understand what it means to enter into the sufferings of Christ. In coming up against deeply entrenched evil within the church and taking her stand against it, she became the target of astonishing lies, vicious slander, and all manner of verbal abuse. Her very ministry was in question. Weary beyond belief at the strength and the length of the battle, she despaired of surviving the onslaught. *She had strong prayer partners, however, who were standing with her as the battle grew more impossible.* Then as we (the PCM team) came together in prayer with them, we received these incredible words from God. This leader opened her heart and received them, and these words set her back firmly upon her feet and restored to her the vocation (the message of salvation) she has been intrusted with. These are but a few of the words:

Laura [not her real name] is to lift up her voice; she is to exalt the Lord in the assembly of the people. There will be a glorious vindication—her voice is not to be silenced.

There is a new armor for Laura; it is the armor of love God is going to put on her. She is going to be able to face her enemies with a powerful love. She will be overawed at how this love will come through her. She will go forth in this armor. She is not to strive, for she will feel no need to protect herself.

Most who have suffered in the way this servant of the Lord has would feel the need to put up walls and to take protective measures for themselves and their families. But she is not going to. She has entered into the sufferings of Christ. Therefore, she is facing an enemy whose battle plan is designed to stop her mouth from speaking the truth of the gospel and her entire being from living out the truth that Another, the Holy, All Powerful One, is with her. But she has put on the full armor of God, and has asked for and received the gift of battle.

While the archaccuser of our souls, the enemy who would deceive and bring under dark deception even the elect, plans the full destruction of ourselves as persons, we like Laura battle and overcome under the Lord's banner—His holy cross and its way of love (Hebrews 2:10) and not according to the way the world fights:

For though we live in the world, we do not wage war as the world does. The weapons we fight with are not the weapons of the world. On the contrary, they have divine power to demolish strongholds. We demolish arguments and every pretension that sets itself up against the knowledge of God, and we take captive every thought to make it obedient to Christ. (2 Corinthians 10:3-5)

The Scriptures refer to this battle that engages the whole of our being as a good warfare (1 Timothy 1:18-19), and "the good fight of faith" (1 Timothy 6:12). It is against "the world" (John 16:33; 1 John 5:4-5), the flesh (Romans 7:23; 1 Corinthians 9:25-27; 2 Corinthians 12:7; 1 Peter 2:11), our enemies (Psalm 38:19; 56:2-4; 59:3), and ultimately, behind and energizing these things, the archenemy of all that God has created and called good, Satan himself (Genesis 3:15; 2 Corinthians 2:11; James 4:7-10; Ephesians 6:12; 1 Peter 5:8-9; Revelation 12:17).

The Scriptures exhort us to diligence in the warfare (1 Timothy 6:12; Jude 3); and it is to be undertaken with faith and good conscience (1 Timothy 1:18-19), steadfastness (1 Corinthians 16:13; 1 Peter 5:8-9; Hebrews 10:23), watchfulness (1 Corinthians 16:13-14), sobriety (1 Thessalonians 5:6-8), endurance (2 Timothy 2:3, 10), self-denial (1 Corinthians 9:25-27), with confidence in God (Psalm 27:1-3), and with prayer (Psalm 35:1-3).

In the ministry God has entrusted to us on the Pastoral Care Ministries Team, we never cease to be amazed at the myriad and unexpected ways God protects (Psalm 140:7), delivers (2 Timothy 4:18), helps (Psalm 118:13; Isaiah 41:13-14), comforts (2 Corinthians 7:5-7), encourages (Isaiah 41:11-12; 51:12; 1 John 4:4), and strengthens (Psalm 20:2; 27:14; Isaiah 41:10; 2 Corinthians 12:9; 2 Timothy 4:17) us in the midst of spiritual battle—even the worst warfare. It is not unusual, when ministering to the most injured, those just coming out of sinful and perverted lifestyles, to see God deliver several hundred people at one time out of the worst sicknesses of mind as well as the related condition of being seriously demonized. Here we are faced with many caught up in the worst spiritual darkness, having lost the battle due to sin and being outside of Christ. In such moments, we know not only the holy Presence of God and His mighty power at work, but at times our eyes are opened and we see the heavenly host working with us! And we are shown different kinds of angels! For example, at times in helping women severely wounded through misogyny, two of the most unusual angels come! We have to go back to the books of Ezekiel and Daniel for the words and images to describe them! These are powerful angels, and they are apparently especially concerned with the evil that women sustain in war and through misogyny. They are there helping us when these women are to be set free! We see through a glass darkly now, but someday our Lord will explain all these things to us. In the meantime it suffices to say that we, as the Body of Christ, have hardly started to draw on the divine resources our God longs to send. There is joy and victory in the midst of real battle and real suffering.

When the Enemy Is the Beloved Enemy

For a son dishonors his father, a daughter rises up against her mother, a daughter-in-law against her mother-in-law—a man's enemies are the members of his own household. (Micah 7:6)

Often the enemy takes advantage of opposition that arises within our most intimate circles—our close relatives or friends in the Body of Christ—to stir up the most heart-rending kind of spiritual warfare. This especially occurs where an effective ground-breaking ministry is at stake. Always in such demonized warfare, there will be slander and lies. I've yet to see a case like this where a root sin of envy did not have to be exposed and reckoned with as well. Oddly enough, that dread vice is rarely recognized for what it is today.

The tenth chapter of Matthew is concerned with this kind of opposition. When I first began to teach on the healing of relationships through forgiveness of sin, I experienced the most bizarre and irrational opposition, lies, and slander from certain quarters. I would never have expected it to come from that source. The situation was rife with demonic spirits, which also surprised me. Until we've been in the ministry for a good while, we seem to expect these kinds of fierce, obviously demonically inspired battles to happen to other people— not ourselves. I went flat on my face before God. Spiritual battle brings all manner of confusion, so I had a lot of "thinking through" to do with God; and of course I had to forgive and keep on forgiving the same persons, and to intercede and keep on interceding for them. In order to do all this and to keep track of the understanding God was giving me through the Scriptures and the ways He was leading me to pray, I set aside in my prayer journal an entire section entitled, "Beloved Enemies." This section is filled with Scriptures that deeply ministered to me and with prayers God gave me to pray for these dear ones. I can call them that with all sincerity, for they are loved. Had I not learned to pray for them and for the situation effectively, I do not believe I would be able to make that statement. Perhaps I would not have been able to stand in the ministry at all, for the enemy's plan was to bring it down through discouraging me personally. The nature of the warfare would most surely have done that had I not learned to pray for my beloved enemies—those closest to me who opposed the work God has called me to do.

"Painting the Dragon Red"

The Lord delights in showing us how to pray. The earlier we get around to asking Him in each situation, the better off we'll be. When I seemed to be getting nowhere in my battle, I finally cried out in desperation, "Lord, what and how am I to pray for my enemies? Those beloved ones who slander me and the work You've given me to do?"

And God promised to give me a blueprint! Several days later, as I was praying, He did. We on the team call this our "paint-the-dragon-red" prayer. We've helped many other Christians embroiled in spiritual battle by sharing it with them. It contains sound principles that everybody seems to need once the battle is joined:

1) Pray that the eyes of all who surround these persons be opened to see the situation as it really is.

2) Pray that their associates will be given ways to speak truth and light into the situation.

In these first two steps, we are praying for godly illumination and wisdom for the persons who can minister truth and peace into the situation, while at the same time we are praying for their safety. We are asking that these stable people be spared from getting caught up in the dark net of spiritual confusion and deception—a very present danger in spiritual warfare—and that they be enabled to aid others who are ensnared.

As I meditated on these first two ways of prayer, the Lord greatly ministered the story of David and Goliath to me, this truth from 1 Samuel 17:47 in particular: " . . . it is not by sword or spear that the Lord saves; for the battle is the Lord's. . . ." I then asked, "Jesus, what is the smooth stone, slung at your command that will stop the Goliaths of envy, slander, murderous hate, all that is the enemy of Your cross, Your message?"

And immediately I heard in my spirit, "Truth, truth will out—it will hit the mark." Then the following instruction is what caused us to name this way of interceding the "paint-the-dragon-red" prayer:

3) Pray that any demonic power within these persons or within these situations manifest itself—that it may be clearly discerned and seen by all the people.

The Problem of Pain, p. 28

C. S. Lewis has rightly said that "Love is something more stern and splendid than mere kindness."[5] This is terribly hard on the "beloved enemy," but it is the only way he will be healed. In answer to this prayer, God causes the real enemy of all our souls to be revealed for all to see.

There will, of course, always be some unwilling to see and repent. They blind themselves by continuing to rationalize their sin. It is here that the root sin of envy will often be revealed—the sin that has opened the door for the demonic dragon to enter and has provided a nest from which it can strike within the Kingdom, a nest that can also harbor others of its demonic kind. When this happens, we invoke and practice the Presence of God and find that, "Wherever Jesus is, the storms of life become a calm."[6] We find also that He is doing a work within ourselves that could never have been done apart from the disciplines learned through sustained spiritual warfare.

After this third point, the Lord quickened 1 Samuel 14:15 to me. That Scripture verse gave me further insight into the model for taking the offensive in intercessory prayer. I saw that Jonathan and his armor-bearer, only two men, put the entire Philistine army to flight as they fought for God's people. They stepped out in faith, speaking the word of truth, and the Lord worked with them: "Then panic struck the whole army . . . and the ground shook. It was a panic sent by God."

Here we see so clearly what it means to be used by God in *His* (not our) battlings. When we step out at His command, He sends the panic or whatever else is needed. There is an illusory nature to evil. It attempts to win through bluff—through puffing itself up to horrendous size. One word of truth, spoken in the power of the Holy Spirit, solid as a rock and splendid as eternity, flies swift as the surest arrow to puncture evil's swelled balloon of lies, posturing, and bravado. Then panic sets in. There are times when we pray, "Send Your panic, Lord," and He does. We do not fight with words—we speak and live the truth, and God does the fighting.

The fourth step the Lord gave in this "paint-the-dragon-red" prayer is ever so important. It underlines the fact that our battle is against sin and not against the sinner:

4) Ask that what can be salvaged (in this situation and in the lives of your enemies) be saved, humbled, blessed by the Spirit of God.

With this, I wrote out these instructions from the Lord:

Pray for the health, the wholeness, of your enemies. Pray for the salvaging of all that is good, beautiful, and true within them. I do a great work, one that will amaze you. Be at rest now from all that besets, offends, attacks—love, write, pray, live in peace in My Presence. Enter the timelessness of My joy and peace.

That our God is faithful to hear and answer all prayer, including these prayers, is something I want to shout from the housetop. With the prophet Micah, I was given the grace to say: "But as for me, I watch in hope for the Lord, I wait for God my Savior; my God will hear me" (Micah 7:7).

And He did. If we are obedient and stand in Him, our God has an incredible way of turning our battle wounds into healing power for others even while He is yet pouring His healing grace and light into the worst of our gashes.

PRAYER

Lord bring us, especially those of us called to lead in the church, to the point where we can truthfully say with St. Paul: "We put no stumbling block in anyone's path, so that our ministry will not be discredited. Rather, as servants of God we commend ourselves in every way: in great endurance; in troubles, hardships and distresses; in beatings, imprisonments and riots; in hard work, sleepless nights and hunger; in purity, understanding, patience and kindness; in the Holy Spirit and in sincere love; in truthful speech and in the power of God; with weapons of righteousness in the right hand and in the left; through glory and dishonor, bad report and good report; genuine, yet regarded as impostors; known, yet regarded as unknown; dying, and yet we live on; beaten, and yet not killed; sorrowful, yet always rejoicing; poor, yet making many rich; having nothing, and yet possessing everything." (2 Corinthians 6:3-10)

CHAPTER 13

Cosmic Dimensions of Spiritual Warfare in Christian Organizations

Dear friends, although I was very eager to write to you about the salvation we share, I felt I had to write and urge you to contend for the faith that was once for all entrusted to the saints. For certain men whose condemnation was written about long ago have secretly slipped in among you. They are godless men, who change the grace of our God into a license for immorality and deny Jesus Christ our only Sovereign and Lord.

(Jude 3-4)

Love is something more stern and splendid than mere kindness . . .

(C. S. Lewis)

*F*rank Peretti's novel *This Present Darkness* has brought home to many the cosmic dimensions of spiritual warfare and the nature of the suffering that accompanies intense spiritual conflict. In this book and its companion volume *Piercing the Darkness*, Peretti has given back to many Christian minds, formed by twentieth-century materialism, a vital part of their Judeo-Christian symbolic system. These Christians can now "see" the holy angels as well as their fallen, demonic counterparts, and the readers' imaginations are furnished with lively images of the cosmic battle going on "in the heavenlies." Their hearts now have pictures of the way our earthly rulers and institutions are invaded and influenced by the god of this present world. As a result, these Christians no longer abstract away unseen realities. They have a renewed understanding of the value of prayer, the critical part it plays in spiritual warfare. In a manner of speaking, they are enabled to taste again the incomparable "simplicity that is in Christ" (2 Corinthians 11:3, KJV) as they move forward in listening obedience:

> Simplicity is the secret of seeing things clearly. A saint does not think clearly for a long while, but a saint ought to see clearly without any difficulty. You cannot think a spiritual muddle clear, you have to obey it clear. . . . When the natural power of vision is devoted to the Holy Spirit, it becomes the power of perceiving God's will and the whole life is kept in simplicity.[1]

This renewed capacity to see more clearly is one of the gifts that novels written by Christians are especially suited to give. The more profoundly these works emerge out of and reflect Judeo-Christian truth and reality, the greater their value. Such works will always image aright some facet of our earthly situation, and do it against the backdrop of a universe capable of receiving into itself a transcendent order, justice, and harmony. That is, Incarnation (*real* Presence) and Christ's cross (redemption and the possibility of re-creation) will implicitly or explicitly be at the heart of these works. All effective art deals in one way or another with the cosmic battle we are involved in, and with the fact that God, a good beyond our present capacity to fully imagine, has won the ultimate victory.

In the spiritual battle raging within the organized church, we find that not a few of our writers and artists have become infected by the god of this world. When immature and sinful, these artists have an uncommon capacity to mislead others and, like those who teach within the church, will find that much will be required of them at the bar of divine justice (James 3:1; Mark 9:42-50; Matthew 23:1-33). Peretti's novels have had such a great impact on Christians because, within the confines of what these works attempt to do, they effectively image Christian reality. They are thoroughly and unabashedly Christian in a day when some Christian novelists are shy about such things as truth and eternal life, being more concerned with the literary aspects of a work and its acceptance by a secularized church and world. Those of us on the front lines of the spiritual battle today are quite heartily sick of these "artsy" works and the sickly cynicism, however subtle, that leaps up from the pages. Their authors reveal their antinomianism or even outright unbelief along with their inability to paint pictures of good winning over evil as Christians persevere. These defects usually dovetail into attempts to resymbolize sin through psychologizing it in some fashion or another.

For those of us fighting for the souls of men and women, the lack of transcendent meaning and the resulting overemphasis reflected in such art—that of man locked into a narcissistic cosmos of desire, feeling, and so on—is utterly *passé*. It is especially to be deplored in its more refined—that is to say, aesthetic and literary—forms.

We celebrate the art that flows out of a truly Christian imagination and intellect, for it has the power to restore to believers a fully Christian symbolic system. In this century, C. S. Lewis and J. R. R. Tolkien are great models. The images of glory, as well those that depict the true nature of good and evil, continue to reflect the enormous gift that great minds and hearts are to us—with their genius and capacity to mirror moral and intellectual, earthly and transcendent realities to us. Christian writers have always been required to portray truth—to line up with the way things really are—and to come up with images that can at least begin to mediate to the present generation the profound meaning and truth to be mined from God's revelation of Himself. At this time when false prophets, teachers, and apostles or bishops abound, Christians in the arts had better repent their aestheticisms and their need to please a secular public and instead take their place among those whose art flows out of prayerful meditation on and experience of the *real*.

Beyond the shallow, incomplete, and immature writing and art afflicting the church today, some within our church structures and programs are actively given over to an apologetic of evil. These persons are attempting to reconcile good and evil.[2] Some have deliberately set out to destroy the historic faith and are—knowingly or unknowingly—in the service of the enemy of our souls. This being the case, it is no surprise that many Christians faint at the sights, sounds, and smells arising out of the nauseating abominations within the organized church today.

> Woe to those who call evil good and good evil, who put darkness for light and light for darkness, who put bitter for sweet and sweet for bitter. (Isaiah 5:20)

Speaking the Truth

> [I]t matters enormously if I alienate anyone from the truth. (C. S. Lewis)[3]

The old verities, the true nature of God and of His revelation to us in and through Christ, can never be compromised, much less surrendered. There are things we can disagree about, and variously stress, but we must always and earnestly contend for the essentials of the faith. Today, little heresies that will grow to be very large later on are popping up in places we'd never expect to find them. Large ones, too. This has been true throughout the ages, and heresies have served the church in that they keep her humbled and alert, studious and prayerful. They force her to clarify and define for each succeeding generation of Christians "the faith once delivered to the saints" (Jude 3).

But what should concern us most is that one of the things characterizing the current scene is the lack of love for truth itself. One devout, highly respected theologian, after trying to deal with certain well-known writers (also ordained clergy) responsible for spreading error, recently said to me in utter amazement, "They do not care about *truth*!"

What these misguided persons did care about were others' feelings, how others thought about *them*, and how things looked to other people. All this reflects the spirit of the age that loudly proclaims there is no ultimate, objective truth to be known. For these persons, there was only the inner and subjective cosmos of the psyche, with its feelings and desires, to be gratified. Their love for Christ and for others had been sentimentalized and could hardly be called love at all. Care for others was reduced to the level of whatever pop psychology ruled the day. They no longer honored and cared for the truth accessible to the hearts of the faithful and to intellects made holy—enlightened by the Spirit of God in and with His people. Christ, speaking truth to those of like mind in His own generation, said:

> Why is my language not clear to you? Because you are unable to hear what I say. You belong to your father, the devil, and you want to carry out your father's desire. He was a murderer from the beginning, not holding to the truth, for there is no truth in him. When he lies, he speaks his native language, for he is a liar and the father of lies. Yet because I tell the truth, you do not believe me! . . . If I am telling the truth, why don't you believe me? He who belongs to God hears what God says. The reason you do not hear is that you do not belong to God. (John 8:43-47)

The harsh but loving truth that Jesus declares is that we live, finally, by the Spirit of God or by the unholy spirit of this age.

Contending for the Truth

> Buy the truth and do not sell it; get wisdom, discipline and understanding. (Proverbs 23:23)

Apart from the fact that some within the church do not hear the truth and have turned from it, we live in a day when many—though they hold to the truth that is in Christ—find it difficult to contend for the faith once delivered. The spiritual, moral, and intellectual sinew needed to confront and replace the false with the true is oddly disengaged; it is simply missing. I've written about this under the rubric of a "crisis in masculinity"[4]—for that is surely in part what it is. It is the crisis of the unaffirmed and of those unable to initiate and stand for the truth. The good news is that there is healing for this condition, as we've shown throughout this book. Such a crisis involves not only an incapacity to rightly love and honor the truth, but to speak and be the truth in this our day.

To be in touch with one's masculinity (be we man or woman) at the highest level is to be empowered with Truth Himself. It is to be enabled to take one's stand no matter what the circumstances against the lies and the illusions of one's individual life and environment as well as the lies and illusions of one's corporate existence and age. This stand will not be without suffering, even as the lives of Christ and the early apostles illustrate.

When we effectively hear and speak the truth as they did, however, suffering not withstanding, we find true power, true joy, even the true peace that overcomes the world. As one of the great prophets of our age, Alexander Solzhenitsyn, said in his Nobel speech, "One word of truth outweighs the world." What greater consolation can there be than that of being a truth bearer? What greater destiny than to be in league with the God of truth—to have Him for our Father, to have Him name us His children.

Overwhelming Nature of Evil Rampant in Society

The wicked freely strut about when what is vile is honored among men. (Psalm 12:8)

Christians are overwhelmed by the nature of the evil and ungodliness that are today so highly energized and powerful as they take over civic, political, and church structures. Recently, Illinois newspapers carried articles about concerned parents finding witchcraft and other such obscenities in school textbooks. One friend in a chaplaincy finds herself on a hospital staff with other chaplains who either practice sexual perversion or openly approve it in others. Some of them have an acknowledged and overt hatred of God, and one way this is manifested is through (even as the Beast of Revelation) their blasphemies and slanders against the name of God. This situation, a deeply entrenched one, is in a "Christian" hospital. Unfortunately, such a situation is not rare today and is usually "politically" protected. This chaplain is in the midst of a truly terrible warfare. She sees the unmet needs of the sick and the dying, and when she ministers to them the healing words of Christ's gospel, she receives against herself the bitterest hatred, derision, and persecution. Her situation is desperately difficult, but she is called to be there and is a faithful witness in that place. *She stands firm in the truth she speaks.*

Two other friends, active in a church diocese full of the same darkness and blasphemy, find themselves having to stand alone, often on powerful committees, where not only is sexual perversion approved, but there is continual lobbying for the ordination of actively homosexual priests. All of this is in the face of rampant HIV positive cases and full-blown AIDS among homosexually active clergy who are already illegally ordained.

The experiences of these Christians and of the seminarian quoted in chapter 11 demonstrate that we are not doing very well in the spiritual warfare centered in organizational structures. These precious brothers and sisters in Christ, stepping into these structures where we have hardly even begun to fight the battle, are called to stand in the power of the Holy Spirit and speak truth into the dark heart of demonized warfare. It is not easy, and it can even be, as we saw in the case of the seminarian, very dangerous. As Dr. Richard Lovelace writes, one's authority in spiritual conflict takes

> on a new significance which is much broader than individual defensive spiritual warfare. Not only can we expect to carry out offensive warfare which takes ground away from Satan in the exorcism of persons, we can also undertake, when we have liberty from God to do so, the exorcism of structures occupied by demonic forces—not only fallen structures in the church in the process of reformation and revival, but also fallen structures in society which are instruments of injustice.[5]

The Seminarian's Crisis in Masculinity

We can see the spiritual and physical wear and tear that spiritual warfare inflicts on one such as the young seminarian. In the midst of his conflict and resulting illness, I realized that one of the reasons his blood pressure shot up so high was that he was forced into a situation where his true masculinity and therefore his true self were not only being seriously repressed but killed outright. He went in as a fairly knowledgeable and mature Christian, but due to mistakenly putting himself under the unholy and misguided "law" of that seminary, he reduced himself to an immature and powerless state, and he felt bereft of all moral and spiritual power. He believed he could only wait out his time there. Because he was a mature man, however, one endowed beyond the ordinary with masculine giftedness, he was even more damaged than he would have been if he had lacked true power. By not being free to be himself in Christ, he did grave psychological harm as well as spiritual and physical damage to himself. God has now rectified that and is in the process of turning his wounds into a most effective power to heal others, but his understanding of the psychological damage that occurs when a Christian isn't free to stand and speak the truth is only now becoming clear to him.[6]

Just before his blood pressure shot up, an incident occurred in his CPE (work with hospitalized persons) training, a required course for seminarians. Students from several schools came together in the course. Contrary to what one would expect, the course was not primarily designed to help the students minister to patients in crisis situations. Though they did spend time on the floors with the patients, the real emphasis was on the "confrontational" group sessions they daily had among themselves. Their questions and concerns and encounters with the patients provided the subject matter the students, as "presenters," brought before the group. The object of these daily sessions was not to get at objective ways of ministering truth and reality to patients, but in the manner of twentieth-century insanity, to get in touch with the student presenter's subjective feelings brought up by the encounter with the patient. As one might imagine, this was a way of corporately indulging in the "disease of introspection,"[7] and it had the usual frightful impact. The students and their supervisors questioned, probed, and challenged the presenter's motives and self-perceptions while seeking to discover the root of his or her feelings. The efforts were, as the seminarian said, at best amateurish and at the worst brutal and dangerous. He could hardly believe the amount of emotional pressure brought to bear on the presenter as he or she sat encircled by a group that challenged every response and motive. In every case exposure, not healing, was the goal. He said:

> Oftentimes, I had the feeling that we had laid someone out on an operating table, undressed him, sliced him open, pulled out his guts, and then left him there as we walked out congratulating ourselves on what a fine job we had done. It was assumed that the individual could restore his entrails to their proper places, suture his own wounds, get dressed, and get back on his feet by himself. If this proved too difficult, psychiatric therapy was available at discount rates.

The crowning incident occurred as one student—who had been insecure in his sexual identity and had entered the course hoping to find help—told of trying to help a patient with like difficulties. He told the group that during the patient encounter he had finally realized that he was indeed secure in his heterosexual identity, but he was now deeply fearful that out of his experimental homosexual liaisons (which had been encouraged by his peers in other sessions) he had contracted AIDS. With this admission, the advanced students and supervisors began to berate him severely and almost gleefully for denying his "obvious" homosexual orientation and his alleged fear of admitting it. Their message to him—after an hour of tears and emotional exchanges as he attempted to defend his heterosexual position—was that he should admit he was indeed homosexual and should commit himself to that lifestyle, thus facing "his real fear." At one point, and this seems a scene right out of hell, the student was writhing on the floor, and my friend said it was as if the group had turned into demons, gleefully dancing around this prostrate person, all the while naming him homosexual.

This is a nightmare the likes of which Freud could never have envisioned as coming out of his methods for helping analysts to self-understanding. But this is what spiritual warfare not only *is*, but looks like, and it is flagrantly stepped up within the church today. This warfare is widespread in organizations that purport to be Christian and among those whose vocation it is to prepare church leaders.

My friend, the seminarian, wrote: "My shame to this day is that although I did not enter into the frenzy, I was too intimidated by the process to speak out in his defense." In obeying the law of an apostate structure where profanity and unbelief were the order of the day, he was forced to deny his true masculinity—indeed even his identity as a person and as a Christian in whom the Spirit of God dwelt.

When the great majority of Christians find the above unthinkable, much less acceptable, why do we allow destructive programs and practices in our churches and schools? Why do we permit what is flagrantly sinful and opposed to all that is Christian, moral, or even reasonable? Why do we suffer moral and political conditions known to be destructive? Why, when dioceses are full of this, do we, year in and year out, allow these conditions to prevail?

Sometimes, it is said that we must suffer these things in order to obtain some good—for example, to maintain a degree program. Using the corrupt CPE program as an example, there is nothing inherently wrong with the idea of such a program. But it must be profoundly Christian if seminarians are to be part of it. In this particular case, if we care little about the trainees, we yet have an obligation to the sick and dying in the hospitals where these training courses take place. We cannot idly stand by and watch souls at their most vulnerable left without a witness, much less left in danger of being brought into spiritual warfare, and perhaps even left to die without the help our Lord has died to give them. This will involve creative thinking (listening prayer!) on our part. It also absolutely requires that we understand and admit (rather than deny) not only the fierce spiritual warfare raging in church and political structures, but also our almost total impotence in that warfare. Like the young seminarian, we have been losing the battle, rendered unable to *speak truth* powerfully into it.

We must learn to pray effectively, and then to speak the truth in such a way as to see Christian institutions and programs delivered from the demonic.

Practicing the Presence of the Holy Spirit, the Spirit of Truth

> When the Counselor comes, whom I will send to you from the Father, the Spirit of truth who goes out from the Father, he will testify about me. And you also must testify, for you have been with me from the beginning. (John 15:26-27)

When we find ourselves in decidedly unholy situations, ones rife with and energized by the lies and activities of demons, it is then that—in God's Presence and power—we stand. And it is wonderful at all times, but especially in these hard moments, to reflect on the fact that the Holy Spirit sent to us by Christ is the Spirit of Truth.

In writing on the practice of the Presence of God the Father, the Son, and the Holy Spirit, I've perhaps said less in regard to specific special ways of practicing the Presence of the Spirit. But increasingly, as in situations I've just mentioned, I find myself invoking the Holy Spirit and praising Him as the Spirit of Truth. And this is what I find myself saying over and over again to precious beleaguered brethren: "Do you know that the Holy Spirit is the Spirit of Truth? Invoke His Presence! Speak His truth. It may not be accepted right now, but it will sit on the heads of these people until they acknowledge it." True enough, some will not be converted by what they hear, but one day even they, as the Scriptures say, will bow before God and confess that Jesus Christ is Lord.

What a wonderful and mysterious power truth is. How it sits atop the most resistant head and darts into the darkest heart. That head and heart may not choose to act on the truth or to acknowledge it. The person may even repress it very deeply, but once truth is spoken, there is a place in the human heart that knows it has heard truth, and it will have to wrestle with it from then on. It is the truth, and Truth Himself, who changes people, structures, and nations.

Jesus answered, "I am the way and the truth and the life. No one comes to the Father except through me" (John 14:6). Over and over again, He who is the Truth prefaced His sayings with, "I tell you the truth . . . I tell you the truth . . . I tell you the truth."

In spiritual warfare, those who oppose the truth will nearly always be found reviling His name. The following prayer is a wonderful way of practicing the Presence of Jesus. This prayer is invaluable in all of our life, but particularly in the midst of the cosmic battle.

The Holy Name

To invoke the name of Jesus or to breathe it in prayer (as in the Jesus Prayer that comes to us from the Orthodox tradition) is a special and wondrous way of practicing the Presence. That is because:

The Name is the symbol and bearer of the Person of Christ. Otherwise the invocation of the Name would be mere verbal idolatry. "The letter killeth, but the Spirit giveth life." The presence of Jesus is the real content and the substance of the Holy Name. The Name both signifies Jesus' presence and brings its reality.[8]

The full prayer is: "Lord Jesus Christ, Son of God, have mercy on me a sinner," but it is best shortened to simply breathing the holy name.

Before beginning to pronounce the Name of Jesus, establish peace and recollection within yourself and ask for the inspiration and guidance of the Holy Ghost. "No man can say that Jesus is Lord, but by the Holy Ghost." The Name of Jesus cannot really enter a heart that is not being filled by the cleansing breath and the flame of the Spirit. The Spirit Himself will breathe and light in us the Name of the Son.[9]

It is no small joy to leave off breathing the holy name, only to hear the Spirit audibly speak it within.

This prayer, it seems to me, this holding of the holy name, is one of the most precious ways of practicing the Presence. All this was quite forcibly brought to my mind as a way of not only preparing but safeguarding Christians in the advent of persecution for their faith. I had been reading Revelation 13 and 14 and was horrified at the fate of the lost who are destined to wear the name of the Beast on their foreheads:

The beast was given a mouth to utter proud words and blasphemies and to exercise his authority for forty-two months. He opened his mouth to blaspheme God, and to slander his name and his dwelling place and those who live in heaven. He was given power to make war against the saints and to conquer them. And he was given authority over every tribe, people, language and nation. All inhabitants of the earth will worship the beast—all whose names have not been written in the book of life belonging to the Lamb that was slain from the creation of the world. . . .

He [the second beast] was given power to give breath to the image of the first beast, so that it could speak and cause all who refused to worship the image to be killed. *He also forced everyone, small and great, rich and poor, free and slave, to receive a mark on his right hand or on his forehead, so that no one could buy or sell unless he had the mark, which is the name of the beast or the number of his name.* (Revelation 13:5-8, 15-17, italics mine)

After such a terrifying word and image comes this beautiful one. It is for those whose names are written in the Book of Life, those of whom it could be said that "no lie was found in their mouths." "Then I looked, and there before me was the Lamb, standing on Mount Zion, and with him 144,000 who had his name and his Father's name on their foreheads" (Revelation 14:1).

PRAYER

Lord, may Your name be deeply inscribed on our foreheads even now.

And may Your name be as a holy fire within us, one that not only purifies us, but spills over onto all around us.

May Your name be so glorified in us that we can speak Your truth with great authority and effect, even in the face of slander and persecution. In Jesus' name, we pray. Amen.

PRAYER

Lord Jesus, we lift up to You our remaining time and all that it holds. May we be Your witnesses, filled to overflowing with Your Spirit. May we know the Truth, speak the Truth, be the Truth more powerfully and effectively than ever before, thereby lifting high Your cross for the whole world to see. May the world see the Father in You, in us, and reach up their hands to take His Hand.

Father, we thank You that Your arm is not shortened, Your ear is not deaf. Stretch forth Your mighty arm and rescue all who would acknowledge as truth Your Son, our Lord. Hear His intercessions for us, Your people, and strengthen us to do Your fullest will and slightest bidding. It is in His name we exult and pray. Amen.

CHAPTER 14

Wrong Ways to Do Battle

Finally, be strong in the Lord and in his mighty power. Put on the full armor of God so that you can take your stand against the devil's schemes. For our struggle is not against flesh and blood, but against the rulers, against the authorities, against the powers of this dark world and against the spiritual forces of evil in the heavenly realms. Therefore put on the full armor of God, so that when the day of evil comes, you may be able to stand your ground, and after you have done everything, to stand. Stand firm then, with the belt of truth buckled around your waist, with the breastplate of righteousness in place, and with your feet fitted with the readiness that comes from the gospel of peace. In addition to all this, take up the shield of faith, with which you can extinguish all the flaming arrows of the evil one. Take the helmet of salvation and the sword of the Spirit, which is the word of God. And pray in the Spirit on all occasions with all kinds of prayers and requests. With this in mind, be alert and always keep on praying for all the saints.

(Ephesians 6:10-18)

*A*lthough the light of our God shines ever brighter, the darkness has greatly thickened. C. S. Lewis observes this phenomenon, when in his novel *That Hideous Strength,* he puts this observation in the mouth of Dr. Dimble as he converses with his wife:

> Have you ever noticed that the universe, and every little bit of the universe, is always hardening and narrowing and coming to a point? . . . Good is always getting better and bad is always getting worse: the possibilities of even apparent neutrality are always diminishing. The whole thing is sorting itself out all the time, coming to a point, getting sharper and harder. . . .

Mrs. Dimble replies that all this reminds her:

> . . . more of the bit in the Bible about the winnowing fan. Separating the wheat and the chaff. Or like Browning's line: "Life's business being just the terrible choice."[1]

The battle between good and evil is stepped up in this our day, and we are all involved in it, making the "terrible choice" whether prepared or not. Hopefully we are prepared by having put on the full armor of God (Ephesians 6:10-18) and by having asked for and received the true gift of battle. Once this is done, if we are sensitive to the Holy Spirit's leading, we soon become aware that there are many wrong ways to do battle.

Don't Allow Satan to Choose the Battleground

One of the strong temptations we must eschew is the enemy's attempt to get us to leave the positive work of the Kingdom. He works toward luring Christians from their creative, proper, and redemptive work, and down into battle on his own turf, one charged with his negatives: his accusations, rationale, deceptions, and lies. Nehemiah is a great role model for us here, and his story of intense spiritual warfare is one we should probably reread at times when we find our work withstood by our enemies (Nehemiah, chapters 1-6). Nehemiah's enemies were tireless in their efforts to stop the work God had entrusted to him—that of rebuilding the walls of Jerusalem. But Nehemiah simply refused to climb down from atop the walls where he was busy rebuilding and go down to fight with them. His enemies sent this message:

> "Come, let us meet together in one of the villages on the plain of Ono." But they were scheming to harm me; so I sent messengers to them with this reply: "I am carrying on a great project and cannot go down. Why should the work stop while I leave it and go down to you?" Four times they sent me the same message, and each time I gave them the same answer. (Nehemiah 6: 2b-4)

Note that Nehemiah repeats the same answer over and over again through his messengers. This is an important principle in communicating with persons who are determined to destroy us or the work. We let God give us the one word, that one objective word that is difficult for even an enemy to twist or misquote, and then we simply *keep on saying it.*

After that, Nehemiah's enemies began to slander him, with all manner of malice and deceit. But God was with him, and the walls were rebuilt. He was obedient to God, wise as to his enemies' tactics, and he ended up doing the "impossible" task.

Often we do not have the eyes to see the modern versions of Nehemiah's story, the times in warfare when the enemy attempts in much more subtle ways to lure us down onto his plain. A principle to remember is that our archenemy seeks to bring us into endless dialogue with himself through those persons he has deceived. We learn not to entertain the diabolical presence in this way. Such a dialogue is always carried out on the plane of the mind alone—the unassisted intellect or imagination—and we simply do not speak this reduced, desupernaturalized language. It is a language devoid of transcendent meaning and wisdom.

Besides the fact, therefore, that it is foolish to carry on a dialogue with the devil, we cannot translate our language into his. Sadly, however, more people (even Christians) understand this reduced language than the one containing the symbols that mediate to us ultimate meaning, truth, and glory. This is another way of stating that we as Christians have lost the greater part of our souls, together with the language and imagery with which to express the truths of the transcendent and eternal.[2]

I was asked to speak at a large general conference of a church denomination embroiled in spiritual warfare of the most flagrant kind. It was hoped that I would prevail over other speakers who were advocating the acceptance of sexual immorality within the clergy. I declined the invitation, not because I did not want to speak truth into the situation, but because I knew that many of the very Christians who wanted me to speak for orthodox Christianity would not—once the battle was joined—understand my language. And should God have been pleased to move in power, they also would not have understood or approved of the powerful move of the Holy Spirit that it would have taken to bring in the repentance and the healing necessary to really change things in that group.

I knew they would not be like Nehemiah's messengers with one objective word to impart, but that they would get hopelessly ensnared into "loving dialogue" with the enemy as his intents and purposes worked through those under his deception. Our main difficulty in the church battles of today is often with the well-meaning who have learned a spurious kind of empathy, an ersatz way of trying to love their enemies. In other words, these good folk have lost the words and symbols of the Kingdom and speak only the enemy's reduced language.

Another example is the endless church committees on "human sexuality" that meet year after year, endlessly debating and never, of course, coming to any conclusions other than the rationalizing of sin. These committees are often merely a screen for devising an apologetic for perverted sexual behavior. Only the highly trained and very wise heads, those not intimidated by this worldly logic and terminology, who are skilled in disarming patently false logic wherever it arises, should attempt to be the "salt" on such committees. Even then, such persons will often know that they are wasting valuable time, and that the job will simply have to be repeated again the very next year. The enemy tactic consists in constantly repeating the lie and in endlessly pounding away at the moral and spiritual real. The carnal aim is not to uncover and point up truth, but to dishearten those who stand for it. The aim is, through rationalization, to finally make a large entryway for sin into the leadership of the church, and for this the enemy has all the time in the world. After all, he is not engaged in the substantive, creative work of God's Kingdom—only in establishing himself as god.

Rather than go down on the enemy's turf, then, we band together in prayer and receive our instructions from the Lord. We then may well speak a word of truth into a demonized situation and take authority in Christ's name over demons, commanding them to depart. We are not, however, to wear ourselves out, thereby allowing ourselves to become discouraged or even deceived through fruitless and interminable dialogue—dialogue that only too often ends in compromise. Compromise is said to be the art of politics and diplomacy, but wise governments forsake the art when they are facing a murderous tyrant. Compromise spells the death knell in spiritual battle as we face the archtyrant—*Diabolos* himself.

Over and over again, in trying to help Christians embroiled in spiritual warfare, I find myself saying to them, "You are not to dialogue with the old man in anyone! That is merely to bring you into dialogue with the world, the flesh, and ultimately the devil himself!" The carnal old self in those deceived by the enemy has become a mouthpiece for the enemy's lies, slanders, blasphemies, and accusations. Such persons are used to bring the satanic deception they are under upon others. We not only learn to speak, do, and be the truth, but to dialogue only with the truth in another, that is, with the real person and the situation as it really is. It usually takes a good bit of explaining for this to be understood, and I often have to resort to C. S. Lewis's remarkable sketch about the seedy old actor (*The Great Divorce,* chapter 12) to finally make my point. In this story, the actor's wife, Sarah Smith of Golder's Green, would not dialogue with the old, illusory self in her posturing, self-serving husband. She would only speak to the true self, even though it had become almost nonexistent. It finally disappeared entirely as he chose, time after time, illusion and inessentiality over the radiant and substantive reality of heaven that was being offered him.[3] He simply would not leave off his self-pity, and his propensity, always, for shifting blame onto his wife, Sarah, for his unhappiness. Satan is the accuser, and if he cannot distract us in any other way, he would love to usurp all our time and energies in trying to answer his charges. Sarah Smith of Golder's Green did not waste her time or words.

We Are in a Battle That Is Already Won

One of the things to keep in mind in spiritual battle is that the forces of darkness are already defeated by Christ's death and rising, and the evil one's time is strictly limited. Rather than wrongfully striving with him, we are always to be praising, blessing, and thanking our God; we are to be rejoicing in Christ's triumphal train.

> But thanks be to God who always leads us in triumphal procession in Christ and through us spreads everywhere the fragrance of the knowledge of him.

For we are to God the aroma of Christ among those who are being saved and those who are perishing. . . . (2 Corinthians 2:14-15)

Fr. John Gaynor Banks wrote out the following in his prayer journal after meditating on 1 Corinthians 9:25: "Everyone who competes in the games goes into strict training. They do it to get a crown that will not last, but we do it to get a crown that will last forever." Then he wrote the following, a triumphal picture reflecting the true focus in spiritual battle:

MASTER: The saints were great lovers. Love is creative energy. Their love for Me was drawn inward and upward until they became free to serve the Highest. These holy ones, these athletes (1 Corinthians 9:25) of the Spirit, had their battles of course, but they triumphed not so much by any frantic striving with the forces of evil as by concentrating rather on the Sun of Righteousness. They absorbed the rays of My perennial light and heat, and so they literally transcended their lower selves and entered into oneness with the Divine.[4]

Nehemiah's enemies were outside the covenant and the people of God. All too often, our main onslaughts today come from within the organized church itself. And when this is the case, we have to be doubly careful. We must meditate upon Christ's teaching on the wheat and the tares and on His admonitions in the Sermon on the Mount. In this way, and as we prayerfully listen to God, it is possible to be spared from misjudging others, while at the same time we rightly discern and continue in love and unity with our brothers and sisters in Christ. As important, rather than becoming ensnared in misplaced empathy and sympathy with sin, we will be enabled to face issues squarely and name them for what they are.

Wielding the Sword of Truth, Yet Making Peace

Our Lord taught, "Blessed are the peacemakers, for they shall be called sons of God." Barclay, in his commentary on Matthew 5:9, speaks to this word of truth. First of all, it is in the loving, active *facing* of issues that we *make* peace; we can't evade issues and think we are peacemakers:

There is many a person who thinks that he is loving peace, when in fact he is piling up trouble for the future, because he refuses to face the situation and to take the action which the situation demands.[5]

Peacemaking requires that we get the mind of Christ, His love and wisdom replacing our incomplete knowledge and ignorance. At times, it even requires that we take up a whip—after the manner of Christ in the temple with the money-changers. We do all of this, however, with an eye toward establishing right relationships between man and God, and man and man. We are to love our fellows "with actions and in truth" (1 John 3:18). The following, says Barclay, is what Jesus means in this beatitude:

> The Jewish Rabbis held that the highest task which a man can perform is to establish *right relationships* between man and man.[6]

In doing this, however, as we often discover in spiritual battle, there are

> people who are always storm-centres of trouble and bitterness and strife. Wherever they are they are either involved in quarrels themselves or the cause of quarrels of others. They are trouble-makers. . . .[7]

It is no small thing to speak prophetically and to also make peace. We can't always do it. We can never make peace at the expense of truth. True peace comes only with the truth. May we be uncompromising channels of God's truth as well as His peace. In speaking the truth in love, may we plant deep in the hearts of men and women everywhere the seeds of lasting, even eternal peace.

PRAYER

Lord, preserve us from fighting Your battle in our own strength. May we never pull up the precious wheat with the tares. May we triumph, not by frantic striving with the forces of evil, but by keeping our eyes securely fastened on You.

We ask that You make of us expert peacemakers. Help us, in the power of the Spirit, to clear the path of obstacles to making Your peace—real peace—in Your Body here on earth.

Wrongly Personifying Sin

> Then the Lord said to Cain, "Why are you angry? Why is your face downcast? If you do what is right, will you not be accepted? But if you do not do what is right, sin is crouching at the door; it desires to have you, but you must master it." (Genesis 4:6-7)

Here in this remarkable passage, sin is personified. A Biblical commentator explains the origins of this metaphoric speech: "The Hebrew word for crouching is the same as an ancient Babylonian word referring to an evil demon crouching at the door of a building to threaten the people inside. Sin may thus be pictured here as just such a demon, waiting to pounce on Cain—it desires to have him."[8]

Sin within the human heart is a destroyer, and there could hardly be a better metaphor for evil than we have here. This personification of sin enables us to better comprehend its power to devour, and the Scriptural symbols, metaphors, similes, parables, and figures of speech are invaluable in helping us to express these grave matters in such a way as the heart can fully grasp them.

It is one thing, however, to understand sin as figuratively demonic, and quite another to deal with sin in the human breast as though it were in fact a demonic entity rather than a transgression for which the soul is held responsible before God.

In this day when we are so often ignorant of the soul and its motions, many Christians armed with the terminology of deliverance from evil spirits name these motions of the soul (or lack of them) as demons. They identify an absence of the holy graces, good emotions and feelings, together with a corresponding profusion of sinful vices, fantasies, feelings, and attitudes within a soul as demonic infestations. To do this is not only to fail to discern the problem aright—the sin as well as the psychological deficiencies and problems—but even more seriously it is to fail to see the person needing help as human at all. We become thoroughgoing gnostics who spiritualize away the human element—a grievous kind of ignorance that is nowhere modeled for us in the Scriptures. Jesus dealt with *persons*, men and women with full souls, and He helped these souls name and renounce their sins. He never failed to do these folk the grave and great honor of seeing them as persons.

We are souls, with a spirit at our center that either is or is not linked with Christ. In failing to recognize the full soul that is another person, we in effect X out all that is uniquely human about that person's creation. We delete the human. If we fail to see and revere the unique person in the one for whom we pray, we will fail to help that person deal effectively with the real sin and the real emotional difficulties that are there. We may even, in our ignorance and zeal to help the person, name these things as demons and fancy ourselves as "binding" and casting them out. It is the *sin* that is to be bound and the *person* loosed from it. In contrast, the wounds are to be healed. If these have provided a place for demons to hide, we can easily enough expel them once they are discerned.

In ministry that fails to recognize the above, persons are robbed of the great privilege of coming present to their own hearts and there—in the presence of God—finally coming to understand who they are. Rather than helping such persons recognize their sin and repent of it, change their diseased attitudes and allow God to create in them new hearts, we can be in the unhappy position of casting out nonexistent demons of this or that. We will be attempting to "cast out" character traits and deficiencies. Too, and just as tragically, all that is positive within that soul and unique to its creation as a human being will be overlooked. Through ignoring the good, it will go unaffirmed, and, in effect, denied existence. It will not be called into life. A vital step in prayer for this person's healing will have been missed.

Thus today there are well-meaning Christians whose prayers for others are filled with speaking to demons—mostly nonexistent ones.[9] These people need more instruction in the theology of the cross and repentance, as well as clarification about what an authentic gift of discerning of spirits is. All too often, the authentic gifts of wisdom and discernment have been first obscured and then replaced by a faulty theology, often developed from a mistaken exegesis of the Scriptures. A faulty "methodology" quickly follows.

In any one of the three great barriers to wholeness may be found a demon hiding away in a nest that a sin or wound has made for it. In ministry to the person, these demons manifest themselves, and even as Christ would command, "Come out!" or "Be muzzled!" and always simply, "Depart!"—so do we. This is the easiest part of healing prayer once a person has confessed his sin or been released from the effects of another's sins against him. But grievous hurt is done, and prayers for others are needlessly ineffective when, rather than being able to listen to God and to that unique and precious human soul that is looking up to God, we start clamoring about demons and commanding imaginary ones to depart.

It is this unscriptural *practice of the presence of the powers of darkness* and the very grave dangers involved in such a practice that I want to address next. Also, I want to issue a strong warning about the fact that many (again principally those within certain parts of the renewal movement) are failing to understand the planes of spiritual battle that are properly ours and those that properly belong to God and His angelic hosts. All errors here eventuate, not in a practice of the Presence of God, but in the practice of the presence of our archenemy and his minions. And when we practice his presence long enough and seriously enough, he shows up. In focusing on him, we manage eventually to make a pathway for him to come.

Don't Focus on Satan, Demons, or Principalities and Powers

> There are two equal and opposite errors into which our race can fall about devils. One is to disbelieve in their existence. The other is to believe, and to feel an excessive and unhealthy interest in them. They themselves are equally pleased by both errors, and hail a materialist or a magician with the same delight.[10]

Many today who lecture on spiritual warfare start out with the vital statement that we are not to focus on Satan, but then the overall effect of their teachings lead both themselves and their disciples to do that very thing. Often, by way of warning those they are teaching, they will even quote Lewis in his familiar statement of our well-known predicament quoted above, thoroughly agree with it, and then go on in practice to live out something else.

Two practices, both that focus on the demonic, have come together to do the most mischief. One particularly involves "doing spiritual warfare" *against* principalities and powers, done by those who fail to understand what planes of battle are properly ours and those which properly belong to God and His angelic hosts. The other has to do with the misuse of the terms "binding and loosing"— the misapplying of those terms to demons, and then the resulting mistaken practice of *praying against Satan* rather than *to* God. We pray to God for those souls under Satan's foul aegis, helping them to confess their sins and thereby come out from under the control of principalities and powers. This does not mean that we will not from time to time discern strongholds over persons, nations, cities, and communities. But it means we will be very careful of our focus. It means we will always be found ministering to God—singing and speaking to Him in worship, thanksgiving, and praise. We will always be found practicing the Presence of God. In doing this, as demons, principalities or powers are discerned directly in our path, we speak directly to them, and command them to leave.

Planes of Warfare

Because of ignorance about the true nature of our souls, of misteaching, and of failure to abide by the Scriptural model of the gift of battle, it is amazingly easy for Christians to be confused over what it means to "do spiritual warfare." Any confusion here leaves us thinking the battle is ours rather than the Lord's, and we then battle according to our own understanding and strength. To do this even in part, is dangerous, and there is really no excuse for it. The Scriptures are very clear here, not only with regard to the way Christ and the apostles modeled the warfare for us, but also with regard to the plane of battle that is properly ours, as distinguished from that which properly belongs to God and to His angelic hosts.

A Christian who fails to understand this and who puts these misguided notions into practice can become dangerous to anyone who comes under his influence. The enemy, through gaining that Christian's focus, will have found a "landing platform" through which to "touch down" and bring in all manner of mischief and deception.

I saw a very dramatic instance of this in a large overseas base for training young Christians as missionaries. One of the leaders had been sharing about the unusual amount of spiritual warfare they were unaccountably caught up in and was asking for the prayers of the people in order to discern the cause. Several young men were then invited to stand and pray for the group. These men, obviously still in the throes of the "drive toward power," did indeed pray. But not to God. They faced the four corners of the world and with great voice started commanding principalities and powers. I could see they were quite experienced at this and was immediately alarmed as I realized in my spirit that they had made contact with the evil "principality." Dark power crackled down, and bizarre things happened simultaneously on campus. An explosion occurred in one building, while fire broke out in several places on the grounds. Later, as I talked to the leaders on that base, I shared with them how such a practice makes a landing platform for the enemy. They acknowledged that they had experienced all manner of confusion and warfare in connection with the ministry of these particular young persons.

Perhaps one of the most difficult experiences along this line that we as the PCM team have encountered will reveal even further how very dangerous such practices can be. This situation involved intercession and a seriously misguided group's attempt to "bind principalities and powers over a city."

A number of years back, several Christian leaders approached me within a short time span with a word they had received from the Lord in regard to PCM's need to ask for intercessors. One was awakened in the middle of the night to intercede for us and was given visions of the battle we are in, especially in regard to ministering to persons with sexual neuroses. Another had a specific prophetic word that he spoke over the PCM team, a word to the effect that, from this time on, those persons called to intercede for this ministry will play an increasingly vital and even critical part in the work God has for us to do. Part of that word admonished us to: "Pray that an army of intercessors be raised up, and they will go before you, springing the snares and traps of the enemy."

We did this very thing, and through our newsletter we also asked for intercessors. God mercifully raised up many to pray for us, and only heaven will reveal the incredible blessing this has been. We are amazed to see how faithful God is to spring the snares and the traps of the enemy.

In publishing our need, however, we unearthed the dangerous, unscriptural ways of interceding that some persons have gotten into, and unfortunately, we drew them toward us as well. These misguided ones had one thing in common—the idea that to "do spiritual warfare" was to focus on demons and on principalities and powers over cities and to "bind" them. To "bind" them was to take control over them through verbal assertions—spoken out into the airwaves but aimed toward "them"—i.e., the principalities and powers over cities. These folk, influenced by an extreme teaching (referred to by some as "Faith Formula Theology"),[11] attempt to "control" our Almighty and all-knowing holy God in the same way, believing that if they state their objectives in certain ways and affirm them in "faith," they thereby "force" God to do their bidding. (This is not Scriptural faith, but an inducing of a certain psychological mind-set.) These intercessors see themselves as binding demonic powers by talking to them—in effect praying to demons and by repeating over and over such things as, "I bind you, (whatever name the demon or principality or power appeared to have), and I take authority over you." This is what they called being an intercessor or "doing spiritual warfare."

I've just read John Dawson's book *Taking Our Cities for God: How to Break Spiritual Strongholds*. In it there is no practicing of the presence of demons and praying to them. The misguided intercessors I described are trying to do what John Dawson does and teaches, but unlike him, they focus on the demonic rather than on the sin to be confessed. Dawson faithfully publishes the word of salvation in our great cities, places where unconfessed dark sins have kept people from freedom to grow in righteousness. He helps people to discern and repent of the root sins in their cities. Thereby they loosen the city from the power of demonic principalities and forces that have a right to rule because of unremitted sin. John Dawson speaks and teaches on the healing of communities and cities, indeed, even nations, in the same way as we do of the healing of persons. It is through healing their memories—by confessing the sins that bind them—and by loosing the people and their communities into new, substantive, creative life. He stresses praise and thanksgiving to God—an utter and wonderful practice of the Presence. He speaks of intercessions and of listening to God for the healing word He is speaking for that locale, that city.

All of this John Dawson speaks of in terms of "doing spiritual warfare"— of taking souls from the kingdom of darkness and bringing them into the kingdom of light. And true evangelism such as this will always constellate spiritual warfare. But this can as well be named the ministry of the confessional writ large—a ministry that the church has all but forgotten. There are, therefore, many today who "do spiritual warfare," but rather than following Scriptural principles, focus instead on the forces of evil.

The first time the team and I were exposed to the darkness that comes out of these dangerous prayer practices, we were to minister in a church where many had gathered both to learn to pray for others and for help for themselves. Several teachers of these wrong ways of focusing on the demonic had come— not to learn—but to try to impress me and the team. It did not take long for us to be *impressed* in a most negative fashion, for never have we known, in the context of starting out to conduct a prayer and healing service, the unleashing of such darkness. We knew immediately that these persons had inadvertently first invited and then stirred up the darkness and that their practices were exceedingly confusing and dangerous to any naive soul who might get caught up in them.

Before the first service, their leader said to me: "We pray and fast against principalities and powers [meaning demonic forces], in advance, before we ever go to a place, and we have done this for you. You are now safe because we have accomplished this, we have *bound* the principalities and powers in the high places over this city. . . ."

Right away I knew they were in serious trouble, but I could not help them for they spoke only a bleak "spiritualized" language that was overcharged and left no room for reasoned interaction, communication, or fellowship. For them, there was no room for the truly beautiful, either from the realm of nature and the fully human or from the heavenly. There were only demons, and these were to be sought out and dealt with. With these folk, there was no practice of the Presence—only an imagination filled with the demonic.

Unknowingly, these persons were caught up in a spiritual pride beyond the ordinary. In effect, they said to me, "We are the only ones really who know how to 'bind' the devil, how to deliver the seriously demonized person, etc., and that is because we really know how to do spiritual warfare. We seek and engage the 'biggies' themselves, the principalities and powers. We've come to do this for you and show you how it is done."

Thinking themselves to be intercessors *extraordinaire* and the only ones "doing" spiritual warfare, they were in effect practicing the presence of demons. They had drawn the attention of dark powers toward the Body of Christ in that place by *praying to them* and through pridefully seeing themselves as "binding" them. As it turned out, they had become a channel through which a "principality and power"—a ruling spirit over that city—descended into our midst. It was one meant to be withstood in spiritual battle only by the holy angels as we battled properly for the salvation of souls.

As we began the ministry there, our hearts were opened to discern the huge entity. It named itself and threatened each one of us on the team. There were bizarre happenings and unbelievable confusion as we called on the power of God to quell the dark power.

Needless to say, we were brought into a spiritual conflict of unusual proportions, one that need never have occurred. These folk, thinking they were intercessors, had merely succeeded in informing the powers of darkness in, over, and around that city that we were coming! In listening to them proudly relate all their hair-raising tussles with dark powers, I realized they take this "gift" with them every place they go. The way they pray assures that the persons they are involved with will get into dramatic and terrible confrontations with evil powers, and some of them will come under serious demonic deception. This is dangerous error.

I would not tell of this extreme practice except for the fact that it is no longer a rare circumstance. These practices are spreading (usually in milder forms) to well-meaning persons who intercede daily. Too, as one who helps people to wholeness in Christ, I am aware of the many who attempt to cope with life by (usually unconsciously) striving to control events or persons around themselves—named today the codependent personality. Often these persons, in fear of the demonic, attempt to "control" it in these ways of prayer—and thereby hope to stave off the evil. Thus, "talking to the devil" and practicing his foul presence becomes a dangerous adjunct to the codependence from which these people already suffer. Fearing conflict of any kind, they attempt to safeguard themselves through "controlling" character traits in other persons, traits they may come to perceive as demons.

Some, when shown what they are doing will ask, "But how can I pray?" In other words, there are precious Christian souls out there now who no longer know how to pray without talking to the devil. "How," they ask, when embroiled in spiritual battle with their enemies, "do I pray about this lie," or "this slander," or this darkness of any kind? "Shall I get up an hour early and do spiritual warfare?" meaning, "Shall I arise an hour early and focus on demons and bind them?" No, this is never the thing to do. It is great to get up an hour early and focus on God, affirm the fact that He has won the victory, and ask Him how it is we should trust Him in the face of the darkness and slander coming against us. We have no need to try to control that darkness and slander. He's doing it, and we trust our present and future entirely to Him! It is not by focusing on "demons" of lying, slander, etc., by finding names for them, or by "binding" them continually in prayer—that way only brings one into striving and fear at best, and demonic oppression and even deception at worst.[12] Instead we look straight up to God and talk to Him. Christ has bound the enemy, and ours is merely the mop-up action. In showing us how to pray, the Scriptures record no one focusing on demons. Rather, as Christ taught us, we pray, "But deliver us from the evil one." In other words, "You do it, Lord." We don't get involved in "works" prayers to be free of principalities and powers. We trust God and He sends out His holy angels to do the warfare. If a demonic power happens across our path, once we've discerned it, we command it to leave. Only then do we speak to it—a foul presence that the Holy Spirit has shown us is there. And we expel it with a word: "In Christ's name, be gone!"

We won a great victory in the place where this dark incident happened. God is faithful, and people were reborn, spiritually and psychologically. Many there were coming out of the deep darkness that characterizes our culture today. Included were persons with backgrounds in the occult, witchcraft, sexual perversion, and so on. To these circumstances, of course, we are well accustomed and to dealing with any demonic infestation that might happen to be in their lives. But we paid a much higher price than usual, in terms of the intensity of the battle and the sheer physical and spiritual stress such a circumstance exacts; it was absolutely unnecessary.

Two examples here will show how wonderfully a true intercession works. We were to minister in another country at a well-known but liberal seminary in a city remarkably corrupt even by today's standards. We knew we were entering into great spiritual warfare for the souls within that university, and especially for those training for theological professorships and the pastorate in many other nations. As we confessed the sins of that city and university, known and unknown, and cried out to God for His anointing to preach, teach, and heal in His name, our spiritual eyes were opened. The Lord showed us the angelic battle going on over the seminary where we would be. We saw, as it were, before we ever arrived, the holy angels battling and overcoming the evil angels in answer to our prayers. We had a most incredible ministry there, out of which revival continues to spread, and we did not leave there needlessly weakened physically through unnecessary confrontations with evil forces.

Another example is of a time in England when our full conference was being videotaped before a large group. The Lord was mightily stretching forth His hand to heal and to save. Right in the midst of this, Fr. William Beasley's eyes were opened, and he saw an immense and terrible "principality and power." But it was outside attempting to peer in. It wanted so badly to know what was going on, but it couldn't find out. The holy angels were with us as always, and they had certainly done their part ahead of time. And there had been no misguided group of Christians who—by focusing on this evil entity—had made a pathway for it to insinuate itself into our midst.

Jessie Penn-Lewis's book *War on the Saints,* often called a "classic" on spiritual warfare, has influenced people into these erroneous ways of thinking about and "doing spiritual warfare."[13] One of her theses is that revival does not continue because we do not understand spiritual warfare, and she then proceeds throughout her book to focus primarily on demons rather than on sin. For example, speaking of Israel after the time of Moses and Joshua, she writes, "When these leaders died, the nation sank into darkness, *brought about* by evil spirit powers, drawing the people into idolatry and sin. . . ." (italics mine, p. 28). The Scriptural teaching, of course, is that the sin (apostasy) of the people came first and thereby left them open to the powers of darkness.

This reversal is everywhere apparent in her thinking and runs throughout the book, leaving those who follow her ideas to their logical conclusion with an emphasis always on the demonic. The Holy Spirit's gift of discerning of spirits is apparently not understood, and a tortuous system of "deliverance" through "knowledge" (almost scientism) is given to help the person decide if an idea or a bodily movement is a "counterfeit" and the result of demonic deception. She in effect reduces the soul into a battleground between good and evil forces, while at the same time she minimizes the capacity of the Christian's will to determine which will have the victory. She so emphasizes deception that she leaves the believer in great fear as to the reliability of his own understanding of Scripture or his own ability to hear from the Lord.

Though she liberally cites Scriptures, to use her methods would be to indict any one of the Old or New Testament saints. The knowledge she espouses, unfortunately, is one of doubting and analyzing everything and everyone. Any manifestation of the Holy Spirit or even of natural emotion for that matter, as well as all experience, is immediately suspect; it is to be deemed as counterfeit and caused by demons until it can be proven otherwise. Unfortunately, in her system, hampered as it is by a terrible rift between head and heart, there would never be a way of determining this. The "methods" are those of denial (of emotional and physical needs and their expressions) and of over-spiritualization.

She writes that "the Son of God dealt with the powers of darkness as the active, *primary* cause of the sin and suffering of this world" (italics mine, p. 35). The person who adheres to such a theology and psychology will treat every sin and motion of the soul having to do with suffering as an occasion for contending with a demonic entity. This is what has happened with the practice of "casting out" what amounts to perceived character traits and deficiencies as though these were demons rather than sins to be confessed or deficiencies to be remedied through prayer.

Here again, we have to say no. The Scriptures tell us that these things proceed "out of the heart" of man. It is the unhealed and/or unconverted heart that invites demonic participation. Mrs. Penn-Lewis's teaching leaves people either paralyzed or cut off from what is authentically human and deeply suspicious of it. She holds, as well, what amounts to a Manichaean view of the body (pp. 130ff.), not an incarnational one, and therefore especially warns people about practicing the Presence of God. The effect of her teaching is to disable people from living in the knowledge of the Presence of God with us, while at the same time, they are literally to be conscious always of the presence of demons. A sad irony here is that one loses out not only on Incarnational Reality, the Presence of God with us, but also on the power to discern and to deliver from actual demons.

The dark seeds of many excesses regarding the demonic and spiritual warfare that we see today are rooted in the ideas taken from this one particularly influential book. I have been in the ministry long enough to have seen many truly tragic losses as ministers and whole groups came under serious demonic deception after carrying her teachings to their logical conclusions. A serious study and acceptance of what is in this book leads to seeing demons everywhere and in everyone—a real practice of the presence of demons.

People who thoroughly espouse her teachings are hurt and stymied in every conceivable way—a paranoia strikes at their intellectual as well as their intuitive and imaginative ways of knowing. Their imaginations are finally filled with demonic myths—the very thing Penn-Lewis is attempting to avoid.

In many cases, persons become fearful of others, even paranoid, and the grievous sins of slander and pharisaical pride result, all the evil fruit of fastening one's eyes on darkness rather than on God. Those wishing to know where so many of the slanderous cult hunters get their theology, as well as the blueprint for their witch-hunts, need only look at this book in its unabridged form. Anyone with an incarnational understanding of reality and an understanding of God's power to heal emotional and psychological sicknesses will be attacked by these persons. In this way a very real spiritual battle within the church ensues as the work of the Holy Spirit and the practice of the Presence of God are denied and condemned.

Because the ideas in this book continue to influence thinking in certain fundamentalist, evangelical, and Pentecostal circles, inspiring others to write in the same way, these misconceptions keep spawning movements that deeply trouble the Body of Christ. Mrs. Penn-Lewis's exegesis of the Scriptures is faulty in critical respects. Due to the ongoing influence of her book, I hope that qualified theologians and psychologists will fully critique this work and the teachings that have come out of it. I hope these will be critiques understandable to laypersons, for they have been greatly impacted by Penn-Lewis's teachings.

When she wrote her book, it had some value because she recognized the existence of demons in a time when most of the church thoroughly disbelieved the Scriptures in this regard. Often in stressing a lost or neglected truth, people fall into the opposite error of overemphasizing it. In this particular case, Mrs. Penn-Lewis simply did not have the theological and psychological understanding needed to write on these matters and was reacting in fear to the needs multitudes of people coming into revival had for emotional healing and training. Her writings on the cross of Christ have blessed multitudes of Christians, and it is hoped that this critique of her book on spiritual warfare will in no way disparage the good of her writings.

Finding the right words to explain lost concepts to a particular generation is difficult. We who read Penn-Lewis now can easily understand the cultural blindness she and others wrestled with. For example, we know that her culture profoundly suspected the expression of feeling and emotion. Both were severely repressed. When feeling and emotion burst forward under the influence of the healing work of the Spirit, or when the physical body reacted to God's power and Presence, these occurrences appeared to them as unseemly, even as demonic. Manifestations of God's Presence among them, therefore, had to be filtered through the blinders peculiar to their day and age. We are humbled at this, knowing that none of us escape fully the blindness with which our own age afflicts us.

The great theological and spiritual writers manage to see clearly the mistakes of their age and to transcend them. While recognizing and lamenting their own insufficiencies, they allow other ages and times to speak a corrective word to these. In this day of great spiritual battle, may the Lord bless us increasingly with such writers.

CHAPTER 15

Restoring the Christian Hope of Heaven and the Grace to Persevere

Blessed are those whose strength is in you,
who have set their hearts on pilgrimage. . . .
They go from strength to strength,
till each appears before God in Zion.

(Psalm 84:5, 7)

Dear friends, now we are children of God, and what we will be has not yet been made known. But we know that when he appears, we shall be like him, for we shall see him as he is. Everyone who has this hope in him purifies himself, just as he is pure.

(1 John 3:2-3)

To have the hope of heaven restored to the soul is first of all to regain the great hope of Christ's appearing and the mind-boggling promise that we shall be like Him. The power of hope is mysterious in all the ways it ministers life to us, but in this Scripture we see that this hope "purifies us" even now. This is no small promise at any time, but it is especially important for us who live in these closing days of the twentieth century when institutionalized unbelief, with all its inherent unrighteousness, has made such inroads into the Christian symbolic system and into the Christian soul.

The Scriptures are filled with awesome promises to all who hope in Christ, and thereby overcome. We shall, we are told, be given "the right to eat from the tree of life" (Revelation 2:7), and we will "eat of the hidden manna." One of the promises that speaks to my heart is that of being renamed: "I will also give him a white stone with a new name written on it, known only to him who receives it" (Revelation 2:17). Is this our final naming? Perhaps so, since it is written in a white stone. All Christian healing has to do with calling forth the true self; that is, with being named in the Presence of Christ. We are told that Christ will write the name of God and of the holy city upon us (Revelation 3:12) and that we will "be sons of God" (Revelation 21:7) whom "the second death" will not "hurt at all" (Revelation 2:11). We will have God as our God (Revelation 21:7), and be given "the right to sit with" Christ on His throne (Revelation 3:21). In short, we will "inherit all things" (Revelation 21:7). What a wonderful healing it is to regain the capacity to hope and rejoice in all these things and in all the rest that the Scriptures promise to those who persevere in Christ.

The Miraculous Power God Gives to Persevere

> In this world you will have trouble. But take heart! I have overcome the world. (John 16:33)

> Do not be overcome by evil, but overcome evil with good. (Romans 12:21)

There are few things in life more comforting than Christian friends who understand what ministry on a fallen planet is all about. Through the years, Professor Carol Kraft, who teaches the German language and literature at Wheaton College, has been just such a friend. She is a treasured confidant, one in whom I can confide my deepest concerns, for she is not only a trusted friend, but she has learned how to listen. She really *hears* whatever it is I'm struggling with, and then has the knack of finding something that either exactly expresses it or helps me come to terms with it. She gave me the card reproduced below to illustrate the miraculous as we Christians so often experience it.

© Desclozeaux

This, it seems to me, illustrates the power to persevere that is given us along with the unique and great Christian virtue of hope. Surely, it would be difficult to find a truer picture of the sheer grace God gives us not only to survive but also to overcome the impossible. It depicts the very way this grace is experienced—as we inch a straight and steady line through a fallen, hostile world to our true home.

I'm sure some who read these lines have faced or are even now facing the impossible in terms of what God has called them to do and to be. Perhaps calamity, in the form of circumstances so irrational and dark that they could only have been engineered by the powers of darkness, is even now on their horizon, barreling toward them. The enemy's blow is calculated to maim or to crush— to stop them right in their tracks. But God's message to His own is ever the same: "My power and the strength that I give you are sufficient. Call upon it, ask for it, see if I will not cause all grace to abound toward you!"

St. Paul knew and taught with all his might this great truth: "God is able to make all grace abound to you, so that in all things at all times, having all that you need, you will abound in every good work" (2 Corinthians 9:8). It is no small thing to abound in every good work when boulders the size of mountains hit us, but that is exactly what we can do when we place our trust, not in ourselves or in other created things, but wholly in God. We learn to cry out with the psalmist, "You are a faithful God!"

A word St. Paul uses to describe this kind of grace, the very grace of God, is *polupoikilos* which means many-colored. William Barclay, commenting on Ephesians 3:8-13, says, "The idea in this word is that the grace of God will match with any situation which life may bring us. There is nothing of light or dark, of sunshine or of shadow, for which it is not triumphantly adequate." No matter what we are struggling with, as ministers or as suffering persons who desperately need forgiveness and healing, God's grace is sufficient. Jesus, with implicit faith in the Father, said it all when He looked directly at His troubled disciples and said: "With man this is impossible, but with God all things are possible" (Matthew 19:26b).

Obstacles in the Way of Hope

Some, having read thus far, may be shocked at how passive they are about the eternal and fear that nothing can awaken in them this hope. For other Christians, especially those who have not yet been touched by the Spirit's renewing and who are not living on the cutting edge where they see God deeply touching people and putting broken lives back together, the materialism of the past several hundred years has seeped, almost irreparably it seems, into their souls. As C. S. Lewis has said, it has had the effect of removing heaven from their eyes. For others, the passion for man's approval has dimmed their hopes. It seems needful to look more closely at this dread loss and to assure people that God delights in restoring hope to the soul. The hope of heaven may not be regained on the natural level—but we need only seek Him above all else and earnestly petition Him for its restoring.

There is a sense in which we are all victims of a materialistic age, for in our fallen world there is always some very large exterior obstacle to faith. The largest one, however, is interior. There is that within us that prefers, like Milton's Satan, to reign in hell rather than to serve in heaven. Here, as in all that is amiss with the soul, pride must be confronted. We must fight hard against it in the strength that God gives.

The Passion for Fame vs. the Hope of Immortality

> To those who by persistence in doing good seek glory, honor and immortality, he will give eternal life. But for those who are self-seeking and who reject the truth and follow evil, there will be wrath and anger. (Romans 2:7-8)

A passion for earthly glory wars against and annihilates the Christian's hope of immortality and the legitimate heavenly glory he is to seek. An incredible teaching, this: that eternal life is given to those who by persistence in doing good seek glory, honor, and immortality.

> I tell you the truth, unless a kernel of wheat falls to the ground and dies, it remains only a single seed. But if it dies, it produces many seeds. The man who loves his life will lose it, while the man who hates his life in this world will keep it for eternal life. (John 12:24-25)

Christ's teaching here, as the NIV notes state, "rules out ambition" and reveals in the most emphatic terms that "to concentrate on one's own success is to lose what matters." Rather, our Lord speaks of the honor that comes from God and the conditions for receiving such an awesome thing: "Whoever serves me must follow me; and where I am, my servant also will be. My Father will honor the one who serves me" (John 12:26).

John Milton in Sonnet XXII (on his blindness) refers to fame as "the world's vain mask," and having gained it, he hoped to be led through it. He concerned himself with the classical poets' desire for it, realizing how inferior it was to the great Christian hope of reward. In *Lycidas* he alludes to the ambition for fame as "that last infirmity of Noble mind . . ." and says:

> *Fame is no plant that grows on mortal soil,*
> *Nor in the glistering foil [foil: setting of a jewel]*
> *Set off to th' world, . . .*

Tacitus, in *Histories IV,* speaks of "the passion for glory" as "the last from which even wise men free themselves." Nothing so well shows the sordidness and pride in all this, even the mindlessness of it, as C. S. Lewis's "famous artist" in *The Great Divorce.* A bright and holy Spirit, one of the saints triumphant, was sent to invite him to choose heaven and all its incredible light and beauty, but he is only interested in painting it.

"When you painted on earth—at least in your earlier days—it was because you caught glimpses of Heaven in the earthly landscape. The success of your painting was that it enabled others to see the glimpses too. But here you are having the thing itself. It is from here that the messages came. There is no good *telling* us about this country, for we see it already. In fact we see it better than you do."

But the poor artist cannot be interested in heaven; he can only be interested in his "treatment" of it.

"No. You're forgetting," said the Spirit. "That was not how you began. Light itself was your first love: you loved paint only as a means of telling about light."

"Oh, that's ages ago, . . . One becomes more and more interested in paint for its own sake."

"One does, indeed. I also have had to recover from that. It was all a snare. Ink and catgut and paint were necessary down there, but they are also dangerous stimulants. Every poet and musician and artist, but for Grace, is drawn away from love of the thing he tells, to love of the telling till, down in Deep Hell, they cannot be interested in God at all but only in what they say about Him. For it doesn't stop at being interested in paint, you know. They sink lower—become interested in their own personalities and then in nothing but their own reputations."

The artist, thinking himself to be not "much troubled in *that* way," nevertheless goes on to ask the shining Spirit if he has met certain artists in heaven, persons who are still famous on earth. He is dismayed to hear that if they are there, the Spirit has not yet run across them (after all, there are a lot of people there, many he has not as yet met):

"But surely in the case of distinguished people, you'd hear?"

"But they aren't distinguished—no more than anyone else. Don't you understand? The Glory flows into everyone, and back from everyone: like light and mirrors. But the light's the thing."

"Do you mean there are no famous men?"

"They are all famous. They are all known, remembered, recognized by the only Mind that can give a perfect judgment."[1]

All vain ambition, seeking after the approval and honor that comes from man, is only a substitute for reality: the hope of heavenly glory and immortality. This hope comes with keeping our focus on God, thereby maintaining our first love: "Thou shalt love the Lord thy God with all thy heart and with all thy soul and with all thy strength."

We are saddened from time to time to see the work of Christians who seem to be in the same sort of trouble as the artist in Lewis's story. The proper fear of God or hope of heaven is absent from their "seeing"—at least it isn't reflected in their work. Instead we see complaints about suffering here on earth, an elevation of self-pity, and a willingness to blame God. The real power of God is absent, replaced by a need to reduce God to their own size, intellect, and imagination. Today the odd thing is that so few Christians object. Surely this reflects, besides the loss of Christian hope, the loss of the real Presence of God and the awe and the humility that we as creatures know in such a light.

Have I received a ministry from the Lord? If so, I have to be loyal to it, to count my life precious only for the fulfilling of that ministry. Think of the satisfaction it will be to hear Jesus say—"Well done, good and faithful servant"; to know that you have done what He sent you to do.[2]

What a revolution would come to us all, if it became the one fixed aim and ambition of our lives to stand before God, and to do always those things that are pleasing in His sight.[3]

Hope, what it is and what it means, is surely a mystery. Who can fully understand these words: "Christ within the believer is the *hope of glory*" (Colossians 1:27) or the truth that ours is "a faith and knowledge resting on the *hope of eternal life*" (Titus 1:2). Glory, another part of the authentic Christian mystery, is intertwined with hope. "Eschatalogical glory," as the NIV commentary on Romans 5:2 points out, "is the hope of the Christian." Glorification, as a theological term, is synonymous with immortality. And Christian hope is to be understood only in the context of glory. We will understand more about hope if we meditate upon the Scriptural references to *glory, glorify,* and *glorified.* Together with meditating on Christ's resurrection and the great Christian hope of immortality, we could ask God to increase our desire for heaven and all it contains and for the anticipation of a future state in which we will have a new body patterned after Christ's glorified body. Then, if we have substituted the favor of men and the things of this world for that which is only God's and heaven's to give, we have the great privilege of asking for the grace to deeply repent. We can be turned around to once again face Him. We are no longer compelled to substitute the shadow for the real, our impressions about glory for the thing itself.[4]

PRAYER

O Lord, be glorified in our midst. Enable us with all our might to exalt and glorify Your name and to give thanks. Fill us, O Lord, with thanksgiving. May the hope of glory be awakened in each one of us.

Hope Is Mythic

One of the reasons we can never closely define hope is because it is mythic; it is mythic in its longing for a good too great to put into words. Such words as *hope* and *glory* require an imaginative response, and the Scriptures are full of such responses. Another reason is because you and I too are mythic—more myth than fact, as Dr. Clyde Kilby[5] would say. We have utterly transcendent dimensions, and words such as *hope* and *glory* reflect this fact. The following quotes from the works of Lewis will flood light on these statements:

> It is perfectly easy to go on all your life giving explanations of religion, love, morality, honour, and the like, *without having been inside any of them.* And if you do that, you are simply playing with counters. You go on explaining a thing without knowing what it is. That is why a great deal of contemporary thought is, strictly speaking, thought about nothing—all the apparatus of thought busily working in a vacuum.[6] (Italics mine)

> Human intellect is incurably abstract. Pure mathematics is the type of successful thought. Yet the only realities we experience are concrete—this pain, this pleasure, this dog, this man. While we are loving the man, bearing the pain, enjoying the pleasure, we are not intellectually apprehending Pleasure, Pain or Personality. When we begin to do so, on the other hand, the concrete realities sink to the level of mere instances or examples: we are no longer dealing with them, but with that which they exemplify. This is our dilemma—either to taste and not to know or to know and not to taste—or, more strictly to lack one kind of knowledge because we are in an experience or to lack another kind because we are outside it. . . . You cannot *study* Pleasure in the moment of the nuptial embrace, nor repentance while repenting, nor analyze the nature of humour while roaring with laughter. But when else can you really know these things?. . . Of this tragic dilemma myth is the partial solution. In the enjoyment of a great myth we come nearest to experiencing as concrete what can otherwise be understood only as an abstraction. At this very moment, for example, I am trying to understand something very abstract indeed—the fading, vanishing of tasted reality as we try to grasp it with the discursive reason.[7]

> What flows into you from the myth is not truth but reality (truth is always *about* something, but reality is that *about which* truth is), and, therefore, every myth becomes the father of innumerable truths on the abstract level. Myth is the mountain whence all the different streams arise which become truths down here in the valley: *in hac valle abstractionis.* Or, if you prefer, myth is the isthmus which connects the peninsular world of thought with that vast continent we really belong to. It is not, like truth, abstract; nor is it, like direct experience, bound to the particular.

Now as myth transcends thought, Incarnation transcends myth. The heart of Christianity is a myth which is also a fact. The old myth of the dying God, *without ceasing to be myth,* comes down from the heaven of legend and imagination to the earth of history. It *happens*—at a particular date, in a particular place, followed by definable historical consequences. We pass from a Balder or an Osiris, dying nobody knows when or where, to a historical Person crucified (it is all in order) *under Pontius Pilate.* By becoming fact it does not cease to be myth: that is the miracle. I suspect that men have sometimes derived more spiritual sustenance from myths they did not believe than from the religion they professed. To be truly Christian we must both assent to the historical fact and also receive the myth (fact though it has become) with the same imaginative embrace which we accord to all myths. The one is hardly more necessary than the other. . . . We must not be ashamed of the mythical radiance resting on our theology.[8]

A great many different views on it [myth] have, of course, been held. Myths have been accepted as literally true, then as allegorically true (by the Stoics), as confused history (by Euhemerus), as priestly lies (by the philosophers of the enlightenment), as imitative agricultural ritual mistaken for propositions (in the days of Frazer). If you start from a naturalistic philosophy, then something like the view of Euhemerus or the view of Frazer is likely to result. But I am not a naturalist. I believe that in the huge mass of mythology which has come down to us a good many different sources are mixed—true history, allegory, ritual, the human delight in storytelling, etc. But among these sources I include the supernatural, both diabolical and divine. We need here concern ourselves only with the latter. If my religion is erroneous, then occurrences of similar motifs in pagan stories are, of course, instances of the same, or a similar error. But if my religion is true, then these stories may well be a *preparatio evangelica,* a divine hinting in poetic and ritual form at the same central truth which was later focussed and (so to speak) historicised in the Incarnation. To me, who first approached Christianity from a delighted interest in, and reverence for, the best pagan imagination, who loved Balder before Christ and Plato before St. Augustine, the anthropological argument against Christianity has never been formidable. On the contrary, I could not believe Christianity if I were forced to say that there were a thousand religions in the world of which 999 were pure nonsense and the thousandth (fortunately) true. My conversion, very largely, depended on recognizing Christianity as the completion, the actualization, the entelechy, of something that had never been wholly absent from the mind of man. . . . [I]f the truth or falsehood of Christianity is the very question you are discussing, then the argument from anthropology is surely *a petitio.*[9]

We need to redeem the term *myth.* Many are confused when they hear the term used in a positive way. Christians, for example, think of the warnings in the Scriptures about turning aside to myths, a needed warning, for false religions (the Manichaean, Gnostic, and Jewish occult, etc.) all have their myths—their symbolic systems. But so does the orthodox Judeo-Christian.

> Those who do not know that this great myth became Fact when the Virgin conceived are, indeed, to be pitied. But Christians also need to be reminded . . . that what became Fact was a Myth, that it carries with it into the world of Fact all the properties of a myth. God is more than a god, not less; Christ is more than a Balder, not less. We must not be ashamed of the mythical radiance resting on our theology. We must not be nervous about 'parallels' and 'Pagan Christs': they *ought* to be there—it would be a stumbling block if they weren't. We must not, in a false spirituality, withhold our imaginative welcome. . . . For this is the marriage of heaven and earth: Perfect Myth and Perfect Fact: claiming not only our love and our obedience, but also our wonder and delight, addressed to the savage, the child, and the poet in each one of us no less than to the moralist, the scholar, and the philosopher.[10]

And the serious problem we now face is that the Christian world has lost its symbolic system (its true myth) and more nearly holds to the symbolic system spun out of atheistic materialism—a myth that denies heaven, the unseen real, the transcendent, and the supernatural, along with the moral good.[11]

Our Pilgrimage in Time

Our journey in time is for the special ordering of our lives and passions. The church wisely has set aside a special time-within-time, the Lenten Season, for us to stop and look at our lives in view of eternity and to check our spiritual temperatures for any worldly virus our souls may have caught. It is not accidental that this period precedes Easter and prepares us for the Feasts of Christ's resurrection and ascension that follow:

> *The grace of abstinence has shone forth,*
> *banishing the darkness of demons.*
> *The power of the Fast disciplines our minds.*
> *Lent brings the cure to our crippling worldliness.*[12]

As Fr. Thomas Hopko writes, Lent stands as the great reminder that:

We are in exile. We are alienated and estranged from our true country.

To forget God is the cause of all sins. To be unmindful of Zion is the source of all sorrows. To settle down in this fallen world, which is not God's good creation but rather the Babylon which the wicked have made, is death to the soul.

Christians await the "holy city, new Jerusalem coming down out of heaven from God, prepared as a bride adorned for her husband," which is the true homeland of all human beings (Revelation 21:2). . . . They already live in it to the measure that they have discovered their authentic humanity made in God's image and likeness in Christ.[13]

There is a dangerous forgetfulness on our part that this world is not our true and final home. This has been greatly exacerbated by the fact that our educational systems, drawing their theories from materialist philosophy, have claimed heaven to be off-limits and have taught us to look within ourselves and to this earth for the ultimate good. As C. S. Lewis points out, this progressive subjectivization has resulted in an

evil enchantment of worldliness which has been laid upon us for nearly a hundred years. . . . Almost our whole education has been directed to silencing this shy, persistent, inner voice; almost all our modern philosophies have been devised to convince us that the good of man is to be found on this earth.[14]

I think this explains why we have such difficulty in understanding and celebrating Lent in beneficial ways. We are no longer sure deep down that we are exiles, that this is not the promised home. Therefore, we've accommodated ourselves to Babylon and then are overwhelmed at the sickness, fear, hatred, and violence we see here. It is a strange fact that we Christians continue to be unduly shocked and even overcome by the sight and the extent of the evil we discover in the world—as if we didn't know it to be a fallen one.

Lent is to remind us that it is all too easy to settle in here, to warn us that perhaps a "crippling worldliness" has indeed overtaken us.

See to it, brothers, that none of you has a sinful, unbelieving heart that turns away from the living God. But encourage one another daily, as long as it is called Today, so that none of you may be hardened by sin's deceitfulness. (Hebrews 3:12-13)

This is what the Lenten Scripture readings and teachings are meant to correct in us. They would teach us how we can live in the midst of Babylon and not be destroyed by it, even as Christ prayed:

My prayer is not that you take them out of the world but that you protect them from the evil one. They are not of the world, even as I am not of it. (John 17:15-16)

Spiritual Discipline of Ourselves

The journey through life then, if made successfully, requires that we order our inner and outer lives. We do this through prayer, and keeping an effective listening prayer journal is the best means I can recommend. For those who have difficulty ordering all that an effective vocation has brought into their orbit, or for those who have grown dangerously passive, slothful spiritually and mentally, you may want to read—on your knees—Richard J. Foster's books *Celebration of Discipline* and *Freedom of Simplicity*, or Gordon MacDonald's book *Ordering Your Private World*. It is essential that we order our lives and our "loves" this side of glory—in time.

We are often said to be creatures of time, and that we are. But time too is a creature. It is created. It will not always *be*. This is, for me at least, an overwhelming concept to grapple with and keep before my eyes; it is one I cannot really "think" or fully grasp. But the truth of the matter is, God is outside of time, and not subject to it. Someday we too will no longer be subject to time. Meanwhile in our pilgrimage, it is important to see time as *gift*, as treasure not to be squandered.

Coleridge in an essay entitled "On Method," makes the following remarkable statement:

If the idle are described as killing time, he [the methodical man] may be justly said to call it into life and moral being, while he makes it the distinct object not only of the consciousness, but of the conscience. He organizes the hours, and gives them a soul; and that, the very essence of which is to flee away, and evermore to have been, he takes up into his own permanence, and communicates to it the imperishableness of a spiritual nature. Of the *good and faithful servant,* whose energies, thus directed, are thus methodized, it is less truly affirmed, that he lives in time, than that time lives in him. His days, months, and years, as the stops and punctual marks in the records of duties performed, will survive the wreck of worlds, and remain extant when time itself shall be no more. . . .

Such a remarkable idea! That of taking time into ourselves. May God assist us all as we allow time to live in us.

Reminders of Heaven

As a child I had the great good fortune to grow up in the care of a mother who not only lived the gospel, but every day "sang" it as she went about her household chores. She majored on the hymns that celebrated the cross and the hope of heaven. Though she had to be away from the house earning a living the greater part of the day, when at home—if she was not entirely exhausted—the house would ring with the songs of Christ's Atonement, and of His gracious and loving invitation to sinners:

"When I see the blood, . . . I will pass over you."
"There is a fountain filled with blood, drawn from Immanuel's veins."
"The Old Rugged Cross"
"Jesus Paid It All, All to Him I Owe"

These hymns would then always give way to the songs that celebrate heaven and eternal life. Her voice climbed its highest untrained reaches when she sang (which she often did), "When we all get to heaven, what a day of rejoicing that will be." As she sang, heaven, in a manner of speaking, descended to us, became real to my little sister and me, and we often joined in. Our Saturdays were especially wonderful because Mother would be home for a nice, long stretch of time, and together we would sail through the straightening of the house so she could get to her prayers and preparations for teaching Sunday school the next day. With windows wide open, sunshine streaming in, we would be shaking out bed covers, dusting and sweeping, all the while singing and celebrating the story of salvation and eternal life.

My sister and I knew by heart all the Bible stories the hymns were based on, for Mother had told them to us every night at bedtime. She did it in what I now realize to be unique and creative ways. She was a naturally gifted teacher and disciplinarian (the two gifts go together), and she was always *teaching* us—about God, about others, about everything. I've been surprised to see how often in dysfunctional households the children are not taught in this way—it is almost as if the great things are stingily measured out. There seems to be the notion or even fear that children cannot handle truth. I believe they are starving for great and positive input. Though many seem not to realize it, children are from very early on struggling with good and evil and need ways of understanding these and the power to name them. Nothing seemed too great or too high for Mother to tell. So she passed on to us the profound things—early. In marvelous yet simple, down-to-earth ways, the hope of heaven and the understanding of the eternal (ontological) dimensions of *being*, of what it means to be created in God's image and eternal likeness, were passed on to my sister and me—in words and images we could retain. She had, as a widow in her early twenties, done as St. Paul had admonished Timothy: "Take hold of the eternal life to which you were called" (1 Timothy 6:12). And she passed on to us the knowledge of this in story form, along with the *real thing itself.* She was a sacramental channel of the Presence of God and of a most precious faith and hope.

I've shared the above in order to emphasize our plight as moderns. Even with such a heritage as this, I am a twentieth-century person affected by the age and culture in which I live. It is an age that has lost the hope of eternal life and that cannot put up signposts that point the way to heaven. Such an age has lost the capacity even to speak of the soul's longing for heaven and immortality. Therefore, while persevering, and valuing time as gift, I for one need special reminders of heaven. I need to set up personal signposts, those that remind me to pray always for Christ's appearing and to rejoice in my goal of eternal life in Christ and my full inheritance in Him.

Several years ago, I was deathly tired. I had completed *The Broken Image* and *Crisis in Masculinity,* books that had come out of facing great darkness with large numbers of people, and I had experienced intense spiritual warfare and opposition to the work. As I took the last manuscript to copy and mail off, I remember crying out to God, "Lord, I'm fainting, I need a glimpse, an extraordinary one, of heaven. Please, Lord, if I'm to do what you've called me to do,

I need to walk with one foot in heaven and one here! I need reminders of heaven always before my eyes!"

Then I remember thinking, "You'd better be careful praying like that—you may suddenly get caught up to the third (or was it the seventh!) heaven like St. Paul did, and the contrast might make you decide to stay there—unfit you permanently for here!"

Of course, such an experience would have been incredibly healing, but obviously I was not quite ready to ask God for that and was not sure I should. (I don't usually ask God for experiences, per se, for there are pitfalls in doing so, as I write about in *The Healing Presence.*[15] I trust the Lord for the experiences I need, and then only as He wills.) So I wondered if I had crossed over the line at this point. But He answered my prayer—almost instantly—and in a wonderfully down-to-earth way.

Immediately I was surprised to see a small jewelry shop in the same building—one that had not been there a week or so before. On entering, I saw it did not have the usual traditional array of expensive diamonds, gold, silver, and so on. This one carried the work of innovative artists, and their work was not necessarily in precious gems—but in colorful ones, expertly cut, and set into the most pleasingly designed settings, some round, some square, some oblong. All these shapes and colors immediately took on symbolic meaning for me, meaning having to do with eternal life and heaven.

A ring and bracelet suddenly stood out from all the rest. The ring had one large round stone the color of sunshine and one small round ruby. The bracelet had square-cut stones the same as the ring, with several small, square red rubies. The metal was of beautifully crafted silver, with a tiny thread of gold around the jewels in the ring and a matching thread running the circumference of the bracelet. The rubies symbolized the blood of Christ and His cross—the way into the City, while the stones that reflected the color of sunlight, together with their shapes and the beautifully molded metals, spoke powerfully of the City itself. They also spoke to me of another kind of reward, that of our works that will stand the fires of judgment.

Strongly then, the imagery the Apostle John used to describe the Heavenly City and its gates in the book of Revelation (21:18-21) came to me. These very stones of earth suddenly symbolized for me the greater lights and shapes and highways of that City. They seemed to shine with the glory of heaven. I purchased the ring and bracelet and cherish them—I think I always will—for to me they are at once a pointer and a symbol reminding me daily of our great Christian hope and of our eternal reward.

Often as I'm ministering somewhere and there are hundreds of deep needs before me that I know the Lord wants to transform, the stones of my bracelet and ring will suddenly catch the light and speak to me of heaven. The Presence of the Son of God with us in that place, the very Light of Heaven, blesses the myriad facets of the earthly light in ring and bracelet, and becomes for me an awesome reminder of heaven.

It takes a certain amount of courage to share something like this. The one time I told about this in a group, one man cried out, "Now all our wives will want new rings!" So lest husbands feel suddenly protective of their wallets, let me say that God would not necessarily bless the same symbol to every one! In fact, no one has ever shared a like experience with me. Also, I think that if I had overvalued jewelry in the past or valued it for wrong reasons, God would not have blessed it so as a symbol of heaven for me. But I do think that sheer beauty in color, shape, stone, metal, and artistry is a key here. God loves beauty. He created it. He's pleased with the truly beautiful things we craft from His creation, and these things can symbolize Him and His way of salvation for us. Our symbol-starved twentieth-century hearts need, even crave, vital symbols of the eternal home our hearts were fashioned to know and for which they yearn—our incredible Christian hope.

Beyond the way the colors, shapes, and beauty of well-cut stones impress me, the foundation stones of Scripture speak to me far more than I can understand. They tell ultimately of our Lord, the great Foundation Stone, so there is no end to the meaning of what these symbolize. The great hymn "The Solid Rock" nearly always leaves me in tears. As an organist, one of my favorite prelude and hymn pieces was "Rock of Ages." I can't remember playing it when someone didn't start to weep, and I know that was because the hymn never failed to lift me up into thanksgiving and worship. Another is "The Rock That Is Higher Than I," and a modern version of this hymn touches me deeply. This very day, I am listening to it as I write.

Isaiah, foreseeing the first advent of our Christ, writes:

So this is what the Sovereign Lord says: "See, I lay a stone in Zion, a tested stone, a precious cornerstone for a sure foundation; the one who trusts will never be dismayed." (Isaiah 28:16)

He is the Mighty Rock, seen also as both fountain and cistern, the Stone which at once holds and releases the water of life.

Whoever drinks the water I give him will never thirst. Indeed the water I give him will become in him a spring of water welling up to eternal life. (John 4:14)

They have forsaken me, the spring of living water, and have dug their own cisterns, broken cisterns that cannot hold water. (Jeremiah 2:13)

The ring and bracelet that seemed to me to signify the Heavenly City and our Christ, also spoke immediately of our works in time. St. Paul, speaking of his work in the Kingdom, said:

By the grace God has given me, I laid a foundation as an expert builder, and someone else is building on it. But each one should be careful how he builds. For no one can lay any foundation other than the one already laid, which is Jesus Christ. (1 Corinthians 3:10-11)

He then goes on to describe the work that will last in terms of gold, silver, costly stones. Nothing else will stand the test of fire:

If any man builds on this foundation using gold, silver, costly stones, wood, hay or straw, his work will be shown for what it is, because the Day will bring it to light. It will be revealed with fire, and the fire will test the quality of each man's work. If what he has built survives, he will receive his reward. (1 Corinthians 3:12-14)

It is necessary to petition fervently that our works will stand the fire of judgment—a worthy goal indeed. As stewards of the Kingdom, we are entrusted with the secret things of God; we are stewards of a wisdom "that human wisdom cannot discover." Have we set ourselves to find this wisdom? God promises it to those who ask for it. In this Scripture, the stones symbolize the purity of the word we pass on to others. These stones rest on the Word, the Foundation who is Christ, and the pure words He passed on to His apostles and to us.

I began this book with the darkness and self-hatred that Christians such as my friend and colleague Clay McLean can suffer until they find the healing that we within the Body of Christ are so uniquely graced to minister. Few can write songs such as his that so deeply articulate and celebrate what it means to come out of the darkness and into the light. Everything in this book is written with the goal of bringing hurting people into just such a transformation. So I close by sharing one of his songs as fruit of the ministry of the healing power of our Lord and as a way of encouraging us all to persevere "against the night."

AGAINST THE NIGHT

When men have lost all reason and evil seems to win,
Then compromise is treason and silence is a sin.
Let all who hate the darkness prepare to stand and fight.
The children of the morning must stand against the night.

When all that wisdom treasures is treated with disgrace,
And idols of Damnation are set up in their place,
When every holy symbol is fading out of sight,
The children of the morning must stand against the night.

We'll do the work of heaven against a setting sun
Until the final darkness when no work can be done.

Then watching for the Bridegroom with oil lamps burning bright,
We'll worship in the darkness and stand against the night.

Against the final darkness no earthly strength can stand.
The evil shall be shattered, but not by human hand.
The Maker of the morning will come in Holy Light
That burns in righteous anger and wrath against the night.

Then comes the final morning when all will be restored,
The shadowlands transformed by the glory of the Lord,
When every darkened memory is washed in Healing Light,
Where there will be no warfare, for there will be no night.

Microstar Music © Clay McLean, 1989. Used by permission.

PRAYER

Lord, we would anticipate the very portals of heaven, "each gate made of a single pearl," and what it will mean to pass through such beauty and color and unmitigated light and goodness to receive the reward of those made worthy in the blood of the Lamb. May we pass through with the great hope that our work has survived, that it has indeed been accomplished on and in You, our Great Foundation Stone.

Lord, as You restore our Christian souls, restore to us the hope of heaven. May we once again receive glimpses of the eternal beyond that beckon us as we run this race from the region of time to the healing that only eternity with You can bring. Amen.

Notes

PREFACE

1. Oswald Chambers, *My Utmost for His Highest* (New York: Dodd Mead, 1935), p. 127.
2. F. B. Meyer, *Our Daily Walk* (Grand Rapids: Zondervan, 1951), p. 45.

PART I: The Virtue of Self-Acceptance

1. Richard Lovelace, *Dynamics of Spiritual Life: An Evangelical Theology of Renewal* (Downers Grove, IL: InterVarsity Press, 1979), p. 212.

CHAPTER 1: Self-Hatred: The Traitor Within
When Temptation Comes

1. Oswald Chambers, *Oswald Chambers, The Best from All His Books*, vol. 2 (Nashville, TN: Oliver-Nelson Books, 1989), p. 318.
2. *Ibid.*
3. *Ibid.*, p. 319.
4. *Ibid.*
5. This radical obedience is not one of slavish legalism, but that which describes the "walk in the Spirit," that stance whereby we obey God for the primary reason, that of love and awe of Him.
6. *See* chapter 5, "Creative Power," in my book *The Healing Presence* (Wheaton, IL: Crossway Books, 1989).
7. Chambers, *The Best,* p. 318.
8. I recommend Richard Lovelace, *Dynamics of Spiritual Life: An Evangelical Theology of Renewal* (Downers Grove, IL: InterVarsity Press, 1979).

    Today, it is as if many, including leaders, have a remarkably shallow understanding of the Atonement, especially of what justification and sanctification are all about. Many seem to skip from an initial conversion to matters of power—such as are promised in a baptism of the Spirit and in spiritual authority. When we fully receive and live out the doctrines of justification and sanctification, we find we must seek and gain emotional and psychological healing, and we acquire the concomitant self-knowledge that attends such healing. But having lightly skipped over these matters, these persons are not to be trusted with any kind of power.

    In such cases, for example, there will be an exploitation (a "spectacularization") even of true spiritual giftings to the point that they "clang" and become tools in the enemy's

234 RESTORING THE CHRISTIAN SOUL

hands. Bona fide spiritual power, when in the service of unmet ego needs, quickly becomes corrupted by reason of "admixtures"—i.e., incursions of fleshly and even demonic darkness. The Holy Spirit, offended, does not remain under such circumstances, so that which began in goodness ends in something carnal or even occult. Such Christians are then trapped in a fleshly "drive toward power"—one that has no connection at all with Christ's cross and true spiritual power. In these cases, human pride has been left intact and the extent of sin in the heart unnoticed and unchallenged. One has been too proud to seek and gain the needed psychological and spiritual healing. One has neglected the full message of the cross, and in effect has denied the existence of a Christian soul, one that is in need of restoration.

9. *See The Healing Presence,* chapter 14, "Renouncing False Gods and Appropriating the Holy."
10. Chambers, *The Best*, p. 319.

CHAPTER 2: First Great Barrier to Wholeness in Christ: Failure to Accept Oneself

1. *See* my book *The Healing Presence* (Wheaton, IL: Crossway Books, 1989), chapter 12, "Introspection Versus True Imagination."
2. *See The Healing Presence,* chapter 4, "Separation from the Presence."
3. John Fawcett, a Christian brother and fellow team member who before his healing was trapped in analyzing and hating himself, expresses it this way: "Some who are afraid of the appearance of narcissism in the language of self-acceptance veer dangerously close to self-hatred in their antidote to it, as if a deeper introspective gaze upon our own guilt and sin could bring us to fuller freedom in Christ. But self-hatred is not the opposite of narcissism; rather, it is egocentrism under a different guise—the same mirror of self viewed from another angle. The discovery of the true self encompasses the denial and crucifixion of the flesh, but it is far more than a negative process. We find our true selves positively in relation to God: hearing His loving, affirming Word, we are freed to celebrate the new self He makes. We become enamored not of our own accomplishments nor of our unworthiness, but of the beauty of Jesus. Through His Spirit He descends into us that Christ may dwell in our hearts by faith (Ephesians 3:17), transforming us into His image, from glory to glory (2 Corinthians 3:18)."
4. Michael Scanlon, *Inner Healing* (New York: Paulist Press, 1974), pp. 51-52.

CHAPTER 3: Struggling Through to Self-Acceptance

1. *Die Annahme seiner selbst*, 5th ed. (Wurzburg: Werkbandverlag, 1969), pp. 14, 16. Quoted in Walter Trobisch, *Love Yourself: Self Acceptance and Depression* (Downers Grove, IL: InterVarsity Press, 1976), p. 9.
2. *See* Trobisch, *Love Yourself*; Frank Lake, *Clinical Theology* (Crossroad Publishing); and Hemfelt, Minirth, and Meier, *Love Is a Choice: Recovery for Codependent Relationships* (Thomas Nelson) for solid Christian examples of these writings.
3. Oswald Chambers, *My Utmost for His Highest* (New York: Dodd Mead, 1935), p. 315.
4. C. S. Lewis, *Mere Christianity* (New York: Macmillan, 1960), p. 190.
5. C. S. Lewis, *Experiment in Criticism* (Cambridge: Cambridge University Press, 1969), p. 138.
6. For more on this, *see* my book *The Healing Presence* (Wheaton, IL: Crossway Books, 1989), chapter 13, "Incarnational Reality."
7. Walter Trobisch, *The Complete Works of Walter Trobisch* (Downers Grove, IL: InterVarsity Press, 1987), p. 659.

8. Trobisch, *Love Yourself,* p. 680.
9. C. S. Lewis, *Letters of C. S. Lewis,* ed. W. H. Lewis (New York: Harcourt, Brace and World, 1966), p. 155.
10. *See The Healing Presence,* chapters 8 and 9, "Perceiving God Aright" and "The Imagery Really Matters."
11. C. S. Lewis, "The Weight of Glory" in *The Weight of Glory* (Grand Rapids: Eerdmans, 1972), pp. 8-9.
12. David Seamands, *The Healing of Memories* (Wheaton, IL: Victor Books, 1985), p. 102.
13. As Rebecca Manley Pippert says in *Hope Has Its Reasons,* there is an intentional element in even our worst deceptions, and this is "why we are held responsible for our own condition. We may be deceived, but we are never that deceived." (San Francisco: Harper and Row, 1989), p. 86.
14. There is a good example of this in the life of C. S. Lewis. In his spiritual autobiography *Surprised by Joy,* Lewis describes the grievous effects of losing his mother to cancer (chapter 1). As he writes, his father lost not only his wife at this time, but his sons as well. Lewis struggled for the greater part of his life to understand his deep antipathy toward his father. His life with Mrs. Moore and her family can only be rightly understood as one comprehends the reaction he had to the loss of his mother early in life and then, related to that, the way he could not accept his father. Lewis never had full insight into this, as George Sayer, one of his close and long-term friends, has observed. *See* Fifth Annual Marion E. Wade Lecture, 9/28/79, The Marion E. Wade Center, Wheaton College, Wheaton, IL.
15. Quoted from a lecture given at a Pastoral Care Ministries School.
16. Karl Stern, *The Third Revolution: A Study of Psychiatry and Religion,* Image Books Edition (Garden City, NY: Doubleday, 1961), p. 152.
17. Romano Guardini, *The Virtues* (Chicago: Regnery Company, 1967), p. 6.
18. These would be primarily familial or *storge* needs. For a study of the four basic loves, *see The Four Loves* by C. S. Lewis.
19. *See The Healing Presence,* chapter 12, "Introspection Versus True Imagination."
20. As I show in *The Broken Image,* all categories of homosexuality have this one failure in common—the failure to emerge from puberty affirmed as persons, thereby finding true self-acceptance. All are unaffirmed in their gender identity and have fallen into the wrong kind of self-love.

    As masturbation is always a part of male homosexuality and often a part of lesbian behavior as well, it is extremely important to recognize when this habit is rooted in infantile trauma and is related to severe dread and anxiety. Those feelings accompany the severest psychological injuries in infants. In these cases, a dread-ridden masturbation (in contrast to a merely lustful one) ensues. *See The Broken Image* (Wheaton, IL: Crossway Books, 1981), pp. 54-62, together with pp. 121-136, "Homosexual and Lesbian Behavior Related to Failure of the Infant to Achieve an Adequate Sense of Being" for more on this.
21. Lewis, *Surprised by Joy* (New York: Harcourt, Brace and World, 1955), p. 71.
22. Stern, *The Third Revolution,* p. 149.
23. *Ibid.,* p. 150.
24. *See* my book *Crisis in Masculinity* (Wheaton, IL: Crossway Books, 1985), pp. 130-140 for more on this. When the church faithfully teaches men and women to find their identity in Christ, they will have no difficulty with roles as such. But it is dangerous to teach on the roles of men and women per se.
25. *See The Broken Image,* pp. 121-136.
26. *See The Healing Presence,* pp. 48-54.
27. *See Crisis in Masculinity,* pp. 62-76, for prayers that enable us to forgive even the parent who is the most difficult to honor and forgive.

CHAPTER 4: Affirmation: What It Is and How It Is Received

1. In counseling, it is important to realize that the way of the wounded "inner child" is so often the way of the foolish child: "The way of a fool seems right to him, but a wise man listens to advice" (Proverbs 12:15). We are never to dialogue with that foolishness, but with the authentic person. The writer of Proverbs expresses perfectly what many in counseling desperately need to know and understand: "Do not answer a fool according to his folly [his foolishness], or you will be like him yourself" (Proverbs 26:4).
2. The descriptive term "dry alcoholic" refers to a person who carries the characteristics and personality traits of someone addicted to alcohol. Such a person does not know what normal is, and there may be addiction to other substances. Some of the more obvious traits include manipulative and controlling behavior.
3. Oswald Chambers, *My Utmost for His Highest* (New York: Dodd Mead, 1935), p. 68.
4. *Ibid.*, p. 333.
5. *See* my book *Real Presence: The Christian Worldview of C. S. Lewis as Incarnational Reality* (Wheaton, IL: Crossway Books, 1979), chapter 7, "The Great Dance," for C. S. Lewis on the will; *see* my book *The Healing Presence* (Wheaton, IL: Crossway Books, 1989), p. 64, for a prayer for healing of the will.

CHAPTER 5: Listening Prayer: The Way of Grace and the Walk in the Spirit

1. Dick Keyes, *Beyond Identity* (Ann Arbor, MI: Servant Books, 1984), p. 97.
2. C. S. Lewis, *The Problem of Pain* (London: Collins Fontana Books, 1959), p. 63.
3. C. S. Lewis, *Experiment in Criticism* (Cambridge: Cambridge University Press, 1969), p. 138.
4. C. S. Lewis, *Poems* (New York: Harcourt, Brace and World, 1964), pp. 92-93.
5. Lewis, *The Problem of Pain,* p. 140.

PART II: The Forgiveness of Sin

1. F. B. Meyer, *Our Daily Walk* (Grand Rapids: Zondervan, 1951), p. 142.

CHAPTER 6: Healing of Memories: The Forgiveness of Sin

1. *See* my book *The Healing Presence* (Wheaton, IL: Crossway Books, 1989), pp. 131-32.
2. *Ibid.*, chapter 10.
3. Agnes Sanford, *The Healing Gifts of the Spirit* (Philadelphia/New York: Lippincott, 1966), pp. 126-27.
4. C. S. Lewis, *Letters of C. S. Lewis,* ed. W. H. Lewis (New York: Harcourt, Brace and World, 1966), p. 155.
5. Recommended Reading: chapter 4, "Spirit, Soul, and Body," in my book *Real Presence: The Christian Worldview of C. S. Lewis as Incarnational Reality* (Wheaton, IL: Crossway Books, 1979) and sections entitled "Soul," pp. 1036-37, "Spirit," p. 1041, "Man, Doctrine of," pp. 676-81 in H. D. McDonald, *Evangelical Dictionary of Theology,* ed. Walter A. Elwell (Grand Rapids: Baker Book House, 1984).
6. McDonald, *Evangelical Dictionary,* p. 678.
7. F. B. Meyer, *Our Daily Walk* (Grand Rapids: Zondervan, 1951), p. 169.

8. Robert M. Doran, S. J., "Jungian Psychology and Christian Spirituality: II," *Review for Religious,* 38 (1979/4): p. 510.
9. Karl Stern, *The Third Revolution,* Image Books Edition (Garden City, NY: Doubleday, 1961), pp. 70-71.
10. C. S. Lewis, *Letters to Malcolm: Chiefly on Prayer* (New York: Harcourt, Brace and World, 1963, 1964), pp. 121-22.
11. As an example of a healing of ancestral memories, see David's story in my book *Crisis in Masculinity* (Wheaton, IL: Crossway Books, 1985), p. 51.

     Recommended Reading: David Seamands, *Healing of Memories* (Wheaton, IL: Victor Books, 1985), chapter 1, "The Mystery of Memory," and Lewis, *Letters to Malcolm,* chapter 22.
12. Lewis, *Letters to Malcolm,* p. 109.
13. C. S. Lewis, *The Problem of Pain* (New York: Macmillan, 1962), p. 61.
14. Kenneth McAll's book *The Healing of the Family Tree* was the genesis of this teaching, and *Healing the Greatest Hurt* by Matthew and Dennis Linn and Sheila Fabricant further popularized the notions in McAll's book.

CHAPTER 7: Second Great Barrier to Wholeness in Christ: Failure to Forgive Others

1. For more on this, send for tapes on codependency to Pastoral Care Ministries, P. O. Box 17702, Milwaukee, Wisconsin 53217.
2. Oswald Chambers, *Oswald Chambers, The Best from All His Books* (Nashville: Thomas Nelson, 1987), p. 345.
3. Leanne Payne, *The Healing Presence* (Wheaton, IL: Crossway Books, 1989), p. 89.
4. *Ibid.,* pp. 172-75.
5. Chambers, *Best of All His Books,* p. 345.
6. *Ibid.,* p. 344.
7. For example, *see* my book *The Broken Image* (Wheaton, IL: Crossway Books, 1981), pp. 79-82, "Birth Trauma and Repression of Masculinity," as well as Loren's story, pp. 78-79.
8. *See The Broken Image,* chapter 1, "Lisa's Story: Repressed Memory."
9. Frank Lake, "The Origin and Development of Personal Identity Through Childhood to Adult Life: And Its Significance in Clinical Pastoral Care," Second Year Syllabus, no. 4, Clinical Theology, (The Clinical Theological Assn., Hawthornes of Nottingham Ltd., n.d.), p. 5.
10. *Ibid.*

CHAPTER 8: Prolonged Healing of Memories: Abandonment Issues and the Repression of Painful Emotions

1. Leanne Payne, *The Healing Presence* (Wheaton, IL: Crossway Books, 1989), pp. 173-174.
2. Frank Lake, *Clinical Theology,* abridged by Marin H. Yeomans (New York: Crossroad Publishing, 1987), pp. 4-5.
3. Frank Lake, "Clinical Theological Training and Care," Second Year Syllabus, no. 4 (The Clinical Theological Assn., Hawthornes of Nottingham Ltd., n.d.), p. 5.
4. Lake, *Clinical Theology* (abridged), p. 101.
5. *Ibid.,* p. 41.
6. *Ibid.,* pp. 103-4.

7. The *hysterical* attempt to find or posit an insecure selfhood in another, thus entangling the helper with the sufferer.

8. The inability of the one with *schizoid* tendencies to rest in a healthy interdependence with others.

9. For the fullest, most Christ-centered explication of the personality reactions to the failure to come to a sense of being in the first months of life, I recommend Frank Lake's work *Clinical Theology*, the unabridged edition when available, and the abridged (very fine). The abridged edition omits the excellent work he did on homosexual defense mechanisms. For case examples of these, *see* my book *The Broken Image* (Wheaton, IL: Crossway Books, 1981), pp. 121-136.

10. Lake, *Clinical Theology*, (abridged), p. 99.

11. *Ibid.*, pp. 107-8.

12. *Ibid.*, p. 65.

13. Mira Rothenberg, *Children with Emerald Eyes* (New York: E. P. Dutton, 1987), pp. 27-30.

14. Men who cross-dress, both heterosexual and homosexual in orientation, are typically termed *transvestites*, but *we* use transvestite to identify only those who are homosexual in orientation. According to *Baker Encyclopedia of Psychology,* David G. Benner, editor, homosexuals make up only 10 or 11 percent of those who cross-dress. We use the term *cross-dresser,* then, to refer to the remaining 89 percent who are heterosexual males. Both the cross-dresser and the transvestite receive temporary comfort and alleviation of anxiety when they put on feminine attire. But for the cross-dresser, it is also a fetish—he is sexually aroused by the activity. This is an important distinction in knowing how to pray and in understanding the symbolic confusion in their lives. (We do not find men with homosexual orientation to experience sexual arousal in cross-dressing, but the *Baker Encyclopedia* reports it as a rarity.)

15. At times the heterosexual cross-dresser may deny and camouflage this desire to be a woman. For example, the desire can be covered over by fear and hatred of a mother who cannot love and accept the son, yet who is at the same time possessive, controlling, and overbearing. One cross-dresser I ministered to seemed subconsciously to want to be his mother in order to be strong and enabled to survive the effects of her mental illness. He had a very weak father who could not withstand her or protect his son from her. The son's way of coping with his extreme frustration and pain in dealing with her was finally, in a state of anxiety, to put on her underwear. By putting on her clothes, he was symbolically putting on her "sex." In a manner of speaking, to put on her underwear, was *to be her* in order to survive her. His anxiety at being powerless to withstand her, at being suffocatingly and infuriatingly "under her" (emotionally raped by her), constellated sexual arousal. This eroticism was rooted in anxiety and insecurity. He had overcome his cross-dressing for a number of years, and it wasn't until his fiancée broke up with him that he fell back into the compulsion. Here again, he repeated the pattern. He did not, so far as I know, consciously wish to be woman, but unconsciously he cross-dressed in order to be her (this time, the fiancée). Again, to be her was to have power to withstand her rejection of himself. This understanding, along with healing prayer, freed him.

16. There are transvestites (homosexual cross-dressers) who become female impersonators, and spin a web of delusion about themselves. As they get more deeply into this behavior, they may fall under a demonic deception that they are in fact woman. Such an illusory identity can take on a truly demonic life of its own, and these persons are left grievously demon infested. (See *The Healing Presence*, p. 73 and chapter 9.)

17. Frank Lake, *Clinical Theology* (London: Darton, Longman, & Todd, 1966), p. 9.
    Recommended Reading: Frank Lake, *Clinical Theology* and John Bowlby, *A Secure Base,* Basic Books.

CHAPTER 9: Third Great Barrier to Wholeness in Christ: Failure to Receive Forgiveness

1. C. S. Lewis, *Reflections on the Psalms* (New York: Harcourt, Brace and World, 1958), pp. 31-32.
2. Alexander Solzhenitsyn, *Gulag Archipelago,* ed. Edward E. Ericson, Jr. (New York: Harper and Row, 1985), chapter 7.
3. R. A. Torrey, *How to Pray* (Chicago: Moody Press, n.d.), p. 25.
4. C. S. Lewis, *Letters to Malcolm: Chiefly on Prayer* (New York: Harcourt, Brace and World, 1963), p. 82.
5. F. B. Meyer, *Our Daily Walk* (Grand Rapids: Zondervan, 1951), p. 374.
6. Richard Lovelace, *Dynamics of Spiritual Life* (Downers Grove, IL: InterVarsity Press, 1980), pp. 88-89.
7. *See* my book *The Healing Presence* (Wheaton, IL: Crossway Books, 1989), chapter 11, "The True Imagination," especially pp. 145ff.
8. For an excellent treatment of this topic, *see* Lovelace, *Dynamics of Spiritual Life,* especially chapter 4, "Primary Elements of Continuous Renewal."

CHAPTER 10: Conclusion to Healing of Memories

1. *See* my book *The Healing Presence* (Wheaton, IL: Crossway Books, 1989), pp. 94-95.
2. *See The Healing Presence* in its entirety but especially chapter 9.
3. *See* my book *The Broken Image* (Wheaton, IL: Crossway Books, 1981), chapter 6.
4. *See The Healing Presence,* chapter 12.
5. *Ibid.,* pp. 64, 94-97.
6. *Ibid.,* pp. 182ff.
7. *See* my book *Crisis in Masculinity* (Wheaton, IL: Crossway Books, 1985), pp. 62ff.

CHAPTER 11: The Use of Holy Water and Other Powerful Christian Symbols and Agencies

1. *See* my book *The Healing Presence* (Wheaton, IL: Crossway Books, 1989), chapter 11, for more on the ways our spiritual eyes are opened to see the invisible.
2. For more on the fact that sacramental reality exhibits the principle of the Incarnation, see chapter 3, "Sacrament: Avenue to the Real," in my book *Real Presence: The Christian Worldview of C. S. Lewis as Incarnational Reality* (Wheaton, IL: Crossway Books, 1979).
3. *See The Healing Presence,* chapter 14, for a fuller explication of Jung's gnosticism and its impact on the church.
4. John Richards, *But Deliver Us from Evil: An Introduction to the Demonic in Pastoral Care* (New York: Seabury Press, 1974), p. 28.
5. Phallic demons manifest in the context of Baal worship. *See The Healing Presence,* chapter 14, especially pp. 198-99.
6. Michael Green, *I Believe in Satan's Downfall* (Grand Rapids: Eerdmans, 1981), pp. 141-42.
7. *See The Healing Presence,* pp. 90-94, for a definition of demonic *oppression* as over and against *possession.*
8. Mark Pearson, "Counterfeit Christianity," *Mission and Ministry,* 7, no. 2 (Fall 1989), Ambridge, PA 15003, italics mine.
9. Green, *I Believe in Satan's Downfall,* p. 141.

10. Oswald Chambers, *My Utmost for His Highest* (New York: Dodd Mead, 1935), p. 262.
11. *Ibid.*, p. 291.
12. W. K. Lowther Clarke and Charles Harris, eds., *Liturgy and Worship: A Companion to the Prayer Books of the Anglican Communion* (London: Literature Association of the Church Union, London SPCK, 1932), pp. 472-615.

CHAPTER 12: The Gift of Battle

1. Oswald Chambers, *My Utmost for His Highest* (New York: Dodd Mead, 1935), p. 19.
2. *Ibid.*, p. 196.
3. Donald Bloesch, *Crumbling Foundations* (Grand Rapids: Zondervan, 1984), p. 125.
4. *Ibid.*
5. C. S. Lewis, *The Problem of Pain* (New York: Macmillan, 1962), p. 28.
6. William Barclay, *The Gospel of Matthew* (Louisville, KY: Westminster John Knox, 1975), p. 318.

CHAPTER 13: Cosmic Dimensions of Spiritual Warfare in Christian Organizations

1. Oswald Chambers, *My Utmost for His Highest* (New York: Dodd Mead, 1935), p. 258.
2. *See* my books *Real Presence: The Christian Worldview of C. S. Lewis as Incarnational Reality* (Wheaton, IL: Crossway Books, 1979), "Appendix: The Great Divorce," and *The Healing Presence* (Wheaton, IL: Crossway Books, 1989), chapter 14, "Renouncing False Gods and Appropriating the Holy."
3. C. S. Lewis, *The Problem of Pain* (New York: Macmillan, 1962), p. 85.
4. *See* my book *Crisis in Masculinity* (Wheaton, IL: Crossway Books, 1985).
5. Richard Lovelace, *Dynamics of Spiritual Life: An Evangelical Theology of Renewal* (Downers Grove, IL: InterVarsity Press, 1979), p. 384. *See* pp. 381-386.
6. *See* my book *Crisis in Masculinity*, chapter 4, "What Is Masculinity," for more on the tie-in between true masculinity and the power to speak the truth.
7. *See The Healing Presence*, chapter 12, "Introspection Versus True Imagination."
8. A monk of the Eastern Church, *On the Invocation of the Name of Jesus* (London: The Fellowship of St. Alban and St. Sergius), p. 9.
9. *Ibid.*, p. 2.

CHAPTER 14: Wrong Ways to Do Battle

1. C. S. Lewis, *That Hideous Strength* (New York: Macmillan, 1946), p. 283.
2. *See* my book *The Healing Presence* (Wheaton, IL: Crossway Books, 1989), pp. 80-87.
3. *See ibid.*, pp. 178-180 for more on this.
4. Fr. John Gaynor Banks, *The Master and the Disciple* (St. Paul, MN: Macalester Park Publishing, 1954), p. 135.
5. William Barclay, *The Gospel of Matthew* (Louisville, KY: Westminster John Knox, 1975), p. 108.
6. *Ibid.*, p. 110.
7. *Ibid.*
8. *New International Version Study Bible* (Grand Rapids: Zondervan, 1985), p. 12.
9. Even when there is a demonic infestation, the demons are most often not dislodged through this manner of "prayer," or they will return because the sin or wound hasn't been adequately dealt with. We must learn how to discern (that is, move in the authen-

tic gift of discerning of spirits) the presence of the demonic and learn to bring the finger of God to bear on it. The demonic entity cannot stand the light and has to flee at our command. God in His mercy answers all kinds of "misinformed" prayer, but we as Christians are called to wisdom and to understand the human soul.

10. C. S. Lewis, *Screwtape Letters* (New York: Macmillan, 1962), p. 3.
11. A theology derived from E. W. Kenyon.
12. I know and have ministered to people who have come up with entire mythologies of evil powers, and these are spun out of listening to the demons whose presence they learned to practice. They were, therefore, filled with every evil superstition and fear. Some, so deceived, eventually were into a form of "Christianized" witchcraft. Everyone and everything they could not control was eventually named demonic and as "witchcraft," and a demonic myth was then spun around the unfortunate persons who fell prey to them. Deluded persons such as these can become amateur cult hunters, branding true servants of God as acting in the power of demons. Their slander of the servants of God is always of the most destructive kind.
13. To "do spiritual warfare" is to do the works of Christ; it is to preach, teach, and heal in the power of His name (Presence) and thereby bring people out of darkness into the light of God.

CHAPTER 15: Restoring the Christian Hope of Heaven and the Grace to Persevere

1. C. S. Lewis, *The Great Divorce* (New York: Macmillan, 1946), pp. 80, 81, 82-83.
2. Oswald Chambers, *My Utmost for His Highest* (New York: Dodd Mead, 1935), p. 65.
3. F. B. Meyer, *Our Daily Walk* (Grand Rapids: Zondervan, 1951), p. 76.
4. Recommended reading: "The Weight of Glory," an essay by C. S. Lewis published in a book of essays by the same title. Like his novel *The Great Divorce,* this essay is a classic on longing for heaven and immortality and on the honor and affirmation God so desires to give us. For one of the greatest presentations of glory in Western literature, see *The Lord of the Rings* by J. R. R. Tolkien, especially Lothlorien, the crowning of Aragorn, and the return of Gandolf from the dead with a glorified body.
5. *See* my book *The Healing Presence* (Wheaton, IL: Crossway Books, 1989), chapter 12, "Introspection Versus True Imagination."
6. C. S. Lewis, *God in the Dock* (Grand Rapids: Eerdmans, 1970), p. 214.
7. *Ibid.,* pp. 65-66.
8. *Ibid.,* pp. 66-67.
9. *Ibid.,* pp. 131-32.
10. *Ibid.,* p. 67.
11. For those who desire more understanding of myth as a genre in literature, J. R. R. Tolkien's famous essay "On Fairy-Stories," which could as well have been titled "On Myth," is recommended. It is found in *The Tolkien Reader.*

   Lewis and Tolkien excel in the writing of Christian myth. Their novels reflect a Christian cosmos and reality, and their imaginative genius helps to restore a truly Judeo-Christian symbolic system to the modern so in need of it. Most recently, Frank Peretti's books *This Present Darkness* and *Piercing the Darkness* have met a profound need in many Christians. These writings have restored to them the capacity to imagine angelic beings and the Christian supernatural. Many now pray more, and more effectively to our God, knowing that He, in response to their prayers, sends into action even the heavenly hosts! This is the effect of being *remythologized,* of having an imaginative response to our great gospel restored. Also, chapters 8 to 11 of *The Healing Presence,* as well as chapters 10 and 11 of *Real Presence,* deal with this subject.

12. Fr. Thomas Hopko, *The Lenten Spring* (Crestwood, NY: St. Vladimir's Seminary Press, 1983), p. 9.
13. *Ibid.*, pp. 21, 24, 25.
14. *See The Discarded Image: An Introduction to Medieval Renaissance Literature* (Cambridge: Cambridge University Press, 1964), p. 42, and *Real Presence,* "The Whole Intellect."
15. *See The Healing Presence*, "The Presence of God in Contrast to a Sense of the Presence," p. 24.

Index

Abandonment, 27, 41, 52, 77, 83, 97, 103-39
Absolution, 145, 150-51, 154, 157
Abuse, 32, 34, 54, 71, 84-93, 124-25, 176
Affirmation, 21, 28, 31, 33, 39, 40, 45-55, 112, 126, 127
  by a father, 35, 36-37, 38, 40-41, 42, 43, 85-87, 88-91
  by God, 27, 28, 31, 34, 35, 45, 48-49, 52, 90
  by parents, 34, 42, 126, 143
Against the Night (song), 231
Ambivalence,
  same-sex or other-sex, 37, 138, 157
Anamnesis, 74
Approval (or fame), seeking people's, 27, 91, 192-94, 219-22
Arts, the, 192-94
Atonement, 21, 55, 78, 150, 227
Attitudes, 21, 23, 26, 27, 28, 36, 37, 52, 57, 58, 69, 97, 135, 147, 157, 207

Baal, 22, 158, 175, 176
"Bad" mother or father, 37, 123, 124-25, 136-37, 139
Banks, John Gaynor, 73, 205
Baptism, 154, 155, 164, 168, 177-78
Barclay, William, 189, 205, 206, 219
Beasley, William, 33, 177, 213
Being, sense of, 26, 41, 42, 49, 99, 107, 110-36
Bentness, 25, 26-27, 48, 52, 82, 109, 110, 111, 119, 121, 122, 143, 156

Bergner, Mario, 135-36
Beyond Identity (Dick Keyes), 58
Binding and loosing, 92, 153-54, 157-58, 207, 208-12
Birth trauma, 98, 123
Bloesch, Donald, 184
Boerner, Connie, 54
Bond, 37, 99, 109-12, 117-120, 130, 133
  fantasy, 127-32, 134
Book of Common Prayer
Boundaries, 112, 117, 121, 122, 126, 127
Broken Image, The (Leanne Payne), 38, 85, 88, 95, 106, 131, 228
Brokenness, xiii, xiv, 19, 22, 23, 27, 28, 32, 33, 36, 49, 50, 54, 57, 68-69, 71, 72, 73, 75, 76-77, 84, 92, 93, 94, 103-39, 158, 159, 187, 219
Buess, Bob, 35
But Deliver Us from Evil: An Introduction to the Demonic in Pastoral Care (John Richards), 169

Casey, Patsy, 180-81
Celebration of Discipline (Richard J. Foster), 227
Centered (in God), 21, 144, 145
Chambers, Oswald, xiii, xiv, 19, 20, 21, 22, 32, 50, 51, 53, 84, 93, 181, 183, 184, 222
Child, wounded inner, 32, 34, 87, 110, 116, 119, 120, 127
Children
  developmental needs of, 34-35, 36-37, 38, 41-43, 99-101, see *Affirmation*

parents symbolize God to, 34-35, 37, 40-41, 115
Children with Emerald Eyes (Mira Rothenberg), 128
Clinical Theology (Frank Lake), 107, 111, 113, 116-17, 123, 124-25, 139
Codependent, 48, 82, 119, 212
Coleridge, Samuel Taylor, 227
Collaborating with God, 20, 21, 26, 77, 79, 98, 120-22, 127, 135, 153, 155-56, 157, 158-59, 184
Comiskey, Andrew, 33
Communion, 26, 145, 153, 168, 178
Complete Works of Walter Trobisch, The (Walter Trobisch), 33
Compulsions, 22, 49, 76, 85, 108, 112-13, 126, 127, 129, 130, 131, 132, 143, 147, 179
Confession, xiii, 26, 28, 59, 60, 62, 68-69, 73, 74, 77, 81, 82, 92, 94, 96-97, 119, 130, 141-51, 153, 154, 157, 208, 209, 210, 211, 213, 214
Creativity, 20, 21, 22, 33, 91
Crisis in Masculinity (Leanne Payne), 37, 38, 83, 88, 228
Cross (Christ's), xiv, xv, 21, 22, 23, 25, 50, 54, 55, 59, 63, 64, 72, 83, 84, 85, 95, 98, 103, 109, 114, 120, 122, 137, 139, 150, 154, 158, 179, 186, 192, 207, 215, 229
Cross-dresser, 129-32
Crucifix, 63, 150, 156-57, 164, 175, 179-81
Crumbling Foundations (Donald Bloesch), 184

Dawson, John, 210
Defense or coping mechanisms, 28, 29, 98, 107-9, 112-13, 120, 122, 124, 125, 129
Demons, 19, 21, 52, 73, 78-79, 92, 135, 138, 144 , 153-54, 158, 166-70, 172-75, 179-82, 183, 187, 188, 189, 191, 196, 198, 204, 206-12, 214
Denial, 36, 41, 53, 54, 58, 73, 83, 85, 96, 103, 107-9, 120, 128, 129, 132, 143

Deprivation, 22, 26, 37, 41, 64, 70, 76-77, 103-39
Desert Stream Ministries, 33
Discarded Image: An Introduction to Medieval Renaissance Literature, The (C. S. Lewis), 226
Discipling, xiii, 50, 136, 156, 159
Doctrine (theology), false, 59, 78-80, 143, 171, 208, 210, 214, 215
sound, 50-51, 80, 85, 207
Doran, Robert M., 73
Dreams, 94, 96-97
Dying to the old self, 20, 26, 35, 58-59, 62-63, 142, 143, 145, 149, 156
Dynamics of Spiritual Life: An Evangelical Theology of Renewal (Richard Lovelace), 17, 147-48, 196
Dysfunction, xiv, 32, 36, 52, 72, 83, 180

Ego, 39, 123
Evangelical Dictionary (H. D. McDonald), 70
Emotional needs, 28, 31-32, 37, 38, 41, 42, 58, 64, 69, 71, 77, 95, 103-39
Envy, 188, 189

False guilt, 148, 157
Fantasy, 91, 113, 132
bond, 127-32, 134
Favor (Bob Buess), 35
Fawcett, John, 135, 234
Feelings, 19, 21, 23, 24, 34, 36, 58, 68, 71, 72, 73, 74, 83, 88, 90, 97, 99, 103-39, 146, 148, 149-50, 157, 102, 193, 197, 207, 215
split-off, 97, 100, 107, 109, 111, 113, 114-15, 126, 136
shutdown of, 34, 103, 116, 125, 127
Feminine, 36, 37, 38, 41, 42, 49, 91, 118, 128, 129, 130, 132, 143
Fetish, 129, 130, 131-32
Fideism, 59
Forgiveness, 17
receiving, xiii, xiv, 24, 27, 37, 38, 50, 55, 59, 63, 64, 65-80, 82, 94, 95, 141-51, 153-55, 157-59, 167

obstacles to, 141-50
extending to others, xiii, 27, 42, 50, 64, 81-101, 110, 114, 119, 130, 132, 135, 153, 188
Foster, Richard J., 227
Freedom of Simplicity (Richard J. Foster), 227
Freud, Sigmund, 147, 197
Frost, Robert, 35

Gender identity, 36, 41, 42, 85-87, 88-91, 95, 101, 108, 120, 129, 130-31, 132, 137
Gift of battle, 183-190, 202, 209
Gifts of the Holy Spirit, 79, 98, 138, 155, 158, 166, 175, 182, 184, 207, 214
Glory (favor, appreciation), 34-35, 190, 192-93, 203, 220-23
Gnosticism, Gnostics, 179, 207, 225
God in the Dock (C. S. Lewis), 223
God, the Father, xiv, 23, 28, 34, 40, 41, 79, 134-35, 154, 158, 195
    as Affirmer, 34-35, 45, 48, 52, 127
    as Healer, 42, 52
    distorted perception of, 34, 35, 36
Good and evil, line between, 144-45
Gospel of Matthew, The (William Barclay), 189, 205
Great Divorce, The (C. S. Lewis), 204, 220-21
Green, Michael, 175, 175, 179
Grieve, 103, 109-12, 113, 114, 119, 126, 153
Groeger, Guido, 33
Guardini, Romano, 31, 38
Guilt, xiv, 26, 27, 49, 59, 74, 78, 91, 130, 131, 141-51, 157
    false, 148, 157
Gulag Archipelago (Alexander Solzhenitsyn), 144-45

Harris, Charles, 182
Healing Gifts of the Spirit, The (Agnes Sanford), 68
Healing of Memories (David Seamands), 35

Healing of the Family Tree, The (Kenneth McAll), 79
Healing, physical, 72-73, 82
Healing Presence, The (Leanne Payne), xiii, 37, 68, 84, 103, 135, 142, 146, 149, 168, 179, 229
Healing word (God's), 20, 23, 24, 27, 28, 42, 51, 52, 58-64, 86, 87, 109, 137, 158, 169, 211
Heart, xiv, 27, 28, 49, 59, 60, 62, 63-64, 68, 73, 74, 86, 88, 134, 144-45, 147, 157, 191, 206, 207
Heterosexual, 129, 197
Holy Spirit, xiv, 23, 34, 60, 67, 70, 72, 75, 79, 82, 93, 98, 111, 123, 132, 154, 164, 173, 176, 178, 181, 192, 194, 198, 199, 201, 202, 214, 215
    gifts of the, 79, 98, 138, 155, 158, 166, 175, 182, 184, 207, 214
    infilling by, 21, 26, 150, 154, 155, 170, 200
    leading of, 69, 77, 114, 127, 176
    power of, 23, 53, 80, 85, 156, 176, 190, 195
    Revealer, 83, 108, 138
    walking in the, xiv, 25, 27, 53, 57-64, 141-42, 143, 149
Holy water, 163, 164-178, 180, 181, 182
    holy washings, 175-78
    liturgy to bless, 164-65
Homosexuality, 36, 38, 42, 85-87, 91, 98, 108, 129, 142, 170, 195, 197
Hope of heaven, 217-31
Hopko, Thomas, 225-26
How to Pray (R. A. Torrey), 146
Humility, 24, 51, 59, 82, 144, 222
Hysterical (emotionally dependent) personality, 104-24, 126-27

I Believe in Satan's Downfall (Michael Green), 174, 179
Identification process, 37, 38, 39, 40, 99, 116, 129
Identity, xiii, xiv, 21, 22, 26, 31, 36, 39, 42, 45, 50, 53, 62, 63, 69, 84, 89, 99-

100, 119, 120, 121, 137, 139, 145,
  156, 158, 180, 197
Idolatry, 22, 45, 52, 60, 119, 122, 142,
  149, 158, 175, 176
Imagination, xiv, 21, 39, 52, 68, 74, 80,
  85, 86, 179, 192, 211
Incarnational Reality, 71, 72, 79, 109,
  142, 175, 182, 184, 192, 214, 224
Incest, 124, 176
Infants
  needs of, 41-42, 91, 98-101
  emotional damage to, 95, 103-39, 127
Inferiority, 21, 36, 37, 38, 40, 96, 137
Inner Healing (Michael Scanlon), 27
Intercession, 77-78, 185-86, 189-90, 210,
  211, 212, 213
Introspection, 38, 58, 136, 146, 156, 196

Jesus Christ, xiv, xv, 17, 53, 58, 74, 76,
  82, 86, 91, 121, 122, 127, 141, 142,
  147, 153, 154, 155, 158, 176, 178,
  181, 184, 192, 194, 198, 199, 204,
  209, 213, 217, 219, 224, 225, 228,
  229, 231
  atoning blood of, 78, 79
  Bridegroom, 61, 178
  crucified, death of, 21, 22, 23, 33, 34,
    50, 55, 62, 63, 83, 119, 120, 139,
    141, 154, 155, 181
  Healer, 72, 77, 158, 159
  identification with, 32, 62, 63, 84,
    120, 145, 153, 154, 179
  Life, source, center, sufficiency, 26,
    32, 40, 54, 55, 72, 77
  name of, xi, 79, 87, 153-54, 164, 168,
    180, 199-200
  One who frees, 50, 53, 67, 159
  righteousness, the believer's, 51, 64,
    142
  Savior, 23, 24, 53, 64, 79
  submission to, 52, 58, 60, 79, 93
  temptation of, 20
  Word, 42
Jones, Alan, 68
Journal, 20, 23, 24, 35, 45, 46, 58-61, 97,
  185, 226

Jung, C. G., 39, 169, 179
Justification, xiv, 21, 22, 26, 27, 50, 51,
  142, 150, 179

Keyes, Dick, 58
Kierkegaard, Soren, 17
Kilby, Clyde, 223

Lake, Frank, 100, 107, 109, 111, 112,
  123, 124, 139
Language, 81, 194, 203, 206, 211
Law, 26, 51, 53, 57, 141-42, 146, 148,
  196
Lenten Spring, The (Thomas Hopko),
  225-26
Lesbianism, 104-7, 108, 112, 121
Letters of C. S. Lewis (C. S. Lewis), 34,
  69
Letters to Malcolm (C. S. Lewis), 75, 76,
  146
Lewis, C. S., 34, 35, 39, 54, 62, 63, 69,
  75, 76, 78, 139, 144, 146, 189, 191,
  193, 201, 204, 208, 219, 220-21, 223,
  226
Listening prayer, 25, 27, 28, 29, 31, 52,
  53, 57-64, 77, 83, 94, 126, 135, 141-
  42, 145, 146, 148, 155-56, 158, 184,
  198, 204, 208, 211
*Liturgy and Worship: A Companion to
  the Prayer Books of the Anglican
  Communion*, 182
Love (God's), 17, 32, 35, 51, 64, 83, 99,
  109, 115, 116, 122, 123, 126, 141,
  143, 158
Lovelace, Richard, 17, 147, 196
Luther, Martin, 142, 143

MacDonald, Gordon, 227
Manual for Priests, A (Society of Saint
  John the Evangelist), 164, 172
Masculine, 36, 37, 38, 41, 86, 88-91, 95,
  131, 132, 136, 137, 194, 196, 197
Master and the Disciple, The (John
  Gaynor Banks), 205
Masturbation, 38
McAll, Kenneth, 79

McDonald, H. D., 70
McLean, Clay, 19-22, 127-29, 231
Memory(ies), xiv., 26, 27, 28, 32, 34, 36, 38, 42, 50, 64, 65-80, 83, 85, 95, 96, 97, 98, 100, 103-39, 148, 149, 153-59, 176, 180, 211
  ancestral, 69, 74-75, 85, 93-95
  prenatal, 98, 99
Meyer, F. B., xiv, 54, 65, 72, 146, 222
Milton, John, 34, 220
Misogyny, 125, 132, 138-39, 187
Morris, Leon, 35
Mothering, 41, 42, 43, 99-101, 117
My Utmost for His Highest (Oswald Chambers), xiii, 32, 50, 51, 181, 183, 184, 220
Myth, 39, 147, 215, 223-25

Narcissism, 26, 27, 32, 38-39, 40, 192
Nehemiah, 68, 202, 203, 205
New International Version Study Bible, 206
Nouwen, Henri, 159

Obedience, 20, 26, 31, 52, 53, 58, 63, 70, 79, 132, 135, 136, 141-42, 149, 158, 164, 190, 192, 202, 225
Occult, the, 78-79, 94, 166-68, 169, 179, 213, 225
Oil, 151, 164, 168, 170, 174, 178
On the Invocation of the Name of Jesus, 199
Ordering Your Private World (Gordon MacDonald), 227
Oswald Chambers, The Best from All His Books (Oswald Chambers), 19, 21, 22, 84, 93
Our Daily Walk (F. B. Meyer), xiv, 65, 72, 146, 222
Our Heavenly Father (Robert Frost), 35

Pain, emotional, 27, 28, 29, 49, 71, 84, 103-39
Parenting, 34-35, 36-37, 38, 41-43, 83, 99-101
  mothering, 41, 42, 43, 99-101, 117

Pastoral Care Ministry Schools, xiii, 19, 22, 33, 54, 97, 107, 109, 120, 124, 130, 131, 135, 136, 138, 150, 174, 177, 180, 186, 187, 209-10
Pearson, Mark, 178
Penn-Lewis, Jessie, 213-16
Peretti, Frank, 191-92
Perfectionism, 21, 27, 136, 143, 148
Perseverance, 217-31
Perversion, 21, 54, 84, 174, 176, 182, 187, 195, 203, 213
Physical responses to emotional healing, 113, 115, 120, 135-39
Piercing the Darkness (Frank Peretti), 191-92
Pitter, Ruth, 159
Poems (C. S. Lewis), 62
Pomrenning, Mary, 130, 132
Prayer, healing, xiii, xiv, 33, 42, 50, 68, 70, 75, 77-78, 92, 94, 98, 108, 109, 110, 114, 116, 119, 120, 121, 122, 126, 127, 132, 133, 137, 150, 154, 155, 166, 168-69, 174, 182, 208
Prayer, intercessory, 77-78, 185, 189-90, 210, 211, 212, 213
  partners in, 185-86
Prayers, 21, 23-24, 90, 114, 146, 190, 199, 200, 206, 222, 232
  for enemies, 188-90
Praying amiss, 146
Presence of God, Christ, xiv, 21, 22, 23, 28, 31, 34, 41, 58, 68, 70, 71, 72, 77, 82, 84, 85, 86, 93, 95, 98, 113, 123, 126, 135, 137, 138, 142, 153, 155, 157, 168, 179, 180, 184, 187, 189, 190, 192, 198-200, 207, 208, 211, 214-15, 216, 218, 222, 229
Pride, 24, 50-51, 58, 59, 60, 62, 63, 81-83, 96-97, 143, 144, 211, 220
Priesthood of believers, 154, 157
Problem of Pain, The (C. S. Lewis), 63, 78, 189, 191, 193
Projection, 36, 49, 55, 90, 125, 157
Psychotherapy, 98, 108-9, 110, 114, 125, 128, 139, 147, 155, 157, 180

Rationalization, 20
Reflections on the Psalms (C. S. Lewis), 144
Regeneration, 20, 143
Regression, 119, 123, 126-27
Rejection, 19, 27, 31, 36, 38, 42, 45, 50, 64, 74, 76, 91, 94, 95, 96, 99, 118, 119, 125, 126, 130-31, 157, 158
Re-parenting, 110-11, 118, 119
Repentance, 20, 53, 63, 68, 78, 79, 91, 119, 130, 131, 136, 145, 146, 149, 153, 154, 167, 168, 175, 178, 189, 203, 207, 210, 222, 223
Repression, 71, 72, 74, 85-87, 91, 97, 98, 100, 103-39, 146, 147, 199, 215
Resymbolize, 34, 120, 121, 192
Richards, John, 169
Righteousness, xiv, 26, 50-51, 53, 54, 57, 64, 67, 141-43, 145, 149, 205, 210
Rothenberg, Mira, 128

Sacramental, 143, 153, 168, 175, 178, 181, 182
Salvation, xiii, xiv, 21, 26, 53, 64, 70, 71, 141, 150, 179, 181, 212, 227, 230
Sanctification, xiii, 21, 71, 144, 150, 179, 217
Sanford, Agnes, 33, 54, 63, 68, 73, 156
Satan, 20, 22, 92, 142, 153, 154, 166-68, 173, 176, 179, 181, 183, 186, 187, 189, 191, 194, 196, 204, 208, 209, 220
tactics of, 202-4
Scanlon, Michael, 27, 28
Schism between head and heart, 59, 64, 68, 83, 146, 175, 214
Schizoid personality (fearing attachment), 111, 112, 117, 118, 123-25
Screwtape Letters (C. S. Lewis), 208
Scriptures, 40, 49, 58-61, 70, 85, 92, 100, 142, 147, 153, 158, 164, 168, 178, 179, 187, 188, 198, 206, 208, 209, 210, 211, 213, 214, 215, 217-18, 223, 225, 226, 230, 231
Seamands, David, 35
Secular culture and ideologies, 20, 43, 79, 147, 168, 170-73, 179, 191-92, 194, 219, 225, 226, 228
Self-acceptance, xiii, xiv, 17, 22, 25-43, 48, 49, 50, 51, 53, 54, 57, 58-61, 77, 88-92, 97, 132, 138, 142, 143
Self-hatred, xiv, 19-24, 32, 33, 35, 37, 49, 50, 54, 55, 59, 83, 84, 88-92, 138-39
Self-pity, 19, 21, 22
Self-realization or actualization, 32
Separation anxiety, 41, 97, 100, 107, 110, 117, 120, 121, 123, 129, 130, 138
Separation from God, others, ourselves, 69, 70
Sermon on the Mount, 184, 185, 205
Serving God, 20, 26, 35, 59, 63, 88, 154, 158, 176, 222
Sexual neurosis, 36, 38, 42, 85-87, 91, 98, 104-7, 108, 112, 120, 122, 129-32, 174, 176, 179, 210
Sexual sin, 19, 22, 33, 37, 50, 54, 76, 85, 94, 125, 136, 149, 176, 203
Shame, xiv, 21, 22, 54-55
Sign of the cross, 151, 167, 176
Sin, xiii, xiv, xv, 19, 20, 21, 22, 23, 24, 26, 27, 49, 50, 51, 54, 55, 58-61, 62, 63, 64, 65-80, 82, 83, 84, 92, 93, 94, 119, 131, 136, 141-51, 153-59, 168, 181, 187, 189, 192, 198, 206-8, 209, 210, 211, 213, 214, 215, 226
Sinful nature, old self, xiv, 20, 22, 24, 25, 26, 32, 33, 35, 60-63, 143-48, 154, 156, 204
defined, 147-48
dying to, 20, 25, 26, 35, 58-59, 62-63, 142, 143, 145, 149, 156
Social roles, 39-40
Society, evil in, 43, 194-98, 196, 213, 217, 226
Solzhenitsyn, Alexander, 144, 195
Soul, the, xiv, 32, 69, 70-73, 75, 77, 81, 113, 121, 132, 138, 139, 143, 144, 147, 155, 158, 203, 207, 217
Spirit, human, xiv, 69-72, 151, 207
Spiritual warfare, 19, 21, 154, 166-75, 179-216, 228

defined and described, 187
from people close to us, 188-90
in Christian institutions, 169-75, 181, 191-200, 203, 205
planes of, 208-10
Stern, Karl, 37, 39, 74, 109
Storge love, 117
Stringham, James, 74
Submission, 40, 48, 49, 52, 136
Suffering for Christ, 186, 188, 194-95
Surprised by Joy (C. S. Lewis), 39
Symbol, 34, 40, 73-74, 97, 131, 150, 155, 156-57, 163-82, 191-92, 199, 203, 206, 217, 225, 230
Symbolic confusion, 112, 120, 129, 130, 131, 132

Taking Our Cities for God: How to Break Spiritual Strongholds (John Dawson), 210
Temptation, 19-22, 149, 179, 181
Testaments of Love (Leon Morris), 35
That Hideous Strength (C. S. Lewis), 201-2
Thinking, right, 28, 58-61, 148
Third Revolution: A Study of Psychiatry and Religion, The (Karl Stern), 37, 39, 74
This Present Darkness (Frank Peretti), 191-92
Thoughts, diseased, negative, 21, 23, 24, 26, 27, 28, 37, 52, 58-61, 136, 148
Time, 73-78, 94, 115, 158, 227
Timing, 108, 118, 120-23, 126, 157
Tolkien, J. R. R., 193
Tolstoy, 46
Torrey, R. A., 146
Touch, 91, 95, 105-6, 112, 115-16, 117, 120, 126, 127, 138
Transference, 110-11, 116-20, 125, 126, 157
Transsexual, 129, 130, 132

Transvestite, 129
Trauma, 32, 42, 69, 77, 87, 94, 95, 99, 100, 158
birth, 98, 123
infantile, 98, 99, 103-39
Trobisch, Daniel, 36, 37
Trobisch, Walter, 33
True self or center, xiv, 20, 22, 23, 25, 26, 27, 32, 33, 36, 39, 40, 45, 46, 47, 48-49, 52, 53, 61-63, 88, 93, 119, 120, 130, 135-36, 137, 138, 145, 146, 154, 156, 180, 204, 207, 218, 226
Truth, contending for, 185-6, 189-90, 192-200, 205-6

Union with God, abiding in Christ, xiv, 20, 21, 22, 23, 26, 48, 53, 54, 70, 71, 72, 75, 79, 84-85, 130, 143, 159, 184, 186

Virtues, The (Romano Guardini), 38
Vocation, 64, 67, 88, 184, 186, 197, 226
Vows (childhood), 89, 157

Walking in the Spirit, xiv, 25, 27, 53, 57-64, 141-42, 143, 149
War and Peace (Tolstoy), 46
War on the Saints (Jessie Penn-Lewis), 213
Weight of Glory, The (C. S. Lewis), 34-35
Well-being, 19, 41, 99, 110, 111, 123, 129
Will, the, xiv., 20, 53, 68, 85, 86, 143, 148, 149, 156, 168, 214
Womb, emotional damage to infants in, 98, 99
Woundedness, xiii, xiv, 19, 22, 23, 27, 28, 32, 33, 36, 49, 50, 54, 57, 68-69, 71, 72, 73, 75, 76-77, 84, 92, 93, 94, 103-39, 158, 159, 187, 219